HADRIAN'S
EMPIRE

Also by Danny Danziger

The Year 1000
Eton Voices
1215: The Year of Magna Carta
The Cathedral
Lost Hearts
The Noble Tradition
All in A Day's Work
The Orchestra

Danny Danziger and Nicholas Purcell

HADRIAN'S EMPIRE

HODDER

Copyright © 2005 by Danny Danziger and Nicholas Purcell

First published in Great Britain in 2005 by Hodder & Stoughton
A division of Hodder Headline

This edition published in 2006

The right of Danny Danziger and Nicholas Purcell to be identified as the Authors
of the Work has been asserted by them in accordance with the
Copyright, Designs and Patents Act 1988.

A Hodder paperback

3

All rights reserved. No part of this publication may be
reproduced, stored in a retrieval system, or transmitted, in any form
or by any means without the prior written permission of the publisher,
nor be otherwise circulated in any form of binding or cover other
than that in which it is published and without a similar condition
being imposed on the subsequent purchaser.

A CIP catalogue record for this title is
available from the British Library

ISBN 978 0 340 83361 2

Typeset in Sabon MT by
Palimpsest Book Production Limited
Polmont, Stirlingshire

Map by Sandra Oakins

Printed and bound in the UK by
CPI Mackays, Chatham ME5 8TD

Hodder Headline's policy is to use papers that are natural, renewable
and recyclable products and made from wood grown in sustainable forests.
The logging and manufacturing processes are expected to conform to the
environmental regulations of the country of origin.

Hodder & Stoughton Ltd
A division of Hodder Headline
338 Euston Road
London NW1 3BH

For: Rupert and Charlotte de Klee, the very best of friends, and, of course, Lara, Kyle, Ivan, and my godson, Joseph. Also, for Don and Ann Parfet, in a friendship that is always renewed.

ACKNOWLEDGEMENTS

I am very grateful to David McGlade of The Countryside Agency, Val Lowther of One NorthEast (formerly Northumbria Tourist Board), the guide Paul Benians, and especially Tom Keating, whose knowledge and enthusiasm for Hadrian's Wall and the north-east of England is endearing and inspiring.

Also, we would like to thank Hazel Orme for her wonderful work on the text and Caroline Lees for researching, organising, liaising, and mediating.

CONTENTS

INTRODUCTION

Last spring, I went for a walk along Hadrian's Wall. It is a 74-mile-long* stone necklace that stretches across the north of England at its narrowest point – from Newcastle-upon-Tyne westwards to the Solway Firth above the Cumberland plain. This is wild country. Northumbria gives way to Cumbria along the route, and the scenery changes from moorland to mountains. Along the route, bright sunshine turned to needle-sharp rain and even light flurries of snow, and then sparkling sun again, and all the while I could see rainbows arching behind the distant hills. It was a magical, memorable walk. At the end of May, last year, a trail was opened so that walkers can follow the wall for its entire length, and it has become one of the most popular walking destinations in the country.

That magnificent walk inspired me to find out something about Hadrian. I knew almost nothing about him. What kind of man was he? What kind of world did he live in? What sort of place was Rome? What sort of country was this when Hadrian came here in 122 A.D?

By the time Hadrian became emperor in 117 AD, Britain had settled into a regular Roman way of life. Many towns were built and laid out on the Roman grid system (as are New York and Lisbon today). A *forum* (marketplace) and *basilica* (law court) were to be found in all major towns, plus enormous public baths, where washing, exercise, and massage in *gymnasia* introduced a healthier lifestyle to the formerly unwashed and

* Or 80 Roman miles – a Roman mile is roughly equivalent to 1620 yards. The Roman mile was *milia passum*, a thousand paces, a pace being made up of two steps, left and right.

disease-ridden Celts. Native Britons and citizens from all parts of the Roman empire mingled freely and happily, a society that was racially diverse and integrated. Some had even begun to dress as Romans. Tacitus records: 'Our national dress came into favour, and the toga was everywhere to be seen'.

Early in his reign, Hadrian wanted tangible frontiers at the borders of his empire, and after a visit to Britain, his empire's most northern province, in 122 AD, he ordered a wall to be built. It took six years to build. He had already built a wall in Germany, an eighty-mile palisade, though it has left no remains as spectacular as those of the Wall in Britain.

After nearly two thousand years, much of Hadrian's Wall lies in ruin, but there are still around 10 miles of wall as a reminder of what an incredible edifice it must have been. Originally, the wall was over 15 feet high, and in places 10 feet thick. Thousands of native labourers were employed to do the digging and hewing, fetching and carrying. Three legions (a legion consisted of approximately 4200 men), who were already stationed in Britain, were involved with the building. A legion contained within its ranks experts in every field, from clerks to stonemasons and glaziers, architects, engineers and surveyors, and they did all the craftsmen's jobs, assisted by the auxiliary soldiers, the ones who were to be left to patrol the Wall when the work was finished.

The parapet along the top protected troops as they walked along. Built into the wall, roughly equal distances apart, were sixteen large garrison forts. Each of these housed an auxiliary cohort of 1000 men, or a cavalry division of 500 men and their horses. At intervals of one Roman mile were 79 towers called milecastles. Each one contained accommodation for a few troops. Between every pair of milecastles were two turrets, roughly 1600 feet apart. These were used as lookouts, and for sending signals along the Wall. The Roman civil service was inflexible: the milecastles were put in no matter how impenetrable the terrain, and it is difficult to see the purpose of some of them – let alone imagine how difficult they must have been to install. As always, the Roman army consisted of men from all parts of the empire, and one imagines that the soldiers from the warmer climes of the Roman empire, such as Spain and Iraq, must have found the posting a harsh billet so far north in this cold and windswept country.

There is something enormously positive and hopeful about the Wall. It is a reminder of a time when this island was part of an enormous global empire, energetic, vital and self-confident, and this country benefited from the civilising influence of a more sophisticated protectorate, and learned from it, and, ultimately, learned to live without it.

The Roman empire was never as big or as confident as during Hadrian's reign. After that time, Rome relinquished its hold, or lost in battle a great number of client states – although it wasn't for several centuries that the Romans would leave these shores. By the beginning of the fifth century AD, most of the Roman army in Britain had gone, and life suddenly seemed perilous for those British people who now lived as Romans. There was no longer an organised army to defend their way of life. In AD 410, the Britons sent a petition to the Emperor Honorius asking for help from the ravaging Irish and Picts in the west, and the Angles, Saxons and Jutes who were coming over in raiding parties from the European mainland. The emperor replied that they must from now on 'see to their own defences'. A final appeal to Rome was made in AD 446. The monk Gildas, known as the Wise, and later made a saint, sent a poignant letter to Rome, pleading for help. 'The barbarians are driving us into the sea, and the sea is driving us back to the barbarians,' he wrote. 'Two forms of death wait for us: to be slaughtered or drowned . . .' No help came.

Snapped roof trees, towers fallen, the work of the Giants,
    the stone-smiths mouldereth . . .
Came days of pestilence, on all sides men fell dead, death fetched
    off the flower of the people;

Where they stood to fight, waste places, on the acropolis ruins.

This bleak picture of ruin, death and destruction, darkness and plague is a description written a hundred years after the Roman period in Britain. The carefully ordered world of the towns and villas of the Romans had fallen into decay, and Britain was broken up into small kingdoms led by warlords. The Roman roads and bridges and schools and buildings crumbled into dirt.

The Roman empire had imploded. The energy and dynamism of the Roman empire, which had enlightened so many countries in its orbit, was no more. The period which followed, now called the Dark Ages by historians, seemed a step back in time and civilisation. It was to be nearly a thousand years until the Renaissance shook the western hemisphere out of its torpor and into a brave new world.

After several months working on the book, Nicholas and I met in Rome late in February 2004. Rome can be bitingly cold in the winter months, but the night skies are nearly always clear, and the constellations as easy to pick out as they were two millennia ago. Of course, the Romans would have been much more knowledgeable than us about the arrangements of the heavens, and they revered the heavenly bodies – after all, they named the planets after their gods.

I had not been to Rome since a child, so I was looking at that great city with fresh eyes. Nicholas was the best of guides. As we walked the cobblestone Piazza della Rotonda, one could only gasp at the solemn beauty of the Pantheon, quietly illuminated under a soft white light.

The next day, we went to Tivoli, along with six students from the British School in Rome. It was very inspiring to see how Nicholas knows and loves this extraordinary place. Villa Adriana was heavily influenced by Hadrian's journeys around the empire. The massive Pecile, through which you enter, was a reproduction of a building in Athens, and the Canopo is a copy of the sanctuary of Serapis near Alexandria, with a long canal of water, representing the Nile. Most impressive of all within the grounds of the villa is the Teatro Marittimo, an island with an artificial pool, which could only be reached by a retractable bridge for when Hadrian required privacy. Perhaps it is here, in this imposing place, where one best gets a sense of Hadrian the man.

Danny Danziger

* * *

Hadrian was one of the most famous emperors – many more people saw him than saw most emperors. Anecdotes about him turn up all over the place. But there is no complete history of his reign written in antiquity. We have used what remains of the history of Hadrian from the massive Roman History written a hundred years later by a Greek senator at Rome called Cassius Dio. There are a few short biographical accounts, of which by far the best is the Life of Hadrian in a collection of imperial biographies called the Imperial History. Much of this collection is spoof. The author wrote it at the end of the fifth century, when the empire was waning, and decided to pretend to be a committee of six people writing a hundred years earlier. Some of the details are deliberately overdone and bizarre, and the author was quite capable of inventing documents or authors.

Roman towns were as full of inscriptions as modern ones are of road signs: advertisements, epitaphs, notices, edicts, family trees, price lists, whole philosophical treatises, and thousands of formal descriptions of the achievements of people whose statues dotted town centres. Being on stone or sometimes bronze, these often survive, and give another really rich vein of information to mine.

We've drawn heavily on both these types of information. But the other way into Hadrian's world which has helped bring it alive to us is some of the colourful literature written by Hadrian's contemporaries. We've made lots of use of the letters and pamphlets of three Roman senators, Pliny, Arrian and Fronto.

Nicholas Purcell

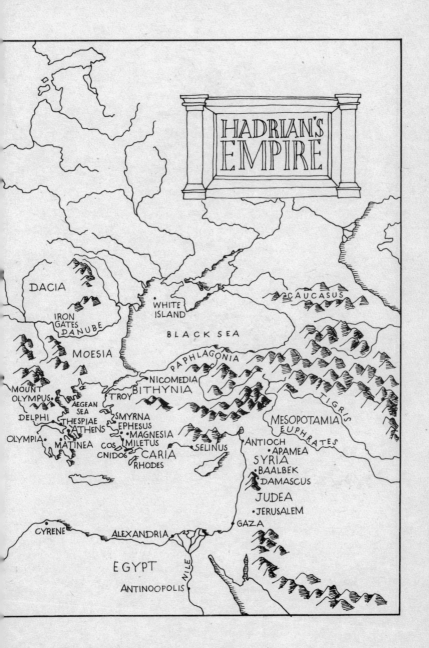

HADRIAN'S EMPIRE

DACIA

IRON
GATES
DANUBE

MOESIA

WHITE
ISLAND

CAUCASUS

BLACK SEA

PAPHLAGONIA

MOUNT
OLYMPUS
DELPHI
THESPIAE
OLYMPIA
MATINEA
CNIDOS
RHODES

NICOMEDIA

TROY

BITHYNIA

AEGEAN
SEA

SMYRNA
EPHESUS
MAGNESIA
COS
MILETUS
CARIA

ATHENS

SELINUS

TIGRIS

MESOPOTAMIA

EUPHRATES

ANTIOCH
APAMEA

SYRIA
BAALBEK
DAMASCUS

JUDEA

JERUSALEM

GAZA

CYRENE

ALEXANDRIA

EGYPT

NILE

ANTINOOPOLIS

I

PUBLIUS AELIUS HADRIANUS

> When playboy Rome has had fourteen kings,
> Sunrise to sunset, enslaving the world,
> A grey-headed man will inherit the throne
> Whose name is the name of a sea
>
> SIBYLLINE ORACLE

In the twelfth year of the reign of Teng, empress of the eastern Han in China, and the sixth of Vologeses III, King of the Parthians; when Vasistiputra had been king of the Satavahana empire in India for fifteen years, 870 years had passed since the foundation of the city of Rome, and eight decades since the crucifixion of Jesus Christ, Publius Aelius Hadrianus became Roman emperor.

Hadrian was born in Rome, on 24 January 76 AD, during the seventh year of the reign of the Emperor Vespasian (69–79). He was a citizen of Rome, born to riches and status, but he had no links to the then emperor, who, anyway, had two adult sons to succeed him. No one can have dreamed that forty years later Hadrian would be the most powerful man in the world.

Normally Roman citizens had three names. The family name was the middle one – Hadrian was an Aelius, his relative Trajan Ulpius, and so on. All men had a first name, from a list of less than a dozen that recurred all the time (there were a few unusual ones in old-fashioned families) – such as Publius, like Hadrian, Marcus, like Trajan, Lucius, Aulus, Gaius and Quintus. To help tell people apart, since a big family might have in it far too many men called Marcus Valerius, they added a nickname, which became part of the family name, like Hadrianus and Traianus. The older ones all had meanings, often rather personal, even rude – Armpit, Squinting, Warty, Red-head, Flop-eared, Big-nose (Ahala, Strabo, Verrucosus, Rufus, Flaccus, Naso). This was starkly different from rich Greek families whose names meant things like Handsome, Best in the War-band, Defender of Men, or Power of the People (Kallias, Aristolochos, Alexander, Demosthenes). Later names became more anodyne, and often derived from family connections with places and people, which was true of Trajan and Hadrian. The prouder a man was of his connections, the more names he acquired. The record is held by Quintus Roscius Coelius Murena Silius Decianus Vibullius Pius Iulius Eurycles Herculanus Pompeius Falco, a senior senator who was to be Hadrian's governor of Britain. Women had only a family name, though they, too, accumulated extras to show off their relatives.

The Aelius family used the name Hadrianus to evoke the town in Italy from which they originally came: Hadria, the river-mouth port in the Po delta, which gave its name to the Adriatic Sea. 'Wherever the Roman conquers, he lives,' they said, and the empire was full of people whose names carried messages of this kind: sometimes misleading or false, since it was easy and desirable to give the impression of being Roman, or of being a Roman of impressive background. It was generations since the Aelii had been based in Italy. Early members of the Aelius family had helped conquer Spain for Rome and had settled in the most fertile part of the new province. Their new home lay on a low hill on the edge of the Guadalquivir plain, a few miles from the city of Seville. It had been founded by the Romans very early in their Spanish wars, in 206 BC, and its name, Italica, proudly announced its links with Italy and Rome.

Italica became a prosperous place in a wealthy region, where Roman families had long lived beside people of indigenous origin. The new landowners invested in agriculture, and the region's natural resources included the rich mines of the Rio Tinto.

Commerce prospered. Hadrian's mother, Domitia Paulina, came from Cadíz, the island port off the coast of Andalucía, which had been founded by traders from what is now Lebanon, roughly a millennium before Hadrian became emperor.

As a citizen-family of Italian origin, and considerable wealth, the Aelii of Italica were in a comfortable position. They were big fish in a small pond, members of the town-councillor élite that dominated each of the hundreds of towns and cities of the Roman world. And these small ponds were fished by the Roman emperors looking for loyal new recruits for a much larger and more important aristocracy in Rome, capital of the empire. Hadrian's grandfather had been recruited in this way. There were two tiers to the imperial aristocracy. The families of the 600 senators were the topmost level. A second rung was the equestrian order, which had 1800 official members.

Recruitment meant taking on official jobs for the Roman state, and becoming a member of the Senate. Hadrian's father, Publius Aelius Hadrianus Afer, was a senator too, so spent much of his time in Rome. The older aristocrats had been purged in the political conflicts of the early empire, forced to commit suicide, or put to death on trivial charges. Nervous emperors had disposed of all possible rivals, until in the Senate that Hadrian joined as a young man there were few whose ancestors had been senators before Augustus invented the imperial monarchy. Newly recruited provincial senators played a full part in the social and political life of the empire's capital, but senators whose families had never left Italy did not forget that these new colleagues were based in remote parts of the imperial fringes. It had been a surprise when Emperor Vespasian won the imperial throne – a man of an equestrian family based in a town sixty kilometres from Rome. No one thought the empire was ready to be ruled by families whose home was 1600 kilometres away across the western Mediterranean.

Hadrian's father died when the boy was nine, and two guardians were appointed. Marcus Ulpius Traianus, his father's cousin, who also came from Italica, was one; twelve years later, known to history as Trajan, he unexpectedly became emperor.

Upper-class Roman children spent little time with their parents: bonding between parents and their offspring was not thought important. When he was only a few days old Hadrian was handed into the care of a wet-nurse, Germana, 'the German girl'. As the wife of a senator living in Rome, Hadrian's mother was probably too busy with social responsibilities to consider the care of her children a priority. Besides, slave wet-nurses were used by most upper-class families, even though some doctors at the time believed there was a danger that the servile nature of a slave might pass to a baby through the milk.

Germana was a slave – a captive from the Rhineland, where Rome had been annexing new territory in the years around Hadrian's birth. The job of wet-nurse was highly prized among female slaves and Germana was chosen because she was strong and healthy. From the wording on her tombstone in Rome, we know that she was eventually given her freedom, had her own children, and outlived her imperial nursling.

Throughout his early childhood Hadrian's day-to-day life and education were managed by senior members of the slave and ex-slave staff of the household. He had only one sibling, a sister Aelia Paulina. The two children are likely to have been educated together and may have shared their lessons with the children of other well-to-do families. The staff supervised manners and deportment, while home tutors took care of Hadrian's formal education, which would have included grammar, poetry and rhetoric. All the signs are that Hadrian was a quick and enthusiastic learner. He developed an early love of music and was particularly fond of singing and playing the flute.

Although the Aelius family had property in Rome as well as a number of country homes in Italy, they also maintained their Spanish estates. As an essential part of his education,

Hadrian first visited Italica when he was fourteen. Little is known about the visit but, like moneyed youths across the empire, the adolescent boys of Italica were taught a mixture of sport and military exercises. Hadrian also hunted. (Indeed, he pursued all of these activities for the rest of his life – and often overdid them.) In fact, he spent such excessive time and energy in the hunt that those close to him became critical, and his guardian quickly brought him back to Rome.

The young Hadrian had many intellectual interests. His education was intended to give him the elaborate skills in formal Latin and in Roman literature that he would need as a participant in cultured upper-class society, and for public life, if he went in for a career as a senator, as his background suggested he would. But Latin authors and Roman learning hardly made sense without the study of Greek literature and philosophy. Roman power had grown up in a Greek world, and half of the empire was more Greek than Roman. The two cultures of ancient Greece and Rome intertwined.

Vespasian's son Domitian, who became emperor when Hadrian was six, was especially passionate about all things Greek. There were influential Greek-speakers among the staff of the Aelius household, and one contemporary biography says that Hadrian had a 'lavish' education in Greek literature. Some of this was in Athens, where many wealthy Romans went to be educated in the Greek tradition. At some point it included singing and medicine, musical theory, geometry, painting, and sculpture in bronze and marble. The result was, even by the standards of the time, an orientation towards Greek culture that singled out Hadrian sufficiently for him to be nicknamed 'the little Greek', Graeculus.

The end of Hadrian's schooling came when he was eighteen, and was asked to sit on a panel of judges in Rome. Two other honorific jobs in the public sphere, which sounded grand but involved little effort, came his way at around this time – jobs that usually went to promising young senators with good connections. One was as a ceremonial official in the equestrian order, the second tier of the Roman élite. The other was more select: every spring, the two chief officials of the old Roman state, the consuls, went together to the sanctuary of Latin Jupiter on the summit of an extinct volcano in the Alban Hills, twelve miles south-east of Rome. They could not abandon the city without leaving a deputy in charge while they were away, and in March 95 the job fell to the young Hadrian. He had now been initiated into the ancient civic traditions of the Roman state and was poised to take the first step up the ladder of a senator's career.

Military service followed. Young senators were assigned to the regiments of citizen-soldiery – the legions – as junior officers, high in social status but low on experience. Hadrian was sent to the garrison of the lower Danube, first to the Second Legion, and then to the Fifth. At the age of twenty-two, he was a bright, ambitious, successful, well-thought-of young officer – a rich, clever young man from a provincial Roman family, devoted to the complexities of Greek and Roman literary culture. Combined with that, he was fit and energetic – and would have been considered likely to have a distinguished senatorial career, governing provinces, and reaching the symbolically crucial rank of consul, perhaps even an adviser to the emperor – always assuming that he didn't fall out with anyone powerful. He also had money, talent and some well-placed relatives. But it was the last advantage that transformed his prospects.

By the time Hadrian had turned twenty, the emperor Domitian had become tyrannical and megalomaniac – one of Rome's most notoriously evil rulers. He had destroyed the last remnants of his own family, suppressed opposition from the Senate, and become a byword for paranoia, cruelty and caprice. On 18 September 96, the emperor was murdered by the palace staff (the perpetrators were then killed horribly by those of the imperial bodyguard who had not turned against the emperor).

An aged senator, Marcus Cocceius Nerva, was chosen as a stopgap emperor until an ambitious senior senator stepped forward as an heir and successor, perhaps a provincial governor with a large army at his command. Marcus Ulpius Traianus, Hadrian's guardian and governor of Upper Germany, got in first. There wasn't any opposition, and on 27 October 97 Trajan was adopted as Nerva's heir. It was a clever way to solve a problem. The blood line did not always throw up the best successor, as Domitian had demonstrated spectacularly. Adoption meant that the best man could be selected, then legitimated by a notional connection with the old regime. That was the theory, anyway . . .

Hadrian's commanding officer on the Danube invited the new heir's cousin to be the messenger who would take the long road to Germany with his regiment's congratulations. He arrived at Trajan's base at Mainz, and was given a third posting of the kind he had had on the Danube in the Twenty-second Legion. Trajan moved down the Rhine to take over the province of Lower Germany. Hadrian's sister Paulina was now married, to a successful senator, Servianus, who had been appointed by Trajan as his successor at Mainz. This was less good for Hadrian than it sounded. Servianus disapproved of Hadrian's frivolous existence and mounting debts – and had said as much to Trajan.

In a very short time news of Nerva's death came in by courier from Rome. Hadrian found himself with an even juicier assignment as the messenger with good news: he had to tell his relative and former guardian that he was now emperor. But Servianus banned Hadrian from undertaking the journey, and even dismantled his carriage to stop him going. But it took more than that to stop Hadrian. His journey was about 150 kilometres but, undaunted, he set out on foot, and arrived at Trajan's headquarters ahead of Servianus' messenger. The message had the desired effect: Hadrian was immediately prevailed on to join Trajan's entourage. He accepted, and entered the world of intrigue that surrounded the homosexual emperor. Quite apart from their shared sexual orientation, Hadrian got on well in this milieu because he had a tremendous capacity for drink, and, it appears, became rapidly involved with the imperial pages.

Two years later, when Trajan finally left Germany for Rome, Hadrian was rewarded for his services with the job of quaestor, the first rung on the senatorial ladder. Each year, twenty young men were selected but the ones who really counted were those, such as Hadrian, deputed to the personal service of the emperor. Among his duties he had to make speeches on behalf of Trajan. On one occasion people laughed at his country pronunciation, a slight he was never to forget.

The important cities of the empire liked to appoint members of the Roman upper classes to their official posts. If the city was distinguished, both parties would be honoured; and the honorand could then be persuaded to spend money on the city, as well as becoming its patron for the future. Athens, most famous of ancient Greek cities, was now enjoying a privileged twilight existence as a heritage centre, but it appointed Hadrian to its ancient office of chief public official in 112; his well-known enthusiasm for all things Greek made this a happy move. The Athenians put up a statue to Hadrian in the Theatre of Dionysus on the slopes of the Acropolis: a standard courtesy in a relationship of this kind. It came with an inscription explaining Hadrian's distinction, which has provided important information about this vital period in Hadrian's life. The widespread habit of engraving such helpful texts on stone or bronze has hugely enriched our understanding of the Greek and Roman world. It consists of parallel texts, in Latin and Greek, detailing his achievements to date – a mini-portrait of the public face of a man who was then five years away from becoming emperor – set out in reverse, ending with the junior judicial job that had started his senatorial career.

To Publius Aelius Hadrianus, son of Publius, Sergian voting-division, consul, member of the Board of Seven for Ritual Banquets, member of the Brotherhood of the Cult of Augustus, governor in lower Pannonia of the emperor Nerva Trajan Caesar Augustus (conqueror of Germany, conqueror of Dacia), praetor and at the same time commander of the First Legion, Minerva's, dutiful and loyal, in the Dacian War, tribune of the plebs, quaestor of the emperor Trajan and his Companion in the Dacian Expedition, decorated by the emperor twice, tribune of the Second Legion, the Rescuers, dutiful and loyal, and of the Fifth, the Conquerors of Macedon, and of the Twenty-second, First-born Fortune's, dutiful and loyal, leader of the squadron of Roman knights, in charge of the city of Rome during the Latin festival, judge of the Board of Ten.

The consulship, grandest and most ancient of the offices of state, comes first. Hadrian got there at the minimum age of thirty-two. In practical political terms, he already had a better title: Companion of the Emperor.

When Hadrian was still quaestor, Trajan set out on a great military expedition. His target was the kingdom of Dacia, in what is now Romania. Civilised and sophisticated, independent, but intermittently aggressive towards Roman interests in the Danube valley and the Balkans, it was also wealthy, and Trajan wanted revenge against a power that had humiliated Roman armies under Domitian. The first war was bloody and spectacular, but it hardly settled the future of the region. A second Dacian war succeeded in its aim of regime change, and Dacia became a Roman province. In the first war, as imperial companion, Hadrian saw a great deal of the fighting; in the second he graduated to commander of the First Legion. Unlike his earlier military experience, this was not routine. Dacia was the most ambitious aggression the Romans had undertaken since the conquest of Britain sixty years before. The decorations he received confirm that Hadrian distinguished himself in action. Before the end of the fighting, he was promoted to the governorship of Pannonia, a command that was strategically vital to the safety of the Roman efforts in Dacia.

However, Trajan's favour could be fickle, and Hadrian sometimes felt insecure. Fortunately he had some useful contacts. He had a close, long-standing friendship with Trajan's wife Pompeia

Plotina, and she arranged, perhaps as early as AD 100, an advantageous marriage with the only available imperial princess, Vibia Sabina, Trajan's great-niece. Hadrian also took over the important job of writing the emperor's speeches.

In 113, after nearly six years of peace, Trajan embarked on another major war, even more ambitious than the annexation of Dacia. The largest organised state known to the Romans outside their empire was Parthia, a loosely structured but populous and wealthy kingdom that stretched across what is now Iraq, from the Roman frontiers in Syria to the mountains of Iran. This region was also the theatre of the most glorious exploits of Alexander the Great, irresistible role-model for conquerors. Parthia had not threatened Rome seriously for years, but was clearly not subject in any way to an empire that liked to think it ruled the whole inhabited world. Earlier Roman wars against Parthia had been either disastrous or inconclusive. And in religion, culture, language and political affiliation, there were no obvious boundaries to Rome's eastern provinces. It was by no means clear that hearts and minds across the region would be more easily swayed by a city on the Tiber than by one on the Tigris.

Hadrian, once again on Trajan's staff, was given the job of governing the important province of Syria, vital to the emperor's war effort as the springboard for the invading armies. In 117 it was announced that Hadrian was to be made consul again, which was a real step up: a second consulship was a sign that a man was getting somewhere – and there had been fewer than a dozen such preferments during Trajan's reign. But several of those were still alive in 117, people of greater distinction, more experience and wider influence than Hadrian.

As in Dacia, the Roman invasion brought early victories, but keeping the conquered Parthian territories in order was a different matter. Trajan reached the Persian Gulf in person, but behind him things started to go wrong. The city of Hatra, in what is now Kurdish northern Iraq, proved especially difficult to control.

Exhausted by the strain of constant fighting, the emperor fell ill, and attempted to return to Rome. On the way home, in August 117, he suffered a stroke and died at Selinus (the name means 'Cow Parsley'), a small town on the south coast of Turkey.

Much later, prophecies were circulated that purported to have predicted the reigns of certain emperors, and Nerva and Trajan were described thus:

> An elderly man will succeed;
> Then a Celt takes the power, who will climb
> On the mountains and speed to the war
> In the east, but he shall not escape
> A terrible doom. He shall die.
> The alien dust will besprinkle his corpse
> In the city whose name is a flower.

The childless Trajan was seventy when he fell ill and speculation was intense as to what he intended to do about a successor. Would he attempt to adopt the best man, as he had been adopted by Nerva? One rumour said that he planned to ask the Senate to supply a list of names to choose from. There were certainly a few senators around who had had distinguished careers, and who had been more influential than Hadrian for much longer. Hadrian had done well, but nothing like well enough to establish him as heir apparent. Or might the family connection count for something? Trajan, though childless, had relatives who were important to him: his sister Marciana, for instance, had been made a goddess after she had died five years before. If family did matter, Hadrian was connected to the dead emperor in his own right, and through his wife Sabina.

And so it turned out. It was announced that in his last hours Trajan had publicly adopted Hadrian. Hadrian received official notice that he had been adopted – and the news that the emperor was dead – at more or less the same time. The army at Antioch hailed him as Trajan's successor on 11 August. There was no effective opposition and Hadrian became Roman emperor.

He had been extremely lucky. Beside the dying emperor's bed had stood his wife Plotina, Hadrian's old ally, and Trajan's niece Matidia, Hadrian's mother-in-law. Since the imperial party were so far from Rome, few other leading citizens were around to observe or intervene. Those present included Publius Acilius Attianus, commander of the emperor's bodyguard. He had been born in Italica, and forty years before, when Hadrian's father had died, had been appointed Hadrian's other guardian. He, too, then, was an interested party. No wonder people thought it was a put-up job. To make matters worse, the letter the Senate received about the adoption was signed by Plotina.

So, although other powerful men might have had their eye on the job, the adoption and its recognition were documented, publicised and accepted with a minimum of trouble. Other emperors made public the name of their successor much sooner, and gave the world a longer time to get used to him. Hadrian was catapulted to the pinnacle of success, converted in a matter of weeks from an ordinary senior senator to ruler of the world. That was certainly a different emotional experience from having been hailed for months as the preferred heir apparent, or born to the succession and brought up to the expectation of absolute power. Trajan's choice was presented as adoption of the best man for the job, but it was clear to all that the relatives of the dying emperor counted for everything. It set an uneasy precedent for the future, and a dilemma for Hadrian, when twenty-one years later he, too, was faced with the problem of a successor.

Although no one else had put in a claim to succeed Trajan, Hadrian was unsure that he could trust those who might have featured on the Senate's list of recommended men. As he journeyed to Rome from the east, some in the capital made serious attempts to find an alternative to him . . . and not much later four senior senators died in mysterious circumstances. Although Hadrian swore it had had nothing to do with him and that, unlike previous emperors, he would not put a senator to death, he never won the Senate's trust.

At fifty-one Hadrian had become the principal public official of the ancient Roman state, recognised by and co-operating with the Senate and people of Rome, a general equipped with the supreme military command held by those who had conquered the world for Rome. At the same time, most of his seventy million subjects – an enormous proportion of the world's population at that time – probably thought of him as some sort of king. Certainly, those who spoke Greek, perhaps a third of the total, *called* him a king (*basileus*). The purple clothing that the emperor wore – coloured with a dye obtained by an extraordinarily intricate and labour-intensive process from the innards of millions of shellfish – was a powerful reminder of his importance. There were other kings, but only the Roman king could decide who was and wasn't royal. 'Honoured by Caesar Augustus with the right to wear royal purple,' says an inscription to one princeling. All the praise of one-man-rule that eight centuries had distilled now devolved on Hadrian, heir to all the monarchies that had gone before, unquestioned ruler of the world.

Roman rulers were iconic, and Hadrian was no exception. What he said, the rumours, jokes and gossip that circulated about him, the official statements of the time, and the judgement of historians influenced the picture people formed of him as an emperor. Portraits of him in stone, bronze, silver and gold, adorned the temples and marketplaces of the empire. He appeared on painted panels in workshops and booths, in cameo and gemstones for the rings of the wealthy, and on hundreds of thousands of coins.

Emperors made sure that they were visible to their subjects, even if they could not be physically present, and every city loyally erected statues of the emperor and his family, as did private individuals. If they could not afford a stone or bronze statue or bust, they commissioned a painted portrait. The images of the emperor were copied from a relatively limited set of originals, then copied across the empire. In Hadrian's case, we have about 355 bases of dedications to him, and around 150 of the portraits that stood on them have survived. This is a good haul for a twenty-one-year reign: 130 of Trajan survive, and about 200 of Augustus, who reigned for more than forty years. There are seven main types, all of which show a mild, attentive, reflective, composed, benevolent man in middle life; he seems active, energetic, good-looking and, perhaps, somewhat younger than he actually appeared.

Earlier emperors made revealingly different choices about their portrait images. The emperor Galba represented himself as severe, old, ferocious, a grim disciplinarian, usually frowning or scowling, his face thin and lined. Vespasian is a man of the people, shrewd, benevolent, with laughter lines, a bald, down-to-earth figure, who made no concessions to fashion or culture: he didn't pretend to aristocratic power, but to practical ability and straightforward merit. Augustus affected an Alexander the Great look, with a swept-aside forelock, deep-set eyes focused on the far eastern horizon, gazing into vistas of what the future could offer.

The fullest literary account of Hadrian's appearance says that he was 'tall, trim, and strong, with soft, wavy hair, and a beard which he grew to hide natural blemishes in his face'. The beard was the most singular element in Hadrian's portrait that set it apart from earlier emperors' images. Beards were not uncommon, but they had never featured in emperors' portraits. Perhaps Hadrian's beard was that of a soldier. Or maybe it related to his sexuality (though Trajan had been depicted as clean-shaven). Was it Greek? A philosopher's beard? If the latter, it is deeply traditional: Hadrian has moved alongside his Greek contemporaries in adopting the look of six hundred years before.

Generally, the older an emperor, the more prestige he could expect. The really bad ones continued to indulge in the vices of youth – pleasure-seeking, anger and impetuosity. Looks mattered – it was believed that character was reflected in the face. When twitching, limping, dribbling, stammering Claudius became emperor, he was laughed at and sidelined from public life by his family.

An individual's luck also determined whether or not he was worth backing. Good luck was not thought to be arbitrary, but a gift. Those who had succeeded largely by luck were considered likely to go on being lucky: they must be favoured by the gods. A person with a lucky streak was good to have around.

By comparison with his predecessors, the chances were high that Hadrian would be a good emperor. Fifty-one was quite old (and he was strikingly grey-haired) but not so old as to make sudden death likely. In fact, his age implied experience and the wisdom that went with it. No one was in any doubt about his intellectual acumen, and when his character was summed up for posterity, it featured prominently, in the formal contemporary accounts of him, the more popular summaries of his horoscope and the oracles that were supposed to have predicted his reign: 'He will be excellent in every respect, and think everything through'; 'thoughtful and well-educated'; 'he will make up for his deficiencies by being careful, far-sighted, magnanimous and adroit' were some of the soothsayers' verdicts.

Other ancient voices speak of Hadrian. The historian Dio tells us that 'he was a really attractive man to meet, and had a real magnetism', while Tertullian, the Christian polemicist, asserts that he was 'the investigator of everything odd'. His biographer reveals his capacity to 'recite from memory books that he had just read, even ones that most people had never heard of'.

A contemporary description of his character declares that:

His was a complex personality, with many strands which took different forms. He had a natural ability to make detached decisions about good and bad behaviour, and could control his feelings by deliberate effort. He cleverly concealed a temperament which was jealous, harsh, libidinous and fixated on showing off. Instead he affected self-control, easy manners and kindness, and kept in check the passion for success which was his dominant feeling. When teased, he answered with real opprobrium.

Another author says he was obsessed with detail, inquisitive and interfering. He retained a childish passion to know more about everything, and be the best at everything he did. He hunted without regard for his own safety, priding himself on killing lions and boars – he broke his collarbone on one occasion, and nearly lamed himself on another.

One of the late Roman biographies of Hadrian lists the accomplishments in which he sought to excel so as to be 'more Athenian than the Athenians' whom he so much admired: singing, both accompanied and unaccompanied, medicine, music, geometry, painting, and sculpture in bronze and marble. The biographer was surprised by the number of accomplishments, and so were Hadrian's contemporaries.

The upper classes found paid work demeaning. Almost anything that required manual dexterity was beneath them, except fighting and agriculture. Certain artistic skills were ambiguous, and of them music, which had always been integral to religious rites, and had been incorporated into philosophical theories of the universe and how to understand it through the study of harmony, was the most respectable. Hadrian's musical abilities were only suspect because music remained a Greek speciality, and because musical talent was uncommon in the Roman upper classes. Mathematics went closely with music, but Hadrian's skill in geometry was perhaps more likely to be connected with his architectural penchant – a less acceptable intellectual taste. Beyond an intelligent concern with planning and its costs, the choice of amenities and adornments, a patron was not expected to become involved in bricks and concrete. The arts that Hadrian is said to have picked up early, sculpture and modelling, lay in a grey area: most artists who did these things were of middling status unless they broke through to celebrity level when their work was hailed as the greatest of the time. But there was a tradition of respectable people who had done these things, reaching back to Socrates, the most famous of classical Greek philosophers.

It is in an anecdote about his architectural interests that Hadrian best reveals his obsessiveness and vindictive self-esteem. His taste was modern. Traditional architecture used columns in long rows and flat ceilings. But new building materials, especially poured concrete, were making it possible to experiment with vaults and domes, and the problems of how to design and build with the new curvilinear forms fascinated Hadrian. He liked to sketch cusped and lobed constructions that resembled fruit and gourds.

Consider this scene at the imperial residence in Rome. Trajan is closeted with his favourite architect, a distinguished Greek from Syria, Apollodorus of Damascus. They are discussing some of the many gigantic and intricate architectural projects with which Trajan was making an indelible mark on Rome. The great patron takes an interest in the work he has commissioned, and for which he is paying. He respects and listens to the best available expert, who has a craftsman's status. Both parties know their place. In comes Hadrian. We can suppose that as a relative he has free access to the most private parts of the imperial palace complex on the Palatine Hill. As yet, though, he is not a certain successor. Anyway, he offers a casual comment on the architectural matters under discussion. Apollodorus is not impressed: 'Go and draw your pumpkins. You don't understand this sort of thing.'

Twenty years later, Hadrian, now emperor, still felt aggrieved by Apollodorus' insult. At this time the huge temple he had commissioned to make his mark on Rome was in progress. It was dedicated to Venus, the goddess from whom Romans were descended, and to the divine spirit of Rome itself, and it was to be the biggest temple in a city of huge temples, with gigantic statues of both goddesses. It was Hadrian's idea, and he had drawn the plans. No pumpkins, this time, so he sent them to Apollodorus to show he could do other things too. Back came the answer – which no one else had dared to give: the colossal statues were way out of proportion. If you imagined the divine ladies getting to their feet from their thrones, they'd go through the ceiling. This was the last straw. It was too late to change the building. Hadrian, humiliated, ordered Apollodorus' death.

But the pumpkins had an important future. Hadrian used complex lobed vaults and domes freely as a major feature of his villa at Tivoli, and it was this style of architecture that produced the greatest of Roman buildings, his Pantheon. In the sixth century, Justinian built Constantinople's own Pantheon, the great domed Church of the Divine Wisdom, Aghia Sophia, to show that his Christian capital could outdo pagan Rome. A millennium later, when Constantinople had become Istanbul, Suleiman the Magnificent built great domed mosques to show that Islam could outdo Christian church architecture. Thus, the centrally planned mosque with its stone dome has a pedigree that reaches back to Hadrian's doodles.

Hadrian could be unpredictable. The greatest doctor of his age, Claudius Galen, recounts how he lost his temper with one of the clerks in his entourage and struck him in the face with a pen in his hand. The clerk lost an eye. Later Hadrian repented and offered the man substantial compensation. All he wanted, the clerk said, was his eye. Even emperors could not achieve complete detachment from the consequences of their actions, and those around them were not always entirely subservient – occasionally they answered back.

Hadrian's dominant characteristic, though, was his interest in everything around him. He was passionately interested in detail, desperate to master things he didn't know about already. And he had an extraordinarily good memory. The curious thing is that the attributes we think would have been commendable in a man governing an empire the size of Hadrian's were regarded by the authors who wrote about him almost as disabilities – that he understood the tax system, for example, was considered not quite the thing for an upper-class Roman.

A senator who was clearly in awe of Hadrian wrote of his love of music, and that he was a hearty trencherman with a taste for rich food. But Hadrian was often, if not always, lacking in humour, particularly in competition, and he did not suffer fools gladly. And his practice of using military messengers to spy on his friends was much resented. He opened private letters, and freely discussed their contents with the recipients. Here is a compulsive, omnivorous egotist who has to know it all.

Hadrian comes across as a loner, a difficult person to live with, even without the constraints and pressures of being Roman emperor. We know little about his wife, but Sabina's life seems to have been unenviable. An imperial couple did not have to live on top of each other, and Sabina managed a household of her own, although she accompanied the emperor on his travels. Hadrian found her gloomy and prickly, and was quoted as saying he would have divorced her had he been a private citizen. But the emperor had to have a wife, and he did not want the bother of finding a new one. When she died in 136, there were those who thought it suicide, induced by the 'abuse almost of the sort that a slave might experience', which Hadrian was said to have inflicted.

A set of school exercises in translating Latin into Greek includes a series of dialogues involving Hadrian. Most were routine exchanges between the emperor and plaintiffs or defendants in the law-courts, or petitioners for favours. But one is a letter from Hadrian to Trajan's widow Plotina in the warmest of terms:

Be cheerful, best and dearest mother: as you pray to the Gods on my behalf, so I do on yours. Your sense of duty and modesty accomplishes everything. I'm delighted, all the same, by Hercules, that my actions are all pleasing and praiseworthy in your eyes. Mother, as you know, today is my birthday, and we should dine with each other, turn and turn about. If you'd like to, then, come in time with my sisters after your bath. Sabina has already started for the villa, but has personally sent a present. Make sure you come quickly, so that we can celebrate this happy day together.

Hadrian's adoption by Trajan made Plotina a second mother, and gave him a new sister in Matidia, neither of whom lived long into the reign of the man they had helped to the throne. Their deaths must have left Sabina isolated, and in a delicate position. Less than five years after his accession, Hadrian – then on the tour that brought him to Britain – dismissed a number of prominent courtiers, including the commander of the body-guard and the chief secretary, 'because their relations with Sabina had been more familiar than the etiquette of the court house-hold required'. This sounds like the wording of the official announcement, and we have no idea what it conceals. The chief secretary in question was in fact Suetonius, whose book *The Twelve Caesars* recounted many of the personal foibles of the first emperors.

Like all emperors and kings in antiquity, Hadrian had a circle of courtiers who were called his friends and companions, members of the imperial council, which included the most senior and responsible officials, such as the commander of the praeto-rians and the prefect of the city of Rome. Most emperors had a few intimate friends among the circle of courtiers, and occa-sionally outside it. Hadrian's brother-in-law, Servianus, came closest, but they had fallen out in Germany in 97, and Hadrian eventually put him to death. Hadrian the intolerant, perfectionist, talented, self-absorbed, critical, versatile, dissatisfied, emotional emperor cuts a rather lonely figure. His most intimate connec-tion by far was with the beautiful young man he met on his travels in the east, Antinous, whom he loved deeply, and whose mysterious drowning in the river Nile has intrigued commenta-tors ever since it took place.

II
ROME

At Rome Hadrian rebuilt the Pantheon, the voting-enclosure, the basilica of Neptune, very many holy temples, the Forum of Augustus, the Baths of Agrippa, and dedicated them all under the names of their original builders.

HISTORIA AUGUSTA

In spring 118, Hadrian came from the east into Italy. He crossed the Alps into the plains around the Venetian lagoon, and headed south for the capital of the empire. His formal entry into Rome and reception by the Senate and people took place in early July.

The Rome he had been brought up in, the capital where he was now emperor, was the largest city in the world. The Mediterranean coastline and the rest of Europe ruled by Rome contained hundreds of cities. Most had populations of up to a few thousand, but there were several huge centres: Carthage, Rome's capital in Africa, near where Tunis is today; Ephesus in western Turkey; Córdoba in southern Spain; and Antioch, in north Syria, where Hadrian had heard about his promotion. Alexandria, capital of the province of Egypt, had half a million inhabitants, but Rome far exceeded it, with around a million.

Over four centuries, Rome had been the base for the conquest and assimilation of the gigantic empire Hadrian had inherited. No other city could provide a better foundation for the legitimacy of a new ruler against political doubts or murmurings. Hadrian took a rapid decision on how to make clear that he and Rome were inseparable ideas. He set in motion a plan for the biggest temple ever built in the city, the temple to the two goddesses Venus and Rome which led to his quarrel with the architect Apollodorus. The site was cleared. This involved moving a hundred-foot-high statue of the emperor Nero in the guise of the sun-god and twenty-four elephants were pressed into service. The colossus was placed between the new temple and the great amphitheatre for gladiatorial games built forty years before – which was how the structure got the name by which it is still known, the Colosseum. On 21 April 121 the dedication ceremony was held (the temple wasn't finished for another fifteen years). The date was the Festival of Shepherds, and it was chosen because that was the birthday of the city of Rome. Hadrian knew his history and his popular tradition: he wanted to show anyone who was inclined to sneer at his family home in the far west of the empire how much he valued the empire's heart and its core traditions.

Most people knew that Rome had conquered the world. They knew when their own area or people had come under Roman rule, and whether their ancestors had co-operated or resisted. Some dreamed of an alternative, but by Hadrian's time most took the empire for granted. The Romans liked to claim that their city and power were invincible and everlasting. Most people probably agreed – the rise of Rome, when they looked at it, seemed predestined and inevitable. The story reached back to the age of the epics and myths of Troy. When the Greeks sacked Troy, the Trojan prince Aeneas (son of the goddess Venus) led a band of Trojan refugees to safety in Italy. It was their descendants who had founded Rome, in the year 753 BC, when what seemed a steady six-hundred-year ascent to universal dominion began.

The Romans told an unsettling story about their own foundation. The founders of Rome, Romulus and Remus, were shepherds – and shepherds were feared in antiquity, rough and uncouth, living in the wilderness, a byword for semi-savagery. Of divine birth – their father was Mars, the god of violent war – the twins had been thrown into the river Tiber because their mother was unmarried. Washed up on the bank, they were suckled in a cave by that most savage of animals, a she-wolf. The twins gathered together a gang of shepherds and runaway slaves – the most villainous element in that part of Italy – and on 21 April 753 BC, founded a new city, Rome, on the hilltop above the she-wolf's cave, with Romulus as king. But Romulus killed his brother in a rage when Remus jumped over the sacred boundary of the new city.

The uncouth shepherds and fugitives were all men. Where to find the other half of the population? Romulus invited the neighbours to a religious festival. Directly afterwards, on a prearranged signal, the Romans seized the women and carried them off – the Rape of the Sabine Women.

This might be fictional, but it is a curious set of tales for Romans to choose to tell about their origin. It contrasts with Greek foundation stories in which cities were founded in heroic circumstances, with valiant deeds on the part of the founder and uplifting interventions by the gods. It's not hard to suspect that it was intended to repel and frighten – these were not people to mess with.

The river Tiber is a key element in the Romulus saga, and it was the secret of his city's success. Rome was one of only a few cities in the ancient world on a major river. Rivers were generally dangerous – both to health and to property when they flooded at the end of winter. Also, few people in antiquity could swim. But the navigable river Tiber gave Rome communications that outweighed its disadvantages. The headwaters of the river and its tributaries covered a huge part of west central Italy and, twenty miles away, the Tiber's mouths (the Roman name was Ostia, which means just that) gave easy access to the sea.

In the eighth, seventh and sixth centuries BC, the Mediterranean was teeming with travellers: sailors, raiders, mercenaries, traders, explorers, pirates, holy men, craftsmen, Greeks, Phoenicians and Etruscans. The banks of the Tiber, at a safe distance from piratical trouble, were just the place for an entrepôt which would be a gateway for all that part of Italy to the humming economies of the Mediterranean rim. The river itself was an artery of communication, and its mouths attracted ships on all the trade routes of the western Mediterranean. The harbour area was thriving already in the sixth century BC. Here stood a wooden bridge, always rebuilt ceremonially to the original design, without the use of metals, a crossing-place of the river as old as the city and as important as the river for communications. By this crossing, the ancient Salt Road took the vital product of the Tiber-mouth saltpans up into the interior, where it was essential for the pastoral economies of all the mountain-dwellers. Salt was a key commodity in the ancient world, and so significant at Rome that they used the word 'salt-money' for army pay – *salarium*, which gives us 'salary'. In Hadrian's time, barges and rafts brought produce downstream to Rome: building stone, firewood, bricks from the riverside claybeds, foodstuffs of every kind. Oxen pulled riverboats against the current from Ostia, bearing all the cargoes of Mediterranean trade, transhipped from seagoing vessels. The river harbours and their huge warrens of warehouses were now one of the wonders of the city. The largest of these warehouses, the Galba complex, had more than 360 storerooms round three immense courtyards, each 140 metres by 185.

The valley of the Tiber was about a kilometre wide at this point, and bounded by steep-sided rocky hills cut into by deep little valleys opening on to the Tiber floodplain. These spurs were thirty to forty metres above the plain, and flat-topped: not very grand scenery, but these eminences became the symbol of the city, the famous Seven Hills. Their tops were waterless and the soil was thin. The clays of the valleys and Tiber plain were more fertile but prone to waterlogging: there were numerous springs in the hillsides, and natural drainage was poor. The first inhabitants of Rome farmed the land around the city, but it was not as a rich agrarian metropolis that Rome grew in size and wealth. It was the control of the river- and land-routes that transformed its economy and society from the start.

By 500 BC, the Romans had built an impressive city wall and several smart temples, culminating in the astonishing Capitol, the temple to Jupiter, Juno and Minerva, which stood on a giant platform on the hill above the river harbour, and rivalled the biggest temples of the Greek world.

In the story the Romans told, this was the moment when they decided that they had had enough of the kings who had ruled them since Romulus. They set up a system in which the kings' power was divided between two aristocrats, called consuls, elected for only one year, who would stop each other getting too regal. They and other less powerful officials were elected by the people, and advised by a council of ex-officials, the Senate – which means, literally, the Council of Elders. This was so stable and effective a system that it lasted essentially unchanged until the emperors took over nearly half a millennium later. And in fact, in a certain sense, it was still there in the age of Hadrian. Hadrian's own career shows how many ancient senatorial offices survived. The consulship continued to be influential and eagerly sought after. The people were still an important idea, in symbol and constitutional theory. The voting-enclosure where they had once elected officials was one of the grandest *piazze* in Rome, and was lavishly rebuilt by Hadrian, though nothing like democracy now survived. The famous acronym SPQR (*Senatus Populusque Romanus*, the Senate and People of Rome) summed up the Roman state.

During the five hundred years that followed the fall of the kings, some people held the consulship more than once, and others became extra powerful by being more successful at war. As Rome sent more armies into the field, and further away, two consuls were no longer enough. Extra generals with special responsibilities – perhaps for a particular campaign – were added, the proconsuls. Their special field was called a province, and this was the origin of the sub-divisions of the Roman empire. Some proconsuls were hugely successful, but they were always curbed by the law that dictated that power must be surrendered at the end of each year.

That principle was not popular with ever more ambitious Roman statesmen, and when it was eventually abolished, the state altered for ever. It happened like this. Julius Caesar and Pompey came head to head in a struggle for political mastery. Civil war broke out. Caesar won, and turned himself into a kind of monarch (although not an emperor), but when he was assassinated, war again broke out between the two men who called themselves his political heir, Mark Antony and Augustus. In 31 BC Augustus finally defeated Antony, even though he was backed by the diplomatic, military and economic clout of his lover Cleopatra, queen of Egypt. Now without effective rivals, Augustus found ways of making all sorts of different powers and rights permanent, and so invented the office of emperor. The job of proconsul – now held by emperors for life, and giving them direct control of almost all the armies – remained at the core of the monarchic system.

And as Roman armies won more and more battles, and Rome's conquests included first of all Italy, then the whole Mediterranean and much of Europe, the capital naturally went on growing. By the time Hadrian inherited that monarchic system and made his ceremonial entrance to the city, Romulus' city had been developing for about eight hundred years.

Rome was shaped by its site, literally, since it was built out of it. People dug into the soft rock of the hills, quarried the stone to build with, and made sun-dried brick from Tiber clay. Even the venerable temples were made of terracotta, local stone and wood, rather than the shining marble used in Greek architecture, which the Romans only began to admire in the second century BC. This was why Augustus wanted to turn Rome from a city of brick to one of marble, and the huge sums he spent on public buildings made his claim plausible. In Hadrian's time another revolution had happened: brick was now fired in kilns, which made it indestructible. There was masses of marble too, brought from the furthest corners of the empire, but Rome was now brick again – and the massive remains of the ancient city today are mostly built of this kiln-fired brick.

By the end of the fourth century BC, fortifications eleven kilometres long surrounded all the canonical Seven Hills. The walls had last been used defensively in 83 BC in a civil war; since then the population had gone on growing, and they were mostly invisible under what a visiting Greek called Rome's 'endless urban sprawl' (the fortifications that are so impressive a feature in today's Rome were built more than a century after Hadrian). No one had ever seen so much city in one place anywhere else. The densely built-up core was only three kilometres or so across, but the city stretched out across the whole region, through cemeteries, ribbon development on the roads, and thousands of suburban villas and farms.

From the hills around, a sea of tiles filled the view, dominated by towering marble temples on every hilltop. The height of the ordinary buildings was overwhelming: the streets were mostly hemmed in tightly on every side by cliffs of plastered brickwork. By Hadrian's time the low-lying floodplain, the Field of Mars, and the district 'Across the Tiber', open space 150 years before, were now occupied with street after street of tenement blocks. These two areas became the heart of medieval and modern Rome, and the remains of the Roman brick tenements are preserved inside many an apparently much more recent structure.

Multi-occupancy tenements were the hallmark of Rome – there were forty thousand, according to lists made in the late empire. This was where most of the million lived, and for this privilege they paid rent to the investors who developed the tenements. For people who had abundant capital, constructing blocks of apartments, called *insulae*, 'islands', for rent was an excellent investment. Land values meant that the blocks were often of seven storeys or more, and each floor was sub-divided into smaller units for rent; even the cupboard-under-the-stairs counted as a unit with letting conditions recognised in Roman property law, which also makes clear that units could be rented by the day. The nicest and most expensive rentals were on lower storeys in good locations, where streets were a bit wider, or on a hill, which allowed a breeze in summer. Apart from the spaces under the stairs, the worst location was under the tiles (*sub tegulis*), where it was intolerably hot in summer. Some could afford a roof over their heads for only a short time each year, and probably saved for midwinter. Still, today, the homeless freeze to death in the cold snaps of the Roman January.

The tenement blocks were labyrinthine, and occupation density was high. There was no privacy. If there was water at all, it was from a single tap in the courtyard – and in many blocks the only water would have been the public fountain in the street. Everyone cooked in their apartments – the buildings must have been constantly full of smoke. Waste disposal was left to individuals. Personal hygiene was hard to maintain: 'Dreaming that you have a few fleas on your body or in your clothes, and kill them, is good,' says the dream-interpreter Artemidorus of Daldis. 'But to be teeming with them is not – it predicts a long illness, or imprisonment, or great want, since those are conditions in which fleas abound. Expelling tapeworms at the anus or by the mouth means discovering that close associates have done you wrong. Worms,' he went on to say, 'are a normal inhabitant of the body, but do no harm whatsoever to it.'

The blocks housed cookshops, storehouses, and other commercial premises, all of which brought in streams of outsiders, and the din was appalling. The philosopher Seneca, who had been the emperor Nero's tutor, describes what it was like living over a small neighbourhood bath-house:

The more energetic are working out, lifting weights. What groans! They're either working hard or pretending to – puffing and heavy panting as they let out their breath. Or there is the lazier type, not too proud for the kind of massage you get in this sort of place, and I hear the slapping of hands on back changing tone from sticking-out to curving-in bits. The last straw is the ball-player, counting out his throws. Now add catching a clothes pilferer or a shoplifter, and the man who likes the sound of his own voice in the bath, and the characters who leap into the pool with a huge splash of slopped water. At least these all have normal voices. But don't forget the depilator, whining non-stop in a nasal flute how much better his service is – the only time he shuts up is when he's plucking hairs and making someone howl. Or the different calls of the drinks-vendor, and the salami-man, and the pie-seller, and all the tavern hucksters crying their wares, each with his own trademark intonation . . .

The streets were packed, smelly, dirty and dark, confusing, indeed frightening – and dangerous. One visitor's bemused account of the city tells of how unwary outsiders visiting taverns would be lured or driven into the warrens behind, forced to labour for the rest of their lives as slaves at the mills or ovens of the great bakeries that prepared bread for handing out to the poor.

It is often a mistake to apply modern standards of amenity to the distant past, but these conditions seemed awful even to the Romans. Yet premises in buildings like these were all that even quite well-off people could afford. Only the super-rich could buy enough ground to build a family house (the lists counted some 2000, which would offer one each for senators plus enough for 1400 or the 1800 inner-circle men of the equestrian order). The most expensive houses were on the hilltops, especially the Quirinal and Esquiline, because they were cooler in summer, or in the suburbs, where life was quieter and the houses more spacious.

The main feature of a traditional house was a large square space mostly covered except for an opening in the centre. This was the *atrium*, and the family hearth was here. It was the symbolic focus (the Roman word for 'hearth' is *focus*) of the house, which was reinforced by the *lararium*, the shrine of the deities of the building and the family, the *lares* and *penates*, and, in an aristocratic house, by a cupboard with busts of the ancestors. The front door led from the street into the *atrium* through a vestibule. This was often the only way in, and policed by a slave – if you were rich enough to have one. Alongside the *atrium* and entranceway there was a substantial reception room, and at least one dining room, some small bedrooms, and a kitchen, store-room and vegetable gardens were tucked away behind the *atrium*. This layout could be elaborated by adding extra rooms and, above all, opening up one or more further courtyards, spacious colonnaded enclosures with a fountain and a garden, and more decorated rooms opening off them. Areas behind the final court-yard were reserved as the family corner of the house. As these extensions became more and more ambitious the old *atrium* often became insignificant except for symbolic purposes, such as receiving dependants paying a respectful morning visit.

The town-house looked entirely inwards. There were few external windows: light came from the *atrium* or the courtyards. Only a few houses – and some public baths – used glass in the windows, usually in tiny panes contained in lead frames. Although it was available, glass was expensive and did not come in large sheets. Most people had shutters over their windows. The street frontages could be fitted up as shops, workshops, or taverns, sometimes brothels. The rent from premises of this kind could be substantial.

Traditionally, the interior was simple: to the Romans the name *atrium* meant 'the smoke-blackened room'. But increasing wealth, and the huge expansion of affordable consumables, meant that it became normal for many houses to contain abundant furni-ture and textiles. It was also normal to plaster the walls and paint them with architectural *trompe l'oeil*, or landscapes, or with figured scenes from literary myth or daily life. Bright paints derived from mineral pigments were available, and at the top end of the scale of sophistication, people displayed exotic colours and rare minerals for their own sake. Terracotta red was one of the favourite backgrounds; glossy black and rich yellow ochre were popular too. A pale sky blue featured commonly, and, in smaller quantities, a much brighter blue made from lapis-lazuli, and a vivid, fiery red derived from mercury ores (*minium*). Painted walls became normal in town, and even poor premises had cheap decorative schemes, sketchily executed in inexpensive colours.

Ancient interiors – temples as well as houses – depended as much on fine textiles, which could be even more expensive. It is mainly from painted, illusionistic interiors that we can sometimes glimpse what the brightly coloured and intricately woven drapes, curtains and awnings might have looked like.

Garden art was closely related to other aspects of interior design, extending rooms and colonnaded walks with rows of trees and shady groves: the summer heat in the Mediterranean made plane trees popular, and richer gardens were full of statuary – cupids strangling geese, deformed children, mythological tableaux. Water was another essential feature. One idea was to have light reflected from water basins in the gardens so that it played over painted walls or richly dyed or embroidered fabrics. The garden offered further places for relaxation and for summer dining. Mediterranean flowers all come together between March and May, and were much admired, but because repeat flowering was unknown, except for certain highly prized roses, they did not form an important element in the garden. In the most careful designs, such as Hadrian's villa, courts and walks were arranged to be at their most attractive in the varying lights of different seasons. Summer and winter dining rooms were arranged respectively for shade and cooling water, or to catch the sun.

The modern idea of domestic space is heavily sub-divided and specialised: dining room, study, kitchen, bedroom, bathroom, and so on. Also, modern Western furniture is traditionally heavy: huge wardrobes, dressers and sideboards, which are not designed to be moved. In traditional interiors the fireplace and chimney-breast are focal points, around which the layout revolves. The logic of Roman furniture was different. It was light, and intended to be portable. The idea was that the family could choose any comfortable and appropriate part of the house for whatever they were currently doing, and whatever they needed could be carried there by the slave staff. Instead of a massive bed that turns a bedroom into the place where you sleep, beds were lightweight and easily moved. They were of a similar shape to a dining couch, with a mattress made from goose feathers or wool. In Hadrian's time a new type of coverlet was designed by a senator close to the emperor: it consisted of a mesh net filled with rose petals, freshly picked from the gardens.

The master could choose where he slept according to the weather or his whim. Slaves usually had no assigned room, but would spread their bedrolls in whichever part of the house the master and his family were not living at the time. Pliny tells of the prophetic dream of one of his freedmen 'who was asleep in the same bed as his elder brother'. Dining was equally flexible. A particular suite would be selected and furniture then carried over there, the couches laid, the textiles and hangings put up. There were no fireplaces: heating came from braziers, and much cooking was done on portable stoves. Only the main kitchens and the baths were purpose-built so that their use was not flexible.

Houses of the traditional type were still common in smaller towns, but in Rome, property values, the constantly changing townscape and different tastes had made them unusual by Hadrian's time. On the one hand, the super-rich had more scope to design spectacular layouts at their country estates, or at select suburban residences on the fringes of Rome, which they called 'market-gardens'. On the other, either in the apartment blocks, which were the normal buildings in the middle of the biggest cities, or in the small gaps between them, ingenious attempts to fit in a nice sequence of designer interiors were as much as even quite affluent people could afford. One beautiful house was built on the flat roof of the huge cisterns that fed Trajan's baths. Many of the two thousand or so spacious detached houses were no doubt very splendid indeed; but here too, as time went on, the traditional *atrium* arrangement tended to be omitted.

Laws prescribed construction standards – building height was limited to seventy feet, for example, and a basic quality was stipulated for timber and brick – but many multi-occupancy developments were little better than shanty towns. (One senator wrote that a building he owned sagged so badly that the mice had left – although the tenants were still paying satisfactorily.) They were also firetraps: every household cooked on charcoal braziers and used olive-oil lamps for light. Conflagrations wiped out large sections of the city in 64, 80 and 191.

If fire didn't get you, the river might. The Tiber was a dangerous neighbour. All the low-lying parts of the city were regularly flooded in winter and spring, when houses collapsed into the freezing, filthy water. The river was also a sewer that was only effectively cleaned in the winter when the flow was strong.

The city had numerous springs and wells, but over the centuries these had been added to by the building of the famous aqueducts that brought rivers of fresh water from the mountains, sometimes from springs as far as seventy or eighty kilometres away. The ingenuity (in calculating gradients), effort (in building arcades for tens of kilometres to carry the water at the right level across the plain) and the cost were outstanding. During Trajan's reign a senator, Sextus Julius Frontinus, commissioner of water, wrote a detailed account of the system, which now had nine aqueducts. He assessed the water supply using a unit of diameter of the lead pipes that drew water off from the aqueduct conduits, clearly hoping for roughly similar flow throughout the system. He gave 14,018 units as the figure for all the aqueducts together, and broke down the usage of this supply as follows:

Delivered outside the city: 4063 units
    to imperial concerns 1718
    to private customers 2348
Delivered within the city, to 247 reservoirs, 9955
    to imperial concerns 1707.5
    to private concerns 3847
    to state concerns 4401
    military bases 279
    75 public buildings 2301

39 ornamental fountains 386
591 cisterns 1335

One of these units amounted to something like 1500 litres per hour, flowing day and night for ever.

This remarkable system mitigated the public-health risks. But much of the water went for display in public places, for fountains or for the baths, and effectively ran to waste: there was never enough to dispose of refuse, or to do much in the way of cleaning so, unfortunately, gastric disease was rife. Even worse, the low-lying plain of the Tiber was malarial, and acute fever was a serious killer until the early twentieth century.

However, aqueducts served some facilities intended to alleviate the problems of sanitation. Communal public lavatories were one of the characteristic features of city architecture in the Roman empire. They were finished to high specifications, and accessible from the colonnades and squares of the city centre; sometimes off the central forum, sometimes in the baths. They could be truly monumental, like the one in a theatre in the city of Side on the south coast of Turkey. It was a vaulted hemicycle, making a curve thirty metres in diameter, with forty or more marble seats arranged along the larger of the two curves. All of these facilities operated in the same way: the seats were arranged over a deep drain, which carried rain or fountain water; running water flowed through a gutter in the floor in front of the seats. Sponges on sticks were made available by the staff, which were dipped into the water flowing through the gutter in front. It is hard to imagine that levels of hygiene can have been very high, or that the water supply can usually have been sufficient to prevent the facility becoming noisome. The strangest thing from our angle, though, is the absence of privacy. These places were only used by men, but it remains odd for us today to think of town councillors and civic officials seated in them side by side.

A few wealthy town-houses had *en suite* lavatories, often finished with marble and beautifully appointed. But these, too, can hardly have been nice to visit: scent might have made the air more attractive, but essentially detritus fell into a hole that was not much more than a cesspit. As a result, lavatories were often put at the ends of the corridors or in cupboards under the stairs. Chamber-pots remained overwhelmingly the most frequent indoor arrangement, and were no doubt convenient, given the flexibility of use of domestic interiors and the availability of slave labour.

Rome's sewers, and above all the Cloaca Maxima, were world famous. And Roman town planning regularly included an impressive drainage infrastructure. The sanitary effect was undoubtedly significant, but the culverts were, above all, storm drains, designed to prevent the torrential rain of the Mediterranean winter from damaging buildings. They were not designed like the great sewers of nineteenth-century London or Paris primarily as a way of disposing of human excrement. And in summer, even the run-off of the aqueducts could not have been sufficient for proper cleaning of the drains. Roman streets must have smelt disgusting.

Human excrement, like animal dung, was in great demand as a fertiliser. Urine, too, had a commercial value: it served as an astringent in preparing cloth and was collected in jars that stood at street-corners. But there were sensibilities about pissing: Artemidorus was not surprised when a man who dreamed that he did so in a full theatre, after the audience had taken their seats, found himself breaking the law.

As for diet, in the country most people ate barley bread or cheap wheaten bread, the equivalent of the black breads of central Europe today; bread from the finest varieties of wheat was expensive. All ancient flour contained grit from the quern, which was seriously bad for the teeth, as skeletal remains demonstrate. The Roman state took some trouble to maintain supplies of affordable wheat for the people of the city of Rome, and the emperors organised a sufficient supply to give up to 200,000 citizen householders around 70 kg of free wheat each month. The dole was not means-tested and didn't go far with a family. Later it was made available in bread, wine, oil, and eventually even pork. But quantities were not intended to surfeit the population, and many, especially women and children, did not get enough. Infants suffered from vitamin-deficiency disorders such as rickets. Disease strikes any undernourished population hard.

Despite the doles, money was essential for rent, sufficient food, clothing – even the poorer-quality tunics or dresses of the poor were quite expensive. The emperors took responsibility for minting: the money supply could not be left to anyone else. There were two precious metal coins: the *aureus*, a valuable gold piece, and the *denarius*, a silver one, also of considerable worth. Most transactions, however, were carried out in the extensive range of bronze and copper coins, which were produced in large numbers. The chief bronze coin was the *sestertius*. The *denarius* was worth four *sestertii*, and the *aureus* twenty-five *denarii*.

Prices were variable, according to local availability and overheads. Rome had the reputation of being particularly expensive. A *sestertius* would buy 1.6 kilograms of wheat, or a loaf and a bit; a litre or so of cheap wine; or two goes with a whore.

It would cost someone

~ eight *sestertii* to buy forty litres of wheat in Egypt (enough for one person for a month)
~ four *sestertii* to pay the executioner to put a slave to death
~ 600 *sestertii* to buy 'a slave-girl of not specially good reputation, the sort that sits around in the slums'
~ 1000 *sestertii* for a quarter-hectare of reasonable farmland
~ 2500 *sestertii* for an adult female slave
~ 2000 to 10,000 *sestertii* for a reasonable tomb.

You could earn

~ 4000 *sestertii* a year as a soldier in the praetorian guard
~ 1200 *sestertii* a year as a private in the legions
~ 576 *sestertii* a year as a skilled worker in a mine or quarry.

Sometimes the emperors distributed gifts of cash, which offered huge numbers of people much-needed help. In Hadrian's time the average amount handed out was more than thirty million *sestertii* a year. On the occasion of his adoption of an intended heir at the end of his reign, he gave three hundred thousand to the people of the city and to the army. But normally money had to be earned.

Casual labour was paid by the job or by the day, and eagerly sought after. The city offered plenty of employment in service industries of every kind – although slaves provided much of the labour in these areas – and in building. An inventor offered the emperor Vespasian a revolutionary new crane – which he rejected because it would put so many needy men out of a job. Day labour in building was all that kept thousands of Romans from destitution, but a range of other work was available: professions recorded on Roman tombstones include slave merchant, dealer in bronze and iron, paint retailer, first midwife of her city district, butcher, grain and pulse wholesaler from the Middle Stairway, fruit-seller and sole-maker. Work was regulated. You couldn't work on a festival day, or when a disaster had happened, such as the death of a member of the imperial family; then people were told to stop working, and officials went through the streets to make sure the shops were closed. Similarly, on festival days, it was against religious law to work.

If someone couldn't find work, they could always borrow. Debt was everywhere and, thanks to the penalties for insolvency, a serious worry for city-dwellers. Interest rates were astronomical; the slightly better-off were often heavily indebted to the state. At the beginning of his reign, in a display of magnanimity, Hadrian burned the tax arrears in the forum so that everyone knew their debts to the state had been cancelled. People relished this visible display and trusted in the good faith of the emperor that their record had been among those destroyed.

If you could no longer afford to borrow, there was begging. In Rome, the five places where bridges crossed the Tiber were favourite spots. But able-bodied beggars made decent slaves, so this was a risky strategy (the free were constantly at risk from slave dealers – on an Aegean island a law had once prohibited women from walking around, so much at risk were they of being kidnapped by slave-dealing pirates). And there were more desperate measures. Crime and burglary was an ever-increasing problem in Rome. There was a high level of daily violence – muggings were common. Less illegal, but often no less violent, was trying your luck at the opportunities offered by tavern life – betting, especially on chariot-races and other forms of gambling.

The first bars and cookshops were linked with the baths, and were a perk for city populations, a way of sharing a watered-down version of the life of the rich. Wine mixed with water was drunk by the customers in an echo of an upper-class dinner. Here they enjoyed versions of the entertainment that went with those dinners too – dancers, entertainers, prostitutes and games of chance. To stock and sell wine, cooked meat and simple foods required some capital and premises: premises meant rent. The street-corner tavern was one among many small businesses run with the backing of richer people who made money out of them. The staff were usually ex-slaves, and the clientele the poor (slave, ex-slave and free) of the neighbourhood. What was sold came from the estates of the people who owned the properties, so they gained there too. Graffiti on the walls of these taverns include 'Successus the weaver loves the landlady's maid', and 'I had it off with the landlady'. Women were prominent in the taverns, which were often hard to distinguish from brothels.

Over the centuries, the tavern developed a life and style of its own that appealed to the upper class too. Going the rounds of the bars and picking fights from which they had to be rescued was a pastime of some emperors. Just as quite well-to-do people had to live in apartments, so they did not always turn up their noses at the fare offered in taverns. The emperor Claudius had not been prominent for most of his life before he became emperor, and intervened when the Senate was discussing the regulation of meat and wine sales: 'Who can live without a bite of fast food?' He went on at length about the old taverns in which he had been a regular in his days as a private citizen.

The dice-game *alea* was controlled by law because it was recognised as a source of potential tension and disorder. But this was not a huge deterrent, and the favourite form of gambling was a game for two players called *tabula*, a combination of ludo and backgammon, which involved throwing dice and moving pieces accordingly. It often ended in bloodshed. Artemidorus, the dream-interpreter, said that a dream of dicing meant that one would quarrel over money. But it was not bad to dream of children playing knucklebones because they played all the time.

The boards often bore inscriptions, which contained all sorts of ribald abuse that players hurled at each other as they played. The most common of the phrases was, '*Ludere nescis*', 'You don't know how to play'. Just occasionally the inscriptions showed some awareness of political issues. One board declaims, 'The Parthians have been killed, the Britons have been conquered, Romans play on.'

The sheer number of people was the biggest problem. By Hadrian's time, ten square kilometres of people on top of each other competing for resources and opportunities, many with too little to do, was bound to produce conflict. Apart from a few main streets and the zones of public monuments, Rome was a tangle of alleys, stairways, ramps, bridges, tunnels, level on level of architecture and temporary additions, all teeming with people. There was a clear law on the boundaries between public and private, but in conditions like these it was impossible to enforce. People set up booths, huts and stalls, blocking access and movement along the streets. Periodically they would be swept away by officials – Domitian's court poet hailed one such clearance, 'Rome is restored to itself' – but they always returned. Because of the congestion, wheeled vehicles, except the light carriages used by the women of the imperial family and the vestal virgins, were not allowed in the city during the day.

Even in the free-standing houses of the rich, there was little privacy. A household with four hundred slaves did not have a similar number of bedrooms, so the slaves spread their bedrolls in attics, store-rooms, sculleries and cellars. Another court poet of Domitian, who was a specialist in obscenity, imagined Helen of Troy and her abductor Paris making love while the slaves peered in and masturbated at the spectacularly erotic show. The senator who owned the house was probably a great urban landlord, and not averse to letting his street frontage for shops, bars or brothels. Social zoning was as yet undeveloped.

Life was tough, and people were materialistic and bloody-minded. Aggressive self-help, encouraged by the dangers and difficulties of urban life, might involve magical assistance, such as placing a curse on an enemy. Anyone could do this, or cast a spell, but the material on which the curse was written was crucial to its success. The best were inscribed on gold, but they all had to be written backwards, then nailed to face the wall for only the spirits to read. One lead curse tablet from Rome attacks someone called Malchius fairly comprehensively: 'Eyes, hands, fingers, arms, stomach, penis, legs, income, profit and health: all these things I bind with these tablets.' A curse might improve one's chances in gambling, and it was common to ill-wish horses competing against one's own in a chariot-race.

People saw Rome as a place where friendship was rare and unreliable. Someone wrote on a wall in Pompeii, 'I loathe the poor. Anyone who asks for something for nothing is a moron. If he pays up, he'll get the goods.' Someone else had 'Welcome Profit' written on their hall floor. That was a good omen: anyone who came in was hailed as a herald of good tidings, better times to come, good fortune all round, and profit was a metaphor for this general warm glow. Another revealing doormat slogan was, 'Beware of the Dog': very witty, since although there might really be a guard dog, the 'Dog' was the name of the lowest possible throw at dice. Rome was festooned with good-luck charms: little phalluses protruded from houses, were carved or painted on walls, there were warnings against the evil eye and countless pleas for good fortune. It was all taken very seriously. In an army roll-call, for instance, it was important that the first name read out was a well-omened one, such as Salvius (safety) or Valens (good health). Bad luck was a terrible scourge.

Yet people still felt that something could be had for nothing. After all, there were handouts. Some thought that state or private generosity led to idle, truculent crowds, but the emperors knew they could not afford to stop providing cash, food and distractions if they wanted to avoid riot and maintain the prestige of their capital. In Hadrian's lifetime, emperors set up complex relief schemes, which at least advertised their concern for poverty in Italian towns. Local landowners mortgaged their estates, and the interest provided a small sum each year for a few dozen poor boys and a smaller sum for poor girls.

The Roman state was suspicious, and tried to prevent potentially seditious gatherings. In one of Pliny's letters to Trajan, he asked whether the people of Nicomedia might have a fire brigade. There had been a bad blaze, and most of the locals had stood around watching rather than helping to put it out. Trajan turned down his request. Although some cities did have licensed fire brigades, the Romans did not want to encourage such groups, in case they proved subversive. For all that, there were clubs and societies; some helped with funeral costs (another financial nightmare) or provided annual festivals, and helped in times of need. Some reflected employment, and the infrastructure that supported the city. Trajan licensed an organisation for the bakers of the city, giving them the right to hold meetings and build a clubhouse. This was an innovation: a college of bakers may not sound a radical step, but the Roman authorities were uneasy about any organisation apart from their own. They had to be small in membership and could not meet in secret: their aims and rationale should be straightforward. They had to support the city – like the bakers – and not be in a position to hold it to ransom. There are few accounts of organised labour causing problems for the state, but there was serious protest, almost a revolt, by the key artisans who ran the imperial mint. The trouble started after supervisors discovered that hundreds of workers had been involved in a scheme to devalue the currency by diluting the precious-metal content of the coinage. When the plot was discovered, the workers ran riot and were joined by local inhabitants. On the whole, though, the professional associations were a success, as far as public order was concerned. They acquired high-ranking patrons who could pass petitions up the chain of authority and acted as benefactors in other ways.

However, the emperor did not rely on the good will of his subjects. Compared with the concentration of soldiers elsewhere in the empire, Rome was a military zone. The élite praetorian guard, twelve thousand strong, had a fortress on the outskirts of the city. Its main function was to protect the emperor, but it also helped keep order in the city. There were units of lower-status troops specifically for the job of keeping order, the urban cohorts; and the numerous watchmen (*vigiles*), recruited from ex-slaves, who policed the city by night, and dealt to the best of their ability with fires – mainly through demolishing buildings in the path of the flames. In this empire armed force was prominently displayed, and most of all in the capital city. The population density was reflected in the heavy provision of soldiery. Most other cities employed security personnel to patrol the wilder boundaries of their territory and control banditry.

Some associations were neighbourhood-based – little societies that gave their members a sense of belonging and protection. The inhabitants of a particular tenement block, the residents around a certain public monument or crossroads, made contributions to and felt secure in being part of an official local organisation. The names of some neighbourhoods give a vivid picture of the scenery: 'At the Sign of the Grass-eating Elephant', 'Fountain of the Four Fishes', 'Oak-Grove Street' and the 'Face of Africa'. The state recognised these street-corner arrangements:

ward officials were appointed, and were expected to demonstrate their loyalty to the emperor by leading worship in honour of the domestic gods and the emperor. The officials reflected the composition of the populace: most were ex-slaves, though probably of the more prosperous kind, set up by their former owners as shopkeepers or tavern-owners.

Other associations linked people from distant parts of the empire. Like immigrant communities in modern cities, people from a particular area of the Mediterranean would congregate in a certain neighbourhood. Each Jewish group had its synagogue and, in Hadrian's age, the state was especially suspicious of their intentions – and those of the still closely related Christian groups, which became increasingly ambitious in setting up financial support for their adherents.

The fact was that most residents in this overcrowded, disaster-prone city had not been born there but had moved to Rome – or been moved there as slaves – from elsewhere in the empire. This was one of the main reasons why urban life was so volatile. People from all over the empire, and even from outside it, were kidnapped or sold into slavery by desperate relatives, and ended up on the markets of Rome. So many came from the east Mediterranean that Greek was as commonly spoken in Rome's streets as Latin. But people came voluntarily in large numbers from the rest of Italy, and from every province, near and far. They came in hope and out of opportunism, because it was the capital of the Roman world and home to the emperors: an Eldorado.

The emperor's presence in the city fostered such dreams. Imperial spectacle displayed the status of the home of the conquerors of the world and the exceptional prestige of their ruler. Imperial power made possible all the free entertainment and gifts. Spectacle, prestige, display also meant work – the opportunity to make money. For all the shocking conditions of life in the city, it must have seemed a better bet than what was on offer in the countryside. So much so that Rome went on growing right up to and beyond Hadrian's time, even though disease and accident carried off so many of its inhabitants.

But the terrible living conditions, the difficulty of realising the optimistic prospects that had brought them to the city and, above all, the abnormally high mortality rate meant that people didn't settle. Rome was not a welcoming place for the outsider who wanted to move in and put down roots. Everything indicates a quick turnover of population.

Only the conquest of the world can really explain why Rome attracted so many hopeful immigrants. And only a conquered world could go on for century after century keeping around a million human beings alive in a malarial desert. The world paid tax to Rome. The amounts levied were not high, but extra was often extorted by the collector, and collection was often brutal. The very poor paid no tax, so the burden fell on the rich and the middling. The tribute of the empire, monies paid by those who had been conquered, funded the doles and other amenities, such as the aqueducts. The emperors maintained Rome out of the proceeds of empire: the tribute, indirect taxes on the sale of slaves, customs duties, income from estates, mines and properties. They spent huge sums on the maintenance of their own establishment, which benefited thousands of members of their household. They were also responsible for much of the spectacle the city populace enjoyed.

The emperors recruited new senators and equestrians to the public service from citizen families scattered all over the empire – the practice that had brought the Aelius and Ulpius families to prominence. These people formed an upper class for the whole empire, linked by involvement in government, which brought them to Rome. So, the wealth of prosperous places the world over was spent in the capital – these were the inhabitants of the two thousand free-standing private houses, and many of the best apartments. They spent much time and money in the city. A large proportion of senators were local magnates in self-governing Italian cities, some of which were just an easy day's walk from

Rome, and their wealth was based on estates in the Italian countryside. Pliny, the letter-writing governor who came from Como in the shadow of the Alps, was typical of them: a great benefactor to Como, he also had substantial estates in several other districts and a house in Rome. Much of the senators' wealth was consumed in court and city life, in keeping their place on the ladder of prestige and in helping their *protégés* to do likewise. The opening of the Senate, and the equestrian class, to rich provincial families from everywhere between Spain and Syria meant that patrimonies from all over the empire produced goods to be sold and money to be spent in the capital.

These men and women did more than just spend. To be part of the imperial circle was regarded as a business opportunity. From the emperor down, they were the large-scale landlords who owned most of the property in the city and they could sell their country produce. Private business played a major role in the outpouring of imperial largesse, and the activities of the Italian and provincial élites in Rome. Apart from the risk of dying of malaria or typhoid, life in the empire's capital was a win-win arrangement for the upper classes.

Rome offered a major economic opportunity to the rich as to the poor. The building industry was in private hands and employed the free poor, so the vast sums expended on the creation and maintenance of gigantic building projects boosted the city's economy. Even the officially managed wheat supply was largely in the hands of private dealers and ship-owners. They were partly compelled, partly persuaded with incentives to supply Rome rather than other cities; and only some of the grain consumed in Rome came through official channels.

It was an attractive market, whether you were selling cheap wine or the most expensive luxuries from the Indian Ocean trade. Some of the astonishing array of goods available in Rome made their way out of the imperial bazaar into other trade networks. To the author of the Book of the Apocalypse – also known as Revelation, the last book of the New Testament –

Rome was an image of wanton imperial domination, but also of the corruption that derives from trade:

> the great whore that sitteth upon many waters . . . upon a scarlet-coloured beast full of names of blasphemy, having seven heads and ten horns . . . the seven heads are seven mountains, on which the woman sitteth . . . the waters where the whore sitteth are peoples and multitudes and nations and tongues . . . The merchants . . . which were made rich by her shall stand afar off . . . saying Alas, alas, that great city that was clothed in fine linen and purple and scarlet and decked with gold and precious stones and pearls . . . And every shipmaster . . . and as many as trade by sea stood afar off and cried when they saw the smoke of her burning, saying What city is like unto this great city! . . . Alas, alas that great city, wherein were made rich all that had ships in the sea by reason of her costliness. For in one hour she is made desolate.

Finally, Rome was the last word in the service industry: all the raw materials that were brought here – by the sea-captains of that terrible prophecy – were transformed into the requisites for a life of luxury, or a version of it, which trickled down to the woman in the street. Clothing, theatre sets and props, pipes for the baths, shoes, books and cosmetics, furniture and *objets d'art* all had to be made, repaired and reworked at every level in the social scale. Rome in the reign of Hadrian's successor Antoninus was called 'the common workshop of the world'. Just unloading the ships and moving stuff around kept porters employed.

The life of ordinary people in Rome depended on this economy. They were at the mercy of the trickle-down effect, cash fed into the economy by the conspicuous expenditure of the state and the super-rich, and it was on the availability of this money that the appeal of the city to immigrants was based. But what trickled down was not just the price the élite paid for their way of life: thousands of people could share in it. The inhabitants of Rome had a strong sense of their perks – or 'conveniences', as they were called (*commoda*).

Through the handouts, the poor had access to a token amount of the food and cash of the wealthy. In the theatres, to which admission was free, they shared in the musical and dramatic culture. In the amphitheatre, again free, they watched the hunts that were a leisure activity for the upper-class male, or imitation warfare between gladiators – including real death. At the circus, also free, they could enjoy chariot races, like the ones Homer described at the funeral games of Achilles. In the baths, to which admission was very cheap, they relaxed as the powerful did and not far away from them. Many had enough cash to support the taverns, in which abundant cheap wine was to be had. This was not to be taken for granted in all parts of the empire, and observers commented – critically, enviously – on the mass drunkenness in Rome. Sex was a service readily sold by the needy, and available alongside the wine, the cooked food and the opportunities to gamble in the city bars. The latter were cheap and nasty, and owed their existence to the mass market, even though some members of the upper class used them.

All roads led to Rome, and they all brought in consumables: herbs from the Greek islands, pepper from south India, cloth made from the fibres in sea-snail shells, British mastiffs, Spanish fish-pickle, nine kinds of papyrus from Egypt. The staples arrived in enormous quantities – there is a hill thirty metres high and half a kilometre round composed of just the fragments of the jars that the oil-importers used. When an emperor built a new bath complex, forests in the Italian mountains were earmarked as the fuel supply.

To maintain their economic portfolios and their extensive social commitments, the upper class had to support a large household. Rome was a great slave-market, and the labour force was brought in from other slave-dealing centres by members of the élite whose homes were in distant parts of the empire. And if slaves meant less waged employment to go round, their labour was undoubtedly of some help even to the poor – in the exhausting work of keeping the baths heated, for instance.

All in all, there was nowhere on the planet where so many people could be viewed all together as in Rome during Hadrian's reign. And not for much longer: the plague of the next generation caused great mortality, and Rome's population supply dwindled over the following century. The devastation of civil unrest in the eastern Mediterranean had an effect too. But under Trajan, Hadrian and Antoninus, the city was at its most attractive and successful.

At the same time the people were a wonder in their own right: part of the reason for building vast structures in which as many as a quarter of a million individuals might watch the chariot-races was to show off Rome's vast populace to visitors. Population was a good thing in antiquity, the world still being many centuries off the galloping demographic increases of modern times and the evil of overpopulation; indeed, the display of people suggested abundant manpower that could be translated into military might.

But the size of the population was an accidental windfall of empire. Rome was the seat of the emperor and the symbolic capital of the world, but it was not in the administrative sense a regional capital, let alone a national one. Italy, like the rest of the empire, was ruled from and through its cities. Other cities sprang up close to Rome. Ostia, its port, was a self-governing community. Tivoli and Palestrina, only thirty kilometres away, were quite important.

The direct jurisdiction of Rome as a city covered a surprisingly small area: the territory ruled by the Romans before they started extending their empire (just over 800 square kilometres in 500 BC). The result was that the city was curiously cut off from what lay around it. It had little natural hinterland. And neither this nor the city was governed in any special way – this was Rome's original heartland, and the infrastructure that now ruled the empire had originally been designed to run it.

The running of the empire was in the hands of the emperor and moved with him. So the point of Rome was not to maintain machinery of state, though it held record offices and archives that supported the Senate and its officials, the emperor and his rule. Rather, the purpose of Rome was to sum up in one extraordinary place how unusual and magnificent the enormous empire was. That was why vast sums were spent throughout the imperial period in making the city more and more amazing.

Although the people were an essential act in the show that was the city of Rome, they were upstaged by the buildings. Ancient writers frequently said that cities were people, not walls, but nowhere was that less true than in Rome.

The city was summed up in its monumental architecture, which was symbolic, even portentous: buildings embodying the history of the greatness of the Roman people who lived and worked among them. But above all big buildings: deliberately huge masses of highly finished stone- or brickwork, embellished with every decoration imaginable, gold, textiles, painted stucco, carved woodwork, polychrome marble. The size, height and extent of Rome and its buildings were designed to be stupendous. The architectural repertoire was extensive: temples, theatres, porticos, imperial palaces, functional buildings like granaries or cisterns, markets or warehouses, and in all of them daunting scale was part of the design. Their purpose was spelled out by a third-century historian: 'This architecture is intended to inspire religious veneration in those who feel it is theirs, but it is meant to strike terror into enemies.' And it worked. As the British king Caratacus said, when captured and brought to Rome, 'When you've got all this, why did you want our huts?' He was pardoned.

Earlier in Rome's history, public architecture had been the gift of the politically ambitious and moneyed, but by Hadrian's time this had changed. Senators were not encouraged to rival the magnificence of the emperor and his family in the showcase city: display in the ancient heart of Roman power was enough to over-inflate a senator's prestige.

The city's centre was dominated by the Capitol. Here, in one of the most awe-inspiring monuments in the cityscape spectacle and the pinnacle of all imaginable honour, stood the sanctuary of the gods who had been responsible for Rome's long rise to fame and power, and for her continuing security and prosperity. There were three of them: Minerva, Juno and, above all, the supreme deity of deities, Jupiter, Best and Greatest, Jupiter of the Capitol. The ancient temple built by the last kings had been destroyed by fire, and the shining marble version that Hadrian knew had been built in his youth by the tyrannical emperor Domitian, so that, also, had become an emperor's monument. Beneath it lay the Roman forum, the old marketplace. The emperors had transformed this, too, with dynastic images and histories. The square where Senate and people had met since the beginnings of the city was now dominated by temples of deified emperors. The Senate house had become equally a monument to the emperors, built by Augustus, and only dimly reminiscent of the place where the conquest of the Mediterranean had been debated and planned.

And by Hadrian's time the old forum had been eclipsed by no fewer than four new monumental squares, joining it and extending its spaces and facilities. Many governmental and judicial functions had been moved to these grand colonnaded precincts, full of gold, silver, bronze and marble statues, and flanked by the basilicas, great aisled halls where the law-courts met. One porticoed square fronted the especially magnificent Temple of Peace, which the emperor Vespasian had built out of the spoils of Jerusalem. It housed the sacred objects that had been seized from the temple when the Romans razed it to the ground during their sack of the city in 70. The precinct was planted with ornamental shrubs and filled with masterpieces of Greek art, a centre for culture and learning.

The most magnificent extension to the forum, and the newest when Hadrian became emperor, was another victory monument, Trajan's Forum, which commemorated the conquest of Dacia. The largest basilica in Rome, the Basilica Ulpia, 175 metres long and with a daring roof-span of twenty-five metres, was fronted by a vast square flanked by colonnades decorated with statues of Dacian prisoners-of-war. Behind the basilica were Greek and Latin libraries, and the column, which still survives, was a slender thirty-metre-high tower with a spiral staircase inside that figured reliefs in a spiral band round the outside, depicting the subjugation of Dacia, in all its violent detail.

The marvels of Roman architecture spread out over the whole city. There were more than a hundred important temples, and many public buildings that rivalled them in bulk, height and opulence, such as the Colosseum or the 1000-metre-long Circus Maximus where the chariot-races took place. Another speciality was the massive bathing complexes, which the emperors and their families had built for public amenity, starting with Augustus' son-in-law Agrippa, whose baths Hadrian modernised after 150 years of use. Trajan's other colossal contribution to Rome's grandeur was the Thermae Traiani. No one in Hadrian's time could have imagined outdoing or repeating this magnificence, but before two hundred years had passed, other emperors had built *three* complexes on a similar scale, two of which were deliberately larger than Trajan's, though none was appointed with quite the luxury of Trajan's baths, or built to such a high specification.

Lists of the Wonders of Rome were compiled to impress those who had never visited, or to guide those who did. The Curiosum named the most notable buildings in one of Rome's fourteen city districts:

City District 13 Aventine contains:
The Weapon-purifying Place
The Temple of Diana
The Temple of Minerva
The Three Fountains
The Baths of Sura (Trajan's friend and Hadrian's backer)
Trajan's family house
The Golden Kerchief
The Plane Grove
Warehouses of Galba

Warehouses of Anicius
Portico of the Bean Dealers
Stairs of Cassius
The Bakers' Market
In all: 18 neighbourhoods: 2488 tenement blocks, 130 houses, 35 warehouses, 44 bath-houses, 89 cisterns and 20 bakeries.

Another document lists some of the names of the eighteen neighbourhoods:

> Weapon-purifying Place Ward, Corn-dealers' Street Ward, Three Roads Ward, Caesetius Street Ward, Valerius Street Ward, Milestone Cistern Ward, Lucky Street Ward, Rim of the Jar Ward, Three Birds Ward, New Street Ward, Wooden Pillar Ward, Timberdealers' Ward, Cosmetics Street Ward, and the Ward of the Doubtful Fortune.

It is hard to resist the impression that the emperors' architects read such lists and deliberately tried to add their own work to the existing landscape of miracles.

Certainly Nero's architects had set out in building his Golden Palace to make possible what nature had ruled out. Inverting a perceived natural order was a favourite game of aristocratic builders, both in their private estates and in public projects. Building out over the sea, penetrating mountains with tunnels or cuttings, draining lakes or creating open water where dry land had been, bridging huge distances: all these things were more of a challenge to display Roman power than exercises in practical problem-solving, though the result might be functional too.

Rome was the City Impossible – the place that broke all the records, overturned all the rules, extreme and miraculous. Its buildings played all these games with nature and super-nature. Trajan was especially keen on this form of display – bridging great rivers, building new harbours and canals, planning highways. To create his new forum, he had to excavate a spur of one of the Seven Hills to get enough level ground. His famous column was a marker of how high the hill had been before the emperor's orders abolished it, as well as a record of the war against Dacia and the emperor's last resting-place.

The massive architecture shaped people's experience in other ways too. The buildings, for spectacles, recreation, largesse, leisure, even religion, represented the aspirations that had first brought many to Rome. Their lives depended on them too. The streets were notoriously full of the endless traffic that building generated as something was always being repaired after fire, collapse or flood, or because it was old and crumbling. Local people were involved in every project that went forward: without casual labour in the building industry the urban economy would have ceased to function.

At the centre of it all lived the emperor, his family and his huge household. Augustus had lived on the Palatine Hill. The early emperors could not quite behave as kings, with thrones and too much public adulation: they were supposed to be citizens among other citizens, however exalted their achievements and however absolute their power in practice. But they needed privacy and leisure space. By taking over other houses and by building on, the hill turned into a city within a city, a palace quarter, although it never had a perimeter wall to separate it from the city.

However, access was tightly controlled: the Palatine *had* once had a wall, Romulus' first city-boundary, and there were only a few routes up the slopes; the emperors had the benefit of living in a secure compound without the odium. Within the compound, they presided over an ever-growing staff of specialised freedmen and slaves, in which the keepers of the clothing and the stuffers of the fowl, the imperial pages and the managers of boxers (with responsibility for unclaimed shipping) jostled with the assistant to the accounts archivist of the province of Syria.

The imperial household, the *familia Caesaris*, was organised in a way that reminded everyone that the emperor's main concern was the army. The head of household was the 'manager of the camp' and the household accounts department was the 'camp budget'. Posts were minutely graded and the slaves and ex-slaves who did well went through a career structure of posts – head of the glassware section, promoted to brooches, and ending up as senior butler. The domestic side was minutely sub-divided: a prominent part was connected with the putting on of spectacles, or with the emperor's appearance at spectacles laid on by others.

Here is a snapshot of staff from the palace of Rome during the reigns of Trajan, Hadrian and his immediate successors, mostly taken from their tombstones:

Financial secretaries for the imperial revenues of
   the province of Palestine
   the province of Upper Pannonia
   the city of Alexandria (with responsibility for imperial properties in Egypt)
I/c [in charge] gold drinking service
Assistant to the accounts department of the Thisiduo Fund [province of Africa]
I/c the imperial customs house at Zurich
Records-clerk of the villa at Tivoli
I/c marble procurement
Chief cashier of the warehouses of Galba
I/c Latin letter writing
Deputy head of the religious record department [died on the Danube]
Head chef [the pretentious Greek word actually means archmeatcook]
Assistant in the imperial legacies department
I/c theatrical silver
Footman in the luxury section
Chief clerk for the grain supply at Ostia
Drinking manager, i/c the emperor's own jug, chief butler, head lictor, i/c records of imperial liberality [died in the same place as Trajan a few days later]
Bookkeeper for the province of Arabia ['who went on the

Gallic and Syrian Journeys' of Hadrian]
I/c the infirmary for the bedroom attendants

But shyness about displaying regal airs dwindled with successive emperors and the autocratic Domitian built himself an enormous complex, the Domus Augustana, with a public wing that combined throne room and temple. The façade had a great flight of steps, there was a precinct below where an audience could gather – and be controlled – and it was crowned with a great pediment, like a temple. There was a central portal and looming doors. Inside, hall opened out of hall in axial sequence. The point was to showcase the emperor, to provide an opportunity for him and his family to interact with the people as before but in much more controlled, distant, even ritualised fashion. The court-poets describe the feasts for hundreds of people over which Domitian presided – on a dais, in the apse at the far end of the enormous hall.

Subsequent rulers rejected some of the aloofness and hauteur of Domitian's style because everyone knew that such surroundings corrupted people. Trajan's wife Plotina made a hopeful statement as they ascended the great staircase to the palace doors for the first time: 'I wish to leave this building the sort of woman that I am as go in.' The same building was Hadrian's home, when he was not travelling or at one of the imperial villas in the Italian countryside, above all his great estate at Tivoli.

On one side of the palace complex, then, was its public face, above the road that led down to the forum, the ancient civic centre of Rome, steeped in associations with the distant past. Handily for the emperors, terrible fires had obliterated much that would have impeded the development of a new set of symbols, and the forum had become a forecourt for the palace, full of the emperors' monuments. On this side, in the Palatine precinct, crowds would gather for many imperial occasions. But more people saw the other side of the palaces, which backed on to the valley in which stood Rome's chariot-racing stadium, the Circus Maximus. The whole of one side of this vast building was dominated by the imperial palaces. There were terraces and balconies from which the court could watch the spectacles below (although there was, of course, an imperial box, situated opposite the turning-posts where the most exciting moments of the races tended to happen). The linkage was vital: the palace is part of the circus: the circus belongs to the emperor. After Hadrian, Roman emperors spent more time in other cities, even making them their permanent bases, and they re-created this pairing between circus and palace across the empire.

It was not improvements to the imperial palace that appealed to Hadrian, however, when he was deciding what he should contribute to the metropolis that would make his mark and perhaps even surpass the extraordinary monuments of Trajan. The Temple of Venus and Rome was his first plan. In scale, it was worthy of his ambitions, but it was relatively conventional in design. Much more significant, and not only because it survives in such good condition to this day, was his revolutionary and magnificent temple of all the gods, the Pantheon. It is the most complete building to survive from the ancient city, and one of the most remarkable pieces of structural engineering from antiquity. Nothing like it had ever been built before.

The Pantheon today stands amid a tangle of medieval backstreets. When it was new, it was in the heart of a zone of shining marble architecture, another labyrinthine sequence of columned public squares and walkways, filled with works of art and planted with trees and gardens. For 250 years, wealthy Romans had been adding one portico after another, filled with temples and gardens and famous Greek works of art. The Virgin Water, an aqueduct built by Augustus' right-hand man and son-in-law Agrippa, fed Agrippa's public baths and an artificial lake in front of them, which drained into the Tiber through an ornamental waterway. Immediately alongside, Nero had added an even bigger bath complex in the style of a Greek gymnasium, and much more magnificent. The biggest colonnaded space was the Enclosure, a monumental version of the field where the Roman populace had met in ancient times to vote for their officials. It had painted porticos on either side three hundred metres long; by the second century it had become the headquarters of dealers in luxury furnishings.

The idea of a Pantheon was not new. Augustus had built the first Pantheon in Rome, a piece of the religious one-upmanship in which the Romans specialised. All the gods worth worshipping were to be found in Rome already, or would be added to the list one day, but why not simplify matters and have a temple devoted to the worship of them all? There were twelve especially important gods, but the inclusiveness of the project is strongly suggested by the circular design, which in the case of the first temple took the form of a precinct, rather than a roofed structure, and its implicit intention was to set up an ambiguity between the 'gods' who had built the structure, Augustus and his family, and the gods who received cult there. The sanctuary was intended as a counterpoint to the great complex of funeral pyre and mausoleum that Augustus, thinking ahead at the beginning of his ascendancy, had constructed for himself and his family forty-odd years before he made use of it. Dead emperors were a different sort of god from living ones. The temples in which they were worshipped stood alongside the tombs in which they and their families were buried. All Romans went to family tombs to pay respects to their dead relatives. The family tombs of the emperors were a natural place at which to commemorate the imperial succession.

Augustus had chosen a location on the approach to the city from the north. There, he had built a cremation ground, and a huge tumulus in a sacred garden and grove, rising high above the Tiber. The neighbourhood became a good one for later emperors, no longer connected to the founder of the empire by blood, who liked to be associated with his divinity. This was where the temples of the divine ladies of Trajan's family, Marciana and Matidia, were built. For Hadrian, then, rebuilding this temple offered a link with the founder of the imperial monarchy, and a building whose purpose was to celebrate the place of the divine emperor in the world of the gods. Hadrian took thought for his own future after death, and built a mausoleum in the same vein as Augustus', also on the Tiber bank, although even larger and more beautiful. Its core is now the heart of the medieval fortress of the popes, the Castel Sant'Angelo. But the temple built after his death, which celebrated Hadrian's own divinity, was in the same zone as the Pantheon, and its remains can now be seen built into the Italian Stock Exchange. Somewhere in this area, in all probability, was the Athenaeum, the now vanished arts centre, which was one of his most famous contributions to the Roman scene.

The invention and mass-production of kiln-fired brick and the perfection of building in concrete made it possible for Roman architects to attempt experiments with vaults, which departed completely from traditional Mediterranean architecture. It is clear that the Pantheon was intended to be the ultimate development of this domed style of architecture, which in popular story and in the buildings of the villa at Tivoli was closely linked to Hadrian's own curious taste for architecture and its inner workings. And the dome as it was built was an even better symbol of the lofty messages about the complexity and grandeur of the world of the gods than Augustus' circular precinct had been.

It looks as if Augustus' religious experts had said that a temple like this had to be open to heaven: why else was the famous *oculus*, the opening in the centre of the dome, carefully constructed to let in the weather, necessitating drains beneath the temple floor? And a sphere was an even more special sign of the perfection and all-embracing nature of the godhead than a circle: the Pantheon was constructed so that the dome formed half of the sphere, which if extended would touch the centre of the floor. So that the temple should not look too unlike the normal form of Roman temples, the façade was a conventional pillared portico, with gigantic columns of Egyptian granite, quarried and transported across the desert, down the Nile and across the Mediterranean at enormous expense (it seems that the design called for even larger ones, but they were not available, so the elevation had to be modified as the project developed). This had a further effect of baroque surprise. The drum of the Pantheon was wedged in among other public buildings, and much harder to see than it is today now that it is detached from other structures. It was therefore with a sense of wonder that a visitor passed through the porch and into the part of the building that was not at all like any other temple in Rome.

Once built, the temple was, no doubt, used for worship, but Hadrian and later emperors also used it as an audience hall, confirming that the divine majesty of the emperor was the principle theme to express. It was clearly enormously impressive to contemporaries, and we know of imitations both in Italy and in distant provinces – on a smaller scale. Eventually the Pantheon was surpassed by the introduction of a light structure of timber, with a thin outer casing of roof-material, which was used in the domes of late medieval and early modern churches; and naturally overtaken by the light suspended roofs of steel, which make the largest roof-spans in modern architecture. And in this there is an apt metaphor for the empire as it was under Hadrian: it represented an amazing pushing to the limits of the brute-force techniques available at the time.

The whole structure is simple, awe-inspiring and surprisingly strong. It did not necessarily represent the easiest way of doing things, and it was built as a statement of sheer power. At the same time, it was also typical in that it was both a structure whose like had never been seen before and a piece of reinvented past. This was a bit of Augustus' Rome, and the inscription on the front porch tells a celebrated lie: it claims that Augustus' right-hand man and later son-in-law built it. This confused the history of Roman architecture for centuries. But for Hadrian, it was a wonderful piece of ostentatious self-effacement. You build a structure whose point is to assert your own belonging, as the most powerful man in the world, in the company of the gods and in the tradition of the greatest of your predecessors. And you refuse to put your own name on the front out of respect for the achievements of others and the desire not to appear boastful in the city in which you are posing as a public official rather than the king of kings.

Only this carefully elaborate modesty could produce a still greater return of honour for the project. Finally, the welding together of all the divergent elements in ancient religion into a single system, the theological melding, which was shaping a newly popular sense of the transcendence and unity of the idea of God, was precisely the sort of cult that stood for the empire under Hadrian. It was another take on what he had done at Athens with a religious centre for all the Greeks; and, unthinkable though it would have been to Roman senators and Christian community leaders alike, this was the sense in which religious behaviour was developing across the whole Roman world, little by little making possible that harmonisation of ancient religion with Jewish and Christian tradition and doctrine that we call the Peace of the Church.

III

BELONGING

Hadrian took great pains to behave as one citizen among others in
conversation, even when he was talking to the lowest of the low.
He loathed people who begrudged him this humane hobby on the
grounds that it was important to maintain the imperial dignity.

HADRIAN'S BIOGRAPHER

At the centre of Hadrian's empire lay the monstrous, bloated,
inordinately attractive city of Rome, full of buildings
intended to shock, too large to contain with a city wall. The
centre was the product of the empire it ruled, shaped by all the
lands from which its people came. And the nature of the capital
altered the world it dominated.

Hadrian changed the appearance of his capital for ever with
his great temples. But his other monument lay on the edge of
his world, the 74-mile/130-kilometre long military work in
northern Britain that we call Hadrian's Wall, a project as la-
borious and demanding as the Pantheon. The empire whose
capital had no walls had great walls on its distant fringes. The
same futuristic power that had masterminded the moving of the
Colossus or the Temple of Venus and Rome built a solid barrier
through the borderlands of the empire across the mountains
from the North Sea to the Irish Sea. Between the massive buildings of the centre and the far-flung fortifications of the edge
lived Hadrian's seventy million subjects. Where did they feel they
belonged? What was their relationship to Roman power and its
advertisements?

In one way, the world had become a single catchment area.

Mobility had obliterated community. Rome was only the biggest pull in a systematically deracinated world. Everyone, it might seem, was an immigrant. During the lifetime of Hadrian's father, Seneca had written to his mother in Rome:

> Consider the abundance of population which the buildings of this gigantic City can scarcely contain – the greater part of this crowd has no fatherland. There is no people that does not rush to Rome, which pays high prices for virtues and vices alike. Get all these folk to a roll-call, and at each name ask, 'Where's your home?' You'll find that the majority have abandoned their home and come to a city which, though very large and very lovely, is not theirs. Now leave this community, which can, after all, be seen as common to all, go round all the cities – there is not one in which a great part of the population is not foreign. Move on from those whose convenient location or advantageous hinterland attracts large-scale immigration, to remote places and the roughest islands – what could be found as barren as this rock, what so precipitous all round, what more meagre in subsistence, what less hospitable to human life, what more appalling to look at, what less equable in climate? And yet here too there are more outsiders than native citizens.

Citizenship, rather than ethnicity, religion or kinship, was the main way in which people thought about community in the ancient world. Every city had its own citizens, and the Roman citizen body, although it was now far larger than even the imperial metropolis could hold, still resembled the citizenry of smaller cities in many respects.

In ancient societies, the idea of citizenship worked in a different way from any form of belonging that is familiar today. Since ancient Greek times, cities had been the main form of community life, and their basic building block was the household unit. Each household had a head, who was responsible for individual members of the household – male and female, kin and dependants, including slaves. '*Paterfamilias*', a Roman term, means 'father of the household'. In Roman tradition, he was the boss, in custom and in law, and his wife, sons and daughters were as much in his power as his slaves.

The heads of households, adult males in charge of their own unit, formed the community. They took part in certain collective activities, all of which had their characteristic location. People came together as a military levy either for training or to prepare for war; they met to vote on civic leaders or to make communal decisions; they assembled at the temples and altars of the gods.

At Rome the political gatherings in which the *patersfamilias* came together to make decisions about how the community worked were called *comitia tributa*, and their main function was to discuss laws. They met in front of the Capitol, or in the forum outside the Senate house. But by Hadrian's time law came from the Senate or – much more – the Emperor. Even though the voting wasn't democratic, speakers endeavoured to persuade the people whose reaction to proposals mattered.

The levy and military exercises took place outside the sacred boundary of the city. The location was on the part of the Tiber floodplain called the Field of Mars (whence the 'Champ de Mars' in Paris and other French cities). It was known as the Enclosure – one of the monuments embellished by Hadrian. This was where the people met in the *comitia centuriata* to vote for next year's officials, whose main task was to command armies in war.

Romans divided the world into two zones: 'at war', *militiae*, and 'at home', *domi*. The line that separated the two was the *pomerium*, the sacred boundary of the city, which Remus vaulted over to his death. It still existed in Hadrian's time, marked by large stones. Communities placed a high value on self-defence. Householders who could afford to do so bought their own equipment and weapons, and underwent training to defend their community. Hiring security staff to fight for you was nowhere near so good. At the beginning of the campaigning season, in the spring when crops had been planted, and there was more spare time, the act of crossing the sacred boundary and going out to the world of war was marked in a ritually significant way, called *profectio* – which means 'setting out'. In mid-March the Quinquatrus festival was held for Minerva and Mars, the Salian priests danced through the streets of the city, and at a religious ceremony called the Purification of the Trumpets, the *tubilustrium*, the weapons were purified for the fight ahead. The citizen-soldiers assembled, armed, on the Capitol, in front of the Temple of Jupiter, then made their formal departure from the city into the world of war.

The end of the campaigning season was symmetrical. If all went well, the returning army had defeated the enemy and was laden with spoils. Then the procession in which the conquering general and his army crossed the sacred boundary back into home life was called the triumph, the most famous of all Roman rituals. Just as they had started out at the Temple of Jupiter, they brought the spoils and the enemy prisoners back to the Capitoline Hill and commemorated the victory by offering the spoils to the gods who had provided the victory, and by strangling the prisoners or selling them as slaves. The weapons tainted by killing were cleaned at the ceremony of the Purification of Weaponry – in early times the participants tasted the blood of the sacrificial victim.

So, being a Roman citizen involved fundamental participation in the community. It was much more hands-on than modern citizenship. Rome was never a democracy in the sense that Athens had been, where thousands of adult male citizens went to the assembly, listened to speeches for and against policy decisions or practical issues and voted on them. Still less was it a representative democracy of the modern kind. But for all that, its citizens stood for the state in a way that cannot be paralleled in our much larger nation-state communities. And that was indicated by the Roman system of personal names, which was deliberately different from that of any other community.

The most distinctive thing about the Roman citizen community – and one that amazed the Romans – was how big it was.

The fact that there were lots of Romans is part of the secret of Roman success.

People who visited Rome were duly impressed – and envious, because the ancient world, on the whole, was underpopulated, with low birth rates and short life expectancy. Greek cities had been known for exclusive citizenships, which made them vulnerable to demographic decline – the Greek city-state of Sparta, for example, which was very strict about who qualified for citizenship, suffered catastrophic declines in population during the fifth and fourth centuries BC. It was inevitable: people were killed, or they didn't have enough children, and, as we've written, cities were unhealthy places. The Romans realised it was only possible to keep up the population if new blood was brought in. Rome had grown by incorporating other people.

The Romans gradually developed many different ways of incorporating new citizens. Of course, there was much discussion as to whether it was in Rome's interest to incorporate foreigners in the body politic. Even those who thought it was – above all to keep up military manpower – couldn't deny the social problems and tensions that came from competition and jealousy. The potential for 'swamping' the host population was as much an issue then as it is now. In the early eighteenth century, Daniel Defoe argued that Britain's age-old openness to outsiders meant that there was no such thing as a true-born Englishman. It was even truer of Rome. But incorporating people was done strictly on Rome's terms. Citizenship was given as a reward to foreign individuals or communities for loyalty to Rome. Some arrangements offered outsiders a selection of citizen rights in return for hard fighting on Rome's behalf; sometimes only their children or grandchildren would be full citizens. The main consideration was loyalty in war. Hadrian's predecessors had made this a pretty common practice, and each year hundreds of Rome's non-citizen soldiers were awarded citizenship on discharge, and a bronze passport-sized document to prove it. On some occasions citizen privileges (in different packages) were given to many communities in certain provinces.

It was also possible to free slaves in return for devoted service. At first they were afforded second-class citizenship, but by Hadrian's time the only major disadvantage of an ex-slave citizen was to be debarred from most public offices.

But the incorporation of other peoples was not the only factor in Rome's expansion. Three hundred years before Augustus, the Roman state comprised Rome and several hundred thousand adult males who lived in other Roman communities up and down west central Italy. (In 234 BC, 270,773 adult male citizens were counted, and in AD 14, 1,728,000.) That was a radical innovation: the organising principle of most peoples in the ancient world had been the single city. Rome broke this barrier and formed a political community spread across several different centres. This was what made possible the development of a Roman empire centred on Rome but including communities from the north of England to the cataracts of the Nile. With each generation, there were more Romans, and more Roman towns, covering a wider and wider area. A Roman town was one whose form of administration was prescribed by a charter and set up on large sheets of bronze in the town's forum. Some were made up entirely of Roman citizens, in others only the upper class. The first chartered Roman towns outside Italy (such as Narbonne in Languedoc) were set up about a hundred years before Augustus, and by Hadrian's time some even existed in Britain: Colchester was the first, then Lincoln, York, Gloucester and eventually London had the same title that the Romans invented in the fourth century BC for their daughter-settlements in the Italian countryside. Thus Gloucester was the Emperor Nerva's Citizen-settlement at Gloucester, *colonia Nerviana Glevensis*. Little by little, these places came to reproduce aspects of Rome. They might have the same gods as at Rome, particularly the deities of the Capitol, Jupiter, Juno and Minerva. They had a forum, a political meeting-place, and round it a characteristic architecture – council-house, basilica, forum, theatre.

By Hadrian's reign there were fifteen million or so Roman

citizens among the seventy million people in the Roman empire. They could no longer vote for laws or in elections at Rome, but they were still a respected and privileged group. The senior regiments in the army, the legions, were recruited from citizens. The emperors liked to pretend (when it suited them) that they were citizens like anyone else.

It made a lot of difference to your life to be a Roman citizen. Some of the advantages can be seen in the story of the arrest in Jerusalem of St Paul, a Jew from Tarsus in southern Turkey but a Roman citizen: 'and as they bound him with thongs Paul said unto the centurion that stood by, "Is it lawful for you to scourge a man that is Roman and uncondemned?" When the centurion heard that, he went and told the chief captain, saying, "Take heed what thou doest: for this man is a Roman."' Chains and flogging were demeaning for a citizen of the ruling power.

Sociologists say that upward social mobility is good for you, and that societies in which there are opportunities for promotion are stable in proportion to those opportunities. A class system that succeeds in discouraging upward mobility leads to trouble. Hadrian's empire still offered a lot of opportunities for social improvement and becoming a Roman citizen was one. But in the years after Hadrian, there was less opportunity for advancement: after 211 a different status system based on property emerged from the emperors' rulings and the lawyers' interpretations of them. The better-off were called 'more decent folk' (*honestiores*) and all the rest were 'more lowly' (*humiliores*). The better deal that Roman citizens had once enjoyed, even if they were poor, was now reserved for the rich. It wasn't easy to become an *honestior* in this new system. During the third century and on into the fourth, the imperial state succeeded in damping down social mobility even more. It locked people into employment: a blacksmith's son had to become a blacksmith; a farmer's son was tied to his father's plot of land. All sorts of mobility and freedom of choice were thought destabilising, and the imperial state cracked down on them.

So, the Roman empire moved away from opportunity and high social mobility and became a world in which people were locked in, with more tension and civil dissent, plus economic downturn. But Hadrian ruled a world in which things were still fluid and people could hope to better their lot.

'Looking at the scale of your fortune and your spirit, I think that there should be displayed buildings which suit your eternity as much as your fame and will have as much utility as beauty,' wrote provincial governor Pliny to Trajan, about new architecture in an important city. High-sounding stuff – but he was talking about municipal baths.

In this period the world was not egalitarian. Status mattered as much to cities as to individuals. When disaster came, the remedies available were in proportion to the victim's prestige. And Pliny's words show us the anatomy of honour: 'fortune', 'spirit' (which meant ability, talent, charisma and panache combined), 'beauty', usefulness and staying-power. All of those blessings brought more of their kind, and an emperor who scored high on these scales deserved cities and provinces, governors and senatorial officials who did likewise. Then the prestige and honour of the age would shine out in the future. The notion afforded no practical consequences: Trajan and the luminaries of his period would not be available to plead its cause by comparison with other ages, but it was essential to the thought that pervaded this period. Everyone looked over his shoulder at the glories of the past and thought of the future in terms of the example they would set when their children's children looked over their shoulders.

This counting of Brownie points helped people in the Roman empire to make sense of their world. They needed a sense of comparison, of ranking. First in honour were the gods, who were at the top of the pecking-order because they were divine. Closely linked with them was the pinnacle of human excellence, the emperor, than whom no human of higher status could be imagined. He was the arbiter of status, the fountainhead from which flowed the gifts and benefits, penalties and punishments that might change the status of everyone else. More generally, the rich, clever, lucky, well-born and virtuous were good and admirable. The ugly, poor, corrupt, unfortunate and ignorant were bad. House slaves, beggars, shepherds, bandits and barbarians from beyond the frontiers were the lowest of the low. Kings and princes, philosophers and councillors, priests and poets were all off to a good start. A similar scale linked the thinking of the Arab caravanserai owner in Palmyra, the Spanish tenant of an olive estate, the Moorish chieftain in the Roman army's auxiliaries and the siege-engine mechanic on the Danube frontier. Across ethnic and social divides, this status system pulled the empire together. It was accepted by people at every level with few exceptions, because ultimately there was hope of improvement.

Social climbing kept the empire running. It also meant that everyone was personally checking their status – and this was easily done. Status was always on display: from seating in the theatre, food and drink at dinner, clothing and footwear and even the furniture in the house. This perhaps seems incompatible with social mobility: if the world was so fixated on status, how could people break the barriers? The answer was a kind of globalisation. Moving sideways made it possible to move up. That was clear when it came to the social roles of women and men.

In the cities of the Roman empire, free women had more self-determination in their lives than had been normal anywhere before, although that is not necessarily saying much. Roman law had found more of a place for them, notably where owning and managing property was concerned: élite women, especially widows or single women whose fathers were dead, often ran households and took decisions about their day-to-day lives similar to those made by men. They were honoured for their wealth and generosity to their communities, and they often participated fully in the life of Greco-Roman high culture.

Another sort of opportunity was offered in the turbulent, fluid societies of ancient cities, in which women, who were everywhere essential to production as well as to family management, often had a great deal of responsibility within the households of ex-slaves or striving, hopeful immigrants. In these contexts we see them as weavers, in the jewellery trade, or selling food in the streets and, above all, in gender-specific occupations such as midwife, wet-nurse and landlady. However, they were expected to eat less than men and put up with more: they were exposed to marital violence and many other hazards. It never occurred to anyone that there might be equality of opportunity between the sexes, and no man doubted that men were superior: more suited in almost every respect to the public life of their ancient community. People said of the evil emperor Domitian: 'There was no human being that he really loved except for a few women.'

The ancient view was clear: women were an inferior sort of human. They were absolutely disadvantaged in legal and social terms. No ancient experiment in citizen-democracy gave the vote to women, and in many communities their rights were strictly curtailed. Their sphere of operation was the home.

Hadrian's life was touched by some high-profile and important women, especially the two he had to thank for becoming emperor, Trajan's wife Plotina and his own mother-in-law Matidia. The power of the great ladies of the imperial household is intriguing. In 119, when Matidia died, Hadrian made a public speech in her praise:

> She was very dear to her husband, but outlived him in a very extended widowhood, the chastest of women, for all that she was in the very prime of life and had outstanding physical beauty. She was unfailingly obedient to her mother, but the kindest of mothers herself: and an attentive and thoughtful kinswoman, helpful to all, stern in no respect, unkind to none. As for me – she would rather delight in my success than turn it to her profit.

When Plotina died, around 124, Hadrian wore black for nine days, and wrote hymns in her honour. He said of her, 'She asked a lot, but always the sort of thing that I could grant.'

Expectations of the women of the emperor's family, and the constraints on them, were the same as in society at large. In the tale of Trajan's death Plotina and Matidia were on their own turf: away from home, the emperor was cut off from the institutions of the court and the state, and sickness was the preserve of female members of the family. No one would have been surprised or critical to find them prominent in the travelling household, or that they took so much responsibility in caring for the dying man. The difference was that the emperor was so high above all other people that even the women of his immediate family were ennobled far above any other woman: they became goddesses too.

The Romans thought in layers: pecking-orders, rankings, hierarchies were of central significance. So all-embracing was this that no one ever thought of improving the position of women: that presupposes a theory of the equality of humans, which had not been dreamed of in antiquity.

What we do find, though, is an interesting unplanned experiment in social engineering. In a community that remains isolated, simple and static, pecking-orders may be unquestioned for generations. But when horizons widen, and communities make comparisons between themselves or are sub-divided, anomalies and discrepancies occur. If one community is recognised by all as superior, its relatively low-status folk may in fact be higher on the social scale than another's relatively high-status members: if I'm emperor, the slaves who mix with me every day remain slaves but are high in the esteem of many.

By the time of the emperors, the integrated world was so huge that status anomalies of this kind were normal. The basic means of determining who was of inferior and superior status didn't change, but the calculation became infinitely more complex. Many women in the Roman world had benefited significantly from this development. It begins with omnipresent institutional slavery: who wouldn't prefer to be a free woman than a male slave?

Gender split the world in half – of course. It's not the fact of the divide, though, that surprises, but that it was so openly proclaimed as a matter of status. So gigantic were the divisions of status, the gulf between 'quality' and the wretched poor, that they could even neutralise the natural deficiency of being female. Still harder to cope with is the omnipresence of slavery.

The fact of two-tier humanity was inescapable. There were slaves everywhere, and slave-thinking was part of everyone's mental framework. The unfree were deprived of most forms of self-determination by harsh social constraints. They were a saleable commodity, in which there was a vigorous market, with all the extra misery of arbitrary dislocation and brutality connected with the slave trade. But the ancient world went further than other slave-using cultures.

For people of this period slaves were not just a miserable exploited minority, an addition to the labour force: they were a sub-division of humanity, and the barrier between slave and free cut across the human race in the same way as the barrier between the sexes. Slaves and free were as much different kinds of people as men and women. Just as no one dreamed of parity between men and women, no one – not even slaves when they revolted or escaped – dreamed of abolishing slavery.

It is at least imaginable how gender attitudes might pervade every aspect of social and cultural life: everything is sooner or later linked to something that is so fundamental to being human. It is much harder to understand that in the Roman world there was another division between one type of human and another. Everyone learned from infancy to think of the world as split between free and slave. Politically and socially active citizenship distinguished a man from a woman *and* a slave.

The barriers between male and female, slave and free could be crossed. Greeks and Romans were fascinated by gender ambiguity. Either sexual role could be adopted by both genders. They

were appalled and fascinated by hermaphrodites and andro-
gynes: there were special ways to dispose of children who
displayed these irregularities. Hadrian as law-giver was energetic
in forbidding castration. And everyone knew that free people
could turn into slaves through capture in war or by slave-dealers,
or by bandits supplying slave-dealers, or by the trickery of local
leaders, or by parents desperate to raise a little cash. Some people
even sold themselves into slavery. Equally slaves could, and did,
become free, adding to the citizen population.

By Hadrian's time the manumission (freeing) of slaves was
common. This was not altruistic, more often a way of extending
social dependency. A cynical slave-owner could encourage a slave
to collect his or her own replacement price. When (or if) the
slave reached thirty years of age, the owner could graciously
accept it in return for manumission. The money would buy a
younger substitute slave. The new freedman was still obliged to
the former owner by a strong bond of gratitude and duty, enforce-
able in law. Freedmen gained more independence when their
former owners died. Although their own position, as befitted
people who had been subject to the abuses of slavery, was carefully circumscribed by law, their children became proper citizens.

A further peculiarity of Hadrian's world was that the two-tier
system of slave and free was not weakened by the consequences
of regular sexual relations across the divide. Everyone knew that
huge numbers of people were descended from slaves and ex-
slaves. Artemidorus, the interpreter of dreams, suggested: 'Having
sex with your slave, male or female, is a good sign because the
slaves are the property of the dreamer. It also indicates that the
dreamer will get good value out of his possessions, and that they
are likely to increase and become more opulent.' The historian
Tacitus guessed that most of the senators of his and Hadrian's
time had at least one slave among their recent ancestors. During
the reign of the next emperor but one after Hadrian, Marcus
Aurelius, the empire was struck by a deadly, unidentified
epidemic, which caused terrible mortality and, in some ways,

marked an end to the period of general stability that had lasted nearly a century. When it reached Athens, the city petitioned the emperor: they wanted to reduce the number of generations of citizenship required from three to one for service on the city council, so hard was it to find sufficient respectable recruits. The emperor agreed. The councillors of Athens now included men whose grandfathers had been slaves. Significantly, Hadrian was rumoured to have consolidated his position in Trajan's household, which was already strong because of the imperial ladies' support, by seducing powerful male ex-slaves.

There was little fear of a systematic slave rebellion. It had happened, but the slaves who were led to such acts of desperation were the oppressed labour force of the countryside. Most just hankered for the opportunity to be a household slave in a large city.

Slaves' obedience is easily enough explained by the violent coercion to which they were subject. As a form of property, slaves had few rights and their low status meant they were punished in particularly cruel and degrading ways. Hadrian's own rulings in court illustrate that well enough. He established that when a person announced that he was a free man, the enquiry as to his status should always be held first so that he should not be submitted to judicial interrogation (by torture). At the other end of the social scale he exiled Umbricia, an upper-class lady, for five years 'because she had abused her female slaves shockingly on the slightest of pretexts'.

Larcius Macedo was the son of a man who had been a slave, and a more intolerable master as a result. He was in his private bath suite at his villa on the coast when his slaves surrounded him. One stabbed him in the throat, another hit him in the face; a third struck his chest, stomach and genitals. When he seemed to lose consciousness, they threw him on to the heated floor to see if he was alive. He stayed quiet, despite the heat, and was carried out, as if he had expired, and was ministered to by loyal slaves and concubines. He lived long enough to see his attackers condemned. Pliny, who told the story, gives another glimpse of the slave's lot. The same Macedo was in a public bath-house when one of his slaves touched the arm of an equestrian who was in their way to ask him to move aside. The man was outraged, and lashed out – but accidentally hit the unfortunate Macedo, rather than the slave, so hard that he nearly fell down.

Hadrian made another legal ruling in a case like this when he sentenced a maidservant to death:

> As long as they can assist their owners in any way, slaves must not prefer to look after their own skins. It is abundantly clear that the maid who was in the same chamber as her mistress at the time of an assault could have made rescue possible, if not by escaping to raise the alarm, at least by screaming so that those who were in the house or close by it could hear – which was why the attacker threatened to kill her if she cried out. She is the more deserving of capital punishment so that other slaves don't form the view that any of them can look after themselves when their owners are in danger.

In the early empire a city prefect, who had to ensure order in Rome, was murdered by a slave. Rumour, as often in such cases, suggested a *crime passionel*. The law demanded that the whole household was crucified. Even the Senate had doubts about executing four hundred innocent men, women and children, but the argument about security and the need to maintain the slave system through terror prevailed. When the condemned were led through the streets to the place of execution, the crowds – many of whom were slaves or their descendants – were on their side, and it took soldiers to get the job done. The situation, even by Roman standards, had been extreme, but the protest was ineffectual and limited.

Because slaves were kept in households, coercion and control was quite easily maintained within each family, who could have recourse to the public authorities if it was necessary to put a slave to death. Mice in your dreams, according to Artemidorus, meant slaves – since they lived in the same house, ate the same food and were scared. It was a good sign to dream of lots of mice, and to see them playing happily, as this predicted great happiness and a large household of slaves. The more loosely affiliated populace outside the great houses was more of a worry although they had every reason to wish to co-operate.

Prestige, honour and status were not immemorially fixed, like caste. Comparison illuminated them: go to the next town, and see how councillors are more flamboyant than ours; travel to the next province, and see how little sign of the emperor's favour there is. The emperor's power to change status animated the whole system of comparison and competition. And no emperor's power to make these adjustments was as visible and immediate as Hadrian's. He journeyed constantly from place to place, integrating the scattered regions of the empire with every move from one city to the next.

The dispensing of promotions and change in status was among the emperor's principal occupations, and one of the main activities in public life. The great and the good did little governing and were barely involved in politics. But they constantly pushed up their own prestige and status, and one of the ways in which they did it was by helping others rise. Letters of recommendation flew in their thousands along the roads of the empire – there are many examples in Pliny's works. Fashion, in everything from hairstyle to bath-house design, illustrates the imitation, flattery and allusive display of influence that went with the unceasing pursuit of status.

'Whips are differentiated by law in this city, according to the status of those who are to be beaten. There is one sort of whip which is used for the Egyptian population, by distinct penal personnel; another, with flat lashes, is used for Alexandrian citizens – and wielded by Alexandrians . . . some small way of preserving a little dignity, even in disgrace,' wrote a Jewish philosopher, about a century before Hadrian, after an oppressive Roman governor had deliberately humiliated the councillors of the Jewish community by inflicting the Egyptian punishment.

Alexandria was the second city of the Roman empire. It had been founded by Alexander the Great, and ruled for nearly three centuries by the descendants of his general Ptolemy, until Cleopatra's suicide in 30 BC. Ancient Egyptian culture survived, and the temples were still in use by priests who could read the sacred texts in the original scripts. Egyptian was still widely spoken, but Alexander and his successors had encouraged a substantial influx of Greek-speakers, and while there had been no attempt to suppress the indigenous culture, or to introduce an apartheid-style system, the Egyptians were reduced to overtly second-class citizens.

The Ptolemies had pursued an aggressive military policy, and maintained an army drawn from the young adult males of the whole Mediterranean area – Romans frequently served in its ranks as officers, even after Rome's conquest of the rest of the Greek world. In this army, Jews played an important role and were rewarded with privileges that encouraged them to stay in Egypt. By the time of Augustus there were said to be as many as a million in a population of about seven million. The population and wealth of Egypt, especially in wheat for export, made emperors careful in their choice of governors for the province. Indeed, they banned all members of the topmost social stratum, the Senate, from visiting it, and the governors were drawn from the equestrians. Even Egypt, they thought, couldn't elevate an equestrian to a contender for the throne.

Community politics in the capital city Alexandria were violent and confused. The Roman governor had to maintain Rome's ascendancy over the now conquered Greek élite, over the no longer privileged Jewish community and the despised Egyptian majority, all of whom needed little provocation to riot.

The Romans ruled through punishment, as the words of the

Jewish philosopher quoted above make plain, but above all through using punishment to point up status and privilege. The author was little concerned about the pain or the physical damage caused by the different whips, although that differentiated them: it was the issue of honour that concerned him. In being subjected to the Egyptian whip, the councillors were subjected to a double downgrade, which was a terrible blow to their prestige and their community.

The Roman idea of crime, like that of punishment, was closely linked to status – that of the injured party and that of the offender. Offences such as violence, theft, fraud and rape were most likely to come to the attention of the law when they were committed by or against people of high social standing. In the back-streets, at night, or in the countryside, far from witnesses, much that was criminal was unpoliced and unprosecuted. Violence that came to the attention of the authorities was usually suppressed by force without recourse to law. But in the higher social groups and within the cities, many people could call upon it, even though the judiciary was often heavily overburdened – partly because the most powerful men in the empire, including the emperor, heard so many cases in person. The historian Dio noted that when he became consul, there were three thousand outstanding cases. For all that, the interpretation of the law was sophisticated and careful – when you got to court.

In the Roman legal system the purpose of punishment was to make a spectacle of the criminal, addressing their status in the community as well as making them suffer physically. Corporal and capital punishment were the principal sanctions, and the bundles of rods and axes, the *fasces*, carried before officials of the old Roman state symbolised this. Citizens had rights, and the conditions in which they might be exposed to such punishments were hedged by the law. Like the Greeks of Alexandria, Roman citizens were usually spared the more painful, degrading punishments, because their status had to be reinforced for the benefit of those who shared it and had done no wrong.

If someone was to be executed 'in the manner of the ancestors' they were beaten to death in public in a piazza just outside the walls of Rome. They might be thrown from the famous Tarpeian Rock, an outcrop of the Capitoline Hill where the most important gods lived, into the forum beneath – and there were spiky emplacements on the slope to ensure death. The corpses of executed citizens might be dragged through the streets attached to a hook, then thrown into the Tiber.

A parent-killer was sewn into a sack with a dog, a snake and a hen, then thrown into the sea. Hadrian had to rule on the difficulty faced in putting this into effect in cities far from the sea, and decided pragmatically that exposure to wild beasts in the amphitheatre was an adequate substitute.

Most citizen malefactors expected a quick execution, usually by decapitation with a sharp sword. Killing non-citizens was a different matter. Slaves in particular were exposed to arbitrary torture and a horrible death. The principal form of execution for the unfree was crucifixion. Artemidorus' *Dream Book* shows a different sort of matter-of-factness about these terrible punishments.

> Dreaming of being crucified is good for all seafarers. Like the ship, the cross to which such a victim is tied is made of wood and nails, and the mast and boom of the ship look like a cross. It's also a good sign for poor men, as the crucified is raised high, and feeds many hungry creatures. This dream predicts finding lost goods, because a crucified person is very visible. But it's bad for the rich, since in crucifixion you are stripped naked and lose your flesh. This dream drives out anyone who wants to go on living in their own place, cultivating their own land, or who is scared of being thrown out, and will not let them stay where they are – because the cross prevents you keeping your feet on the ground.

By Hadrian's reign, the law had started to infringe on slave owners' rights – no castration and no gratuitous cruelty – so that a case had to be made for execution. The controls had some effect. But how much illegal brutality went unreported? And how much ill-treatment was still allowed? Most of all, what does the legislation tell of slaves' lives before it was enacted?

A document from the time of Augustus records some of the regulations in a public executioner's contract. The successful applicant must supply, according to the law, nails, wood, pitch, ropes, candles – all the routine hardware of dreadful suffering. Public execution was meant to be routine, the unavoidable consequence of wrongdoing, and the Roman authorities applied it without question to hundreds of criminals, if circumstances demanded. If need exceeded the resources of the public executioner and his staff, soldiers helped out.

The executioner's contract is explicit in how the carrying-out of the law must fit with the demands of the status system. His staff must be physically sound. They must not live in the city, or nearer to it than a certain point. They must not use the same baths as the citizens. In the street they must wear red clothing so that they are easily identifiable. A bell must be rung in front of the procession of the condemned on the way to the place of execution to attract attention and warn off those who do not want to be polluted by the ill-omened sight. The spectacle of death was intended to be both normal and repellent: the rituals made it hard to miss and reminded bystanders of how terrible it was to behold. Putting people to death was something which concerned the gods, and which carried the risk of dangerous ritual pollution for the community. The Romans, specialists in religious propriety and in avoiding divine displeasure, were extremely careful to manage executions in a way which minimised this risk.

The status of the victim was displayed clearly in crucifixion. It was also clearly on show in the other public punishment for which Hadrian's world was notorious. Crucifixion was carried out outside a city, on a well-trodden approach to the gates, but the even more cruel criminal executions, with a yet more elaborate demonstration of the victim's downgrading in status, were presented to a more leisured public in the heart of a city. This was execution as public spectacle, which all cities put on to honour the gods or the divine emperor. It took place in theatres, circuses or public squares, but most frequently in the arena, with the architectural form the Romans had invented: the amphitheatre. There, criminals were mauled by beasts, forced to fight each other to death, or burned alive.

There were many different communities in the Roman empire to which Greek culture, language and identity were extremely important, as were local, ethnic or religious identities. But the scene is set by the arena and the cross. Belonging in the Roman world was principally about whether you were ruler or ruled.

In talking about literature and the visual arts, the poet Horace said, in the time of Augustus, 'Captive Greece took Rome captive.' He was right. Most of the past – even for Romans – was Greek. What we call the Greek myths were set in real time. One chronology gave 1184 BC as the date of the Fall of Troy. Cities remembered foundation dates, real or imaginary, from about three hundred years after that. History began to be written seriously from the fifth century BC, and the two greatest historians of the ancient world, Herodotus and Thucydides, made famous the wars they described, in which the Greeks survived invasion by the Persians, and in which Athens and Sparta fought almost to the death. The only events that could compete in celebrity were the successful expeditions of Alexander the Great through what is now Iraq and Iran to Pakistan, and the Roman conquest of the world. All of these components in 'universal' history left their mark, and throw light on Hadrian's age.

Alongside interest in the past, literature of every kind – religious, recreational, philosophical, technical, political and persuasive – was also mainly Greek. Hadrian wasn't the first emperor to draw on Greek themes – Greek was woven so tightly into the cultural tapestry that it would have been impossible not to. Augustus wrote a (bad) Greek tragedy. Caligula seems to have been interested in the way in which the Greek rulers of Egypt married their sisters. Nero posed as a musician and athlete in the Greek mode: the Olympic Games were put on specially for him. Domitian put Rome on the map and into the calendar of Greek international sporting and cultural competitions.

Many people, whatever their mother-tongue and community, knew about the labours of Herakles, the epic exploits of the Greeks at Troy, the battles in which the Greeks had seen off the terrifying armies of Xerxes, and the tragedies of the wars when Greeks fought Greeks. Even more knew about Alexander. It was hard for anyone not to know that at some time, somehow, they had all come under the rule of Rome: greedy, ruthless, arrogant and invincible.

But mother-tongue and community were diverse in Hadrian's empire. In Egypt, the ancient language of the people of the Pharaohs was still spoken, and was soon to be taken up as Coptic. In Gaul, the ancient Celtic calendar was inscribed on stone just like those of Greece and Rome. In Sardinia, tomb-stones bore a modern version of the ancient Semitic language spoken by the island's Carthaginian conquerors eight centuries before. In Cappadocia, Christian missionaries operating there three hundred years later would still find it necessary to preach to the villagers in Cappadocian, a language spoken in the region since the days of the Hittite empire in the second millennium BC. All over the Levant, old languages of the Semitic group, especially Aramaic, the language of Jesus, were widely spoken.

Among these varied communities, millions of people had been brought up to speak the two great languages of the empire: Greek and Latin. In Greece and the Aegean, around the coasts of the eastern Mediterranean, in Sicily and parts of southern Italy, Greek was the norm. In the rest of Italy, and in many cities on the other coast of the Adriatic, in Provence, Languedoc, many parts of Spain and the Maghreb, it was Latin. In most areas local people used their native tongue, which Greek and Latin speakers learned. It was worth knowing both Greek and Latin if you were going to travel widely in the empire, and many cradle speakers of local languages became fluent in Greek and/or Latin. It was a world of linguistic virtuosity.

The ancient cities of Greece, and above all Athens, summed up Hellenism. But the Greece that 'took Rome prisoner', or which inspired so much interest in Hadrian that he was called 'the little Greek', was not just another place and its inhabitants. The Greek language was part of an inheritance of culture that went back to the eighth century BC, and which included a huge amount of intellectual, cultural, political and historical material developed and passed on by thinkers, writers, politicians, statesmen and soldiers, consciously following in the wake of their Greek predecessors. For centuries, culturally, the Greeks were the only show in town in the Mediterranean outside Egypt. They went on thinking that. But several hybrids of the Greek tradition had come into being. Italian peoples, and Rome itself, long before its world conquest, slowly blended Italian and Greek culture. After Alexander the Great conquered western Asia, its peoples also found themselves in much closer contact with Greek ideas. The Phoenician cities on the coast of Lebanon, and Egypt, when it became a Greek kingdom, became quite Greek. The Jews, too, adapted to fit a changing world, although Greek influence was always controversial.

After Rome became unquestioned imperial overlord, the relationship between Greek and Roman culture naturally changed. All educated Romans, by necessity, had a knowledge of Greece. They learned the traditions of oratory, poetry, drama, philosophy and law, and the history of the Greeks as well as their own. It was their intellectual heritage too. Rome constantly reinvented itself in Greek dress. Religion constantly imported new Greek ideas: Roman literature produced new forms of Greek models: Roman government drew on Greek experience. No Roman could escape being soaked in things Greek. That said, Greek culture also gave Romans a powerful idea of how different they were. Hadrian's choice to be so keen on Greek culture was, after all, extreme. People could choose 'Latin' cultural markers as well as Greek ones.

* * *

Hadrian's empire was a conquest state, and the wars of aggression mounted by Trajan reminded everyone of that fact. Visual demonstrations of Roman victory were everywhere, from the fortresses of Roman soldiers to the sanctuaries of the divine emperors. At Aphrodisias in Caria, one such temple was decorated with sculptures showing each of the provinces with the emperor who had conquered it. Britain is a dying Amazon, with Claudius looming over her, heroically nude except for a large helmet. Armenia is a fainting, languid, eastern youth, with a statuesque, muscular Nero beside her. The message that war had shaped the empire was unmistakable.

Political economy was a constant reminder of the new order, too. Everywhere outside Italy, apart from a few privileged communities, paid tribute to Rome, as well as a wide range of other taxes and impositions, levies and compulsory services. Tribute was well understood to indicate subjection. Roman citizens – the resident 'Romans who do business among us' – scattered across the empire had special economic advantages. Also, in city after city across the empire, Rome had succeeded in gaining acceptance because it backed small groups of the wealthy and powerful against their enemies, and especially against popular violence. The rule of the many by the few, the narrowness of local oligarchies, and the often frustrated powerlessness of the people of the cities reminded everyone that they belonged to a coercive state.

There was an oath of loyalty to Rome and to the emperor. The wording varied from region to region because it had to involve the local gods, as well as the emperor-god of Rome. This example was used in the mountains of north Turkey, at the beginning of the empire:

> The oath completed by the people of Paphlagonia and the Romans who do business among them: I swear by Zeus, the Earth, the Sun, all the gods and goddesses, and Augustus himself that I shall be well disposed to Caesar Augustus and his children and descendants all my life in word and deed and thought.

They promised to have the same friends and to 'spare neither body nor soul nor life nor children'. They would have the same enemies, and report any plots or resistance.

> If I do anything contrary to this oath . . . I pray that there may come upon myself, body and soul, children and family, and whatever is useful to us, total destruction until the end of my line and all my descendants, and may the bodies of my family not be received on land or sea, nor may land and sea bear fruit for them.

Most places had joined up to the Roman empire by negotiating what were called 'unequal treaties'. These were the usual result of surrender or defeat in not very violent war. Defeat after heavy resistance usually meant extermination. Only a few privileged peoples or cities had special deals. But the nature of the treaty and its stipulations mattered to a great many people, and were another permanent reminder of the violent times when the place had become part of the Roman empire.

Communities wanted constantly to remind Rome of the occasions on which they or their ancestors had done the right thing: 'A hundred years ago, when there was this invasion, we stood by you . . .' And they were often treated better for such displays of loyalty.

Something similar happened in Caesar's conquest of Gaul. The people who had been staunch allies during the war were the Aedui, in what is now Burgundy: they extracted a favourable deal from the Romans' provincial organisation. If Gauls were needed to take part in ceremonies and public occasions, they were always chosen from the Aedui, and they were awarded tax concessions too. So, favouritism was rampant, and the reverse. If you were a people who had fought Rome and had to be compelled to surrender, you would not get a good deal until you had shown your loyalty on a later occasion.

The conclusion is simple. However much better off the inhabitants of the empire were because of the rule of Rome, they did not usually appreciate it. There was always room to improve your position with the rulers of the world – or, failing that, frustration might lead to violence. Each region's stability was always on a knife-edge.

What was the edge of the Roman empire like and how did you know when you reached it? Not, at any rate, by a red-and-white-striped barrier with Roman guards, as in the *Asterix* cartoons. Hadrian's monumental barrier in northern Britain appears to have made the edge of Roman power very visible. But it was not as simple as that, and the Wall, in any case, was an unusual project.

The southernmost reach of Rome was a place called Holy Mulberry Tree, below Abu Simbel and the first cataract of the Nile, in today's Egypt. For the rest of Rome's African provinces, as in the Arabian peninsula, the Sahara made a fluid but effective marker. Westward, the boundary of the empire was the Atlantic. To the north, the wooded lowlands of northern Germany were socially and culturally like the regions the Romans had conquered west of the Rhine. Beyond the middle Danube and the mountains of Dacia, the vast lowlands were so wet, at least in winter, that they almost constituted a water frontier. Certain routes ran on strips of higher ground, through the marshes and lagoons, and were relatively easy to control, like the points where the roads from desert oases came into more fertile land to the south. All along the eastern frontiers, through the mountains of today's Turkey and the deserts of Syria and Jordan, the peoples and territories directly ruled by Rome shaded imperceptibly into those that acknowledged no overlord, or saw themselves as subject to the Parthian king. At the most frequented crossing-points there were guard-posts and customs houses, efficient at controlling who passed and why, and charging them for the privilege. When the holy man Apollonius crossed the eastern frontier, he responded modestly to the customs officials' question that he had to declare Moderation, Justice, Virtue, Self-control, Courage and Self-discipline. 'Where are the girls?' asked

the bureaucrat, the virtues being common names for the prostitutes in whom a traveller like Apollonius might be expected to
deal. 'They're not slave-girls but ladies,' replied the sage.

The astronomers and geographers of Alexandria had demonstrated four hundred years before that the earth was a globe,
and Rome claimed ambitiously to rule all of it. Hadrian's younger
contemporary Claudius Ptolemy, one of the greatest of ancient
observers, mapped large tracts of the old world, locating thousands of places with co-ordinates of latitude and longitude (the
figures survive, enabling reconstruction of the maps – they show
surprising detail from far outside Rome's political control, from
Ireland or even Malaysia). Yet around the borders, fixed or fluid,
of Hadrian's world there were many mysterious fringes, where
reliable knowledge gave out. What did Romans of Rome think
of the windy hills of north Britain? What accounts did amber-
traders bring back of the woods and heaths of the Baltic shores?
Who lived in the great plains beyond the middle Danube, and
how did they survive, when the winter floods made an inland
sea stretching from Vienna to the Iron Gates (a prominent gorge
on the Danube)? What were the oases of the Sahara like? Or the
fabled islands of the Atlantic, or the wonders of the Indian
Ocean? From time to time emperors sent out military expeditions with the aim of systematic exploration of this *terra incog-
nita*. They never reached sub-Saharan Africa or most of Asia.
The Roman notion of China was simply as an impossibly distant
place where silk was made, and Chinese ambassadors to the west
hardly discovered more about the Roman world even when they
reached Antioch.

One especially intriguing area was the Black Sea. Here, a
waterway, the Dardanelles and Bosporus, led from the most travelled seas into a miniature Mediterranean, where much was
familiar on one coast but alien on the other. The mountains on
the coast of Turkey, and the coasts where the holiday resorts of
Bulgaria now stand, were easy to grasp, but to the north the
steppe of Moldova, the Sea of Azov and the crags of the Caucasus

were a much more hostile environment interrupted only briefly by the Mediterranean 'island' of Crimea. The sea was full of fish, and parts of it froze in winter. Into it flowed a series of huge but enigmatic rivers: the Danube, which the Romans knew well, but the Dnestr, Dnepr, Bug and Don were only resonant names – Tyras, Hypanis, Borysthenes and Tanais. Imagine the North Sea with rivers flowing into it from who knows where! A sense of insecurity followed, from lack of control, lack of boundary and vulnerability. Who might come down those rivers to attack the little cities perched precariously on the northern Black Sea coasts? In what distant mountains did they rise? That question had intrigued Black Sea voyagers since the tale of Jason and the Argonauts was new.

For centuries, the great plains had been known as the home of rapidly moving pastoral societies. The game of making nomads settle, and their eventual displacement again, had been played out many times, and no ancient state had come close to controlling it. The distances were too great for any effective surveillance that would provide the information that was power. Traders could give information, but it was far less systematic than the imposition of roads and milestones, garrisons and watchtowers, and was soon outdated. Curiously, mountains were easier to cope with than plains: like rivers, they gave shape to the terrain, offering strategic points on which attention might focus. The Caucasus were forbidding, but there was one key point on which Rome had focused for a century: the pass they called the Caspian Gates, beyond which they knew another exotic sea lay. The Caspian was at the edge of knowledge: the sheer size of the river Volga flowing into it from the north had led to the supposition that the inland sea might be an arm of the encircling Northern Ocean, as the Black Sea was of the Mediterranean.

Around and between these dimly understood landmarks, the whirl of pastoral life went on, societies competing and changing, displacing each other and being moved on, in a history with no one to narrate it. It was this restlessness that eventually out-manoeuvred Roman authority and overwhelmed the frontiers. Could Hadrian have had any inkling of the threat?

In this corner of the world Roman knowledge had increased dramatically with Trajan's Dacian wars and the creation of a province in what is now Romania. It was in these northern fringes of the Balkans that dealing with moving peoples had become part of the routine needing the attention of military government.

An epitaph for a senator who governed what is now Bulgaria, and who died around the time of Hadrian's birth, shows the priorities:

> To Tiberius Plautius Silvanus Aelianus, Prefect of the City of Rome, Commander and Companion of the emperor Claudius in his expedition against Britain, governor of the province of Moesia. He brought across the Danube into Moesia more than a hundred thousand of the people who dwell on the other side of the river with their wives and children and their chiefs or kings, and made them pay tribute; he put down an insurrection among the Sarmatians in its early stages, even though he had sent a large part of his army to the expedition in Armenia; he induced kings who had been unknown to the Roman People or its enemies to worship the standards on the river bank which it was his job to protect; he returned the sons of the kings of the Bastarnae and Roxolani, and the brothers of the king of Dacia, who had been imprisoned or snatched by enemies; he took hostages from some of these; through all of which he consolidated the security of his province and increased it. He was the first man to increase the corn-supply of the Roman People from that province, sending a large quantity of wheat.

The praises of Silvanus are full of the swagger of Roman imperialism. This is the mood in which Trajan and Hadrian were brought up, in which large populations and powerful rulers were the pieces that provincial governors moved around on the bits of the board assigned to them. Rome's power and knowledge constantly increased: tribute and grain flowed in from new sources; the careers of leading senators took them from one imperial adventure to another.

Dacia, the kingdom that had been Trajan's first military target, had been different – a sophisticated and highly organised state in close contact with the Roman world: it had had developing towns, a more complex economy and its own culture. It was ripe for being attacked, looted, genocided and replaced with a Roman province. But the war had been hard and the collection of settlers from all over the Roman world, and the development of the provincial structure, continued through Hadrian's reign; the spectacular column that commemorated Trajan's extirpation of Dacia was both Rome's newest monument and Trajan's own tomb. So, interest in the north-east was high. But Hadrian's approach was different. On his way from Antioch to Rome in 117–18, he negotiated a peaceful settlement with the same powerful barbarian peoples that Silvanus had dealt with, the Roxolani, who lived next door to Trajan's new province of Dacia.

Hadrian found a governor for the great province of the mountains of eastern Turkey who was keen on making the fringes of empire less mysterious. His name was Arrian, and he wrote for Hadrian a literary version of his more routine report. The document is a marvellous snapshot of the time and its attitudes. His main preoccupation was not the tame kinglets and garrisons of the Black Sea coasts: the Romans were well aware of potential instability in the region, caused by the threatening activities of a powerful confederation of people called the Alans. Of all the events of his reign, this was the crisis that portended most clearly the problems with large, aggressive, wandering communities, which Hadrian's successors would face. And it is clear that Hadrian was informed and concerned.

But it is revealing that he was not too bothered (rightly, as the Alans were effectively neutralised by Arrian). For Hadrian, the land of the Alans was not a place of grave geopolitical moment, a matter for top-level policy-making – but the place his favourite horse had come from. The steed was named after one of the great rivers of the Russian steppe, Borysthenes, the Dnepr.

The emperor had a sense of the wilderness, an affinity with the world beyond civilisation; it was a dangerous place, but not a terrifying alternative to order. In natural, untamed areas the display of power took the form not of conversion into a province or road-building, but of hunting.

Hadrian composed this epitaph in verse for his horse's tomb, beside a villa in Provence:

> Borysthenes the Alan, a russet horse, Caesar's own: across the plain, across the marsh, around the Etruscan tombs he used to swoop, against the boars of the Danube; and no boar dared hurt him with yellow tusk, or even touched the end of his tail with foaming maw, as so often happens; whole and youthful, undamaged in limb, he met his appointed time, and is buried here on this estate.

So, from this it seems that the emperor-poet and the imperial hunter had the barbarian north under control. The plains and the swamps were those of the Italian countryside near Rome, dotted with ancient Etruscan burial mounds – already the countryside of Italy had more antiquities than cultivated farms. The boars were those of the frontier in central Europe and the horse was an exotic from the nomadic east, of the same breed as the outsiders held back on the edge of the empire by Arrian. All of these traditional threats and enemies were reduced to easy prey for the emperor at play, to be made the subject of the melancholic verse he often composed. His sadness was reserved for the mortality that struck the young and healthy as well as the old or injured. He never knew how ironic his huntsman's bravado about the world outside might come to seem.

'Barbarian' was a traditional notion that had belonged originally to the classical Greek period, when it had expressed a fierce hostility between Hellenes and almost everyone else, a splitting of the world in two that had seen its consummation in the stand-off of the great Persian wars (481–79 BC). Barbarian is a Greek onomatopoeic word, a mocking version of the babbling noise that people who don't speak your language make: 'ba ba'. Language remained a shibboleth – only Greek and Latin were civilised. By Hadrian's time the word had lost some of its urgency. But it still mattered. Literacy in Greek and in Latin now defined a culture, an in-group, and beyond it people were outsiders, whose ways were not to be trusted.

The trouble was that so many inhabitants of the empire failed the Greek and Latin grammar test. Long ago both languages had become the languages of the system, which all could and many did learn in order to demonstrate to the Arrians and the Hadrians that they were insiders. Locally, at home, people's languages were different – sometimes variants of Greek or Latin, more often local languages left over from before political subjugation by Greek-using kings or Latin-literate generals. A Wanted notice from Egypt shows the predicament of ordinary people: 'an Egyptian from the village Chenres . . . completely ignorant of Greek, tall, thin, clean-shaven, with a wound on the left side of the head, pale yellow complexion, very wispy beard or beard scarcely present, smooth-skinned, narrow-jawed, long nose. A weaver by trade, given to swaggering about like his betters, prattling in a high-pitched voice. Age about 32.'

And different languages went with different patterns of life. Greek and Roman culture were enormously influential, but the authorities were self-satisfied and inclined to be relaxed about others' odd religions or social behaviour, which showed them for the inferiors they were. It was recorded that when Hadrian's predecessor Trajan was negotiating with potentially hostile communities during his wars against the Dacians, they sent him an urgent message in Latin – but inscribed on a large fungus. What more eloquent sign could they have given that they were wild men of the woods? On the whole, they could be allowed to get on with their lives.

'Greek' and 'Roman' were labels for gigantic systems, and had gone beyond easy identification with an ethnic or even a political group. The people who passed the Greek and Latin grammar tests varied wildly in background, social organisation and world-view. It is hard to find a modern parallel for their allegiance to the empire: the world religions have become too entrenched for 'Muslim' or 'Christian' to be analogous; and while 'Western', 'first world' and 'European' carry the right sense of one-upmanship, they are too urgently political: the Greeks and Romans lived in a world in which those were for a long time the only labels and allegiances of their kind. Beyond them there was nothing on remotely the same scale. To be a barbarian simply meant not having a share in the cultural complexity represented by 'Greek' or 'Roman'.

Outside the empire there were a few powerful states that the Romans found it convenient occasionally to elevate into a 'Foe worth Fearing'. The kingdom of Parthia, centred in what is now Iraq, was the prime example. Parthia was rich and densely inhabited – the Tigris and the Euphrates were as good for agriculture as the Nile in Egypt. In many ways, it was very like the eastern provinces of the Roman empire, but it had its exotic and bizarre features. Where the Kirkuk oilfields are today, crude oil used to seep to the surface naturally – 'The soil is so soaked in pitch that it is too sour for agriculture, and life expectancy is very short, because the pitch in the water settles in the internal organs', one correspondent reported. Parthia had its special wonders, but it was not thought of as representing a different culture, a different big system, that might be an alternative to the hegemony of Greek-plus-Roman. This was a world with a single superpower. Had people in the Roman empire known more about China, things might have been different. As it was, it was really only when a Christian world composed of the fragments of the old Greek and Roman systems was confronted by an Islam that was a culturally self-defining, sophisticated, complex, successful military and political force that 'us and them' entered a different phase. But that was half a millennium and more in the future.

There was, however, one exception to this picture that fore-shadowed the later challenges to the empire: Judaism and its derivative, Christianity. But this clash of values, which was in its first, convulsive phase throughout Hadrian's lifetime, really matters.

There were also myriad other 'thems' to be contrasted with the 'us' who were Hadrian and Pliny and Arrian: above all those disenfranchised through normal, huge-scale slavery. They have a vital part to play in the picture. But they never came near being a threat to the dominance of the system.

On the surface, Hadrian's Roman empire was stable, permanent and victorious, with an all-pervasive view of the world-order. Beneath, despite apparent homogenisation and inclusiveness, there was a world of change, anxiety and enmity, resentment and bristling self-definition. Occasionally the cool of the rulers was shattered by an intervention that belied the peaceful good practice of normality. The Romans had a word for it: 'tumult' (derived from the verb 'to swell'), which they had used to describe the nastiest moments of their earlier history, when particularly savage and disruptive foes had come close to gaining the upper hand. Hadrian's reign, peaceful golden age though it at first appears, was marked by many such events. The choice between peace or unlimited aggression and ceaseless conquest was also less simple than it appeared. Because there were barbarians on the inside. But they were on the outside too – disobedient and unorganised forces of chaos beyond the reach of Rome's network of loyalty gestures or submission to tribute or regulation. Hadrian's late Roman biographer was in no doubt about the purpose and meaning of Hadrian's most famous monument: 'He was the first to build a Wall, eighty miles long, to separate the barbarians and the Romans.' In this period, the empire is likened to a single gigantic city, round which runs a great wall, garrisoned by the armies of Rome that in this age even a Greek could call – for the first time, as far as we know – 'our soldiers'. Solidarity within the empire depended on the exclusion of those who lived outside.

IV
LETTERS

Hadrian's drive to be best was unlimited. So he worked up every skill, including the most trivial – such as modelling and painting. He would claim that there was nothing in peace, war, the office of emperor, or the pursuits of a private individual, which he did not know.

CASSIUS DIO

On 29 August 124 Hadrian was at Ephesus, the great city on the east shore of the Aegean Sea. As usual, he was giving audience to embassies. Three men from high in the mountains 240 kilometres to the south-east came before him. They were Artemon, son of Diogenes Tobolasios, Simonides, the son, grandson, and great-grandson of Simonides, and Mettius Apelles. Their names tell the cosmopolitan story of Hadrian's empire: Mettius was a Roman citizen, Simonides a fourth-generation Greek aristocrat, and Artemon's father had both a Greek name and the 'Tobolasios', which marked him out as a descendant of the pre-Greek local community, which survived in the deep countryside.

They had come to ask the emperor's approval for a new festival of music and theatre. Their fellow citizen Julius Demosthenes – it was no coincidence that he had the name of the most famous of ancient Greek orators – proposed a great benefaction, which would bring competitors from far and near. Every fourth year in July there were competitions (with prize money) for trumpet-players and heralds (200 *sestertii*); for writers of prose encomia (300 *sestertii*); for poets (300 *sestertii*); for flute-playing and accompanying choir (500 *sestertii* first prize, 300 second); for comic poets (800 *sestertii* and 400 for the runner-up); for tragic poets (1000 *sestertii* and 500); and for singers accompanying themselves with the lyre (1200 *sestertii* and 600). There were major sacrifices to the gods, and a tax-free fair; there were entertainers; there were amateur gymnastic contests for the local people. A prominent local man was put in charge of the occasion. For the whole year of the contest he would appear in public in a purple robe with a great gold crown, with Hadrian's portrait embossed on it. He led a procession of ten men in white wearing wild-celery wreaths carrying the sacred objects and especially the images of the divine emperors, followed by twenty stewards dressed in white carrying shields and whips to keep order in the theatre. He paid no taxes for five years.

The regulations for this splendid occasion were all inscribed in minute detail on a stone slab. Most of it survives because the place where the orgy of culture envisaged and funded by Demosthenes was to happen is truly remote. The lyre-players and comic poets, the traders at the fair, the trumpeters and singers had to make their way far up into the mountains to a town which was of very minor status among the hundreds of cities in Hadrian's eastern provinces. When communities wanted to express their pride and individuality, they invariably did so in a shared language, comprehensible across the empire – in Latin, and still more, like this festival, in Greek; that language was what we call Classics, the continually growing, diverse, ancient, rich tradition of music and literature that included poetry, drama and public speaking. This was, in other words, one of the most potent ways of distinguishing the insiders from the outsiders, of asserting membership of the civilised world Rome ruled. The writers and performers were people of high education and therefore must have come from high in the social pecking-order, and from larger centres, but Demosthenes' foundation shows how this culture reached out into the backwoods and how widely it appealed to ordinary folk from the scarcely Greek villages of the mountain pastures.

Everyone wanted a festival like it. In the big cities, numerous far grander competitions were normal. This was the route to one-upmanship, the secret of self-esteem. In the peace and prosperity of Hadrian's empire, such innovations proliferated, and literature flourished as never before. Poetry, first used to recount myths or compose hymns, remained an essential part of religion. Oratory was the principal tool for addressing governors or the emperor. Other forms of literature and music throve too, far more in a world where there were hundreds of small ponds in which to excel, than if the empire had been more centralised.

Hadrian gave personal permission for Demosthenes' festival. It was through these competitions and their management that all the small ponds compared themselves with each other and negotiated with the authorities who ran the empire. The negotiation was performed by representatives of the cities that ran the festivals, by the benefactors who funded them and by the celebrities who won the prizes. Everyone agreed that excellence at the literary, musical or gymnastic games was essential to civilisation. The prizes were far higher than the cash handed out to the victors: cities, benefactors and celebrity competitors were all in a position to ask for further favours or for help in times of trouble from governors or from the emperor. Literature was always useful. The poet Mesomedes was quick off the mark and produced a particularly effective ritual lament for Hadrian's dead favourite Antinous. The governor Arrian included a graceful consolation to the emperor on the death of his heroic lover in his report on the military dispositions of the Black Sea. And for Roman citizens, success in the world of culture was a route to upward social mobility and jobs in the equestrian or senatorial service. Higher learning was also thought desirable for the community.

The holy man Apollonius said that there were five types of learned man: philosopher, historian, barrister, letter-writer and commentator. These represented the world of high literature, which also included the brilliant tradition of ancient poetry, reaching back to Homer. Homer's epics, composed in the eighth century BC, continued to be among the most frequently bought and read texts, and their influence permeated Hadrian's world a thousand years on. But from the Homeric fountainhead, the stream of classical literature had broadened and deepened, and an important branch derived from it in Latin. Throughout the history of this literature great luminaries had developed what they found in the works of the past, and passed on their own contribution to be imitated and embellished, in a constant flow of reworking and reinterpretation, which was at its most vigorous in the second century AD.

The most brilliant success stories in Hadrian's time were those of the orator-philosophers of the cities of the old Greek world who came out of this milieu of cultural self-promotion. They are an uneasy mixture of moneyed excess and literary pretentiousness. Scopelian of Smyrna was celebrated for his survival after being struck by lightning in his cradle when his twin brother was killed. He became the most famous orator of the time, and young men from all over the area to the east of Smyrna wanted to study with him. His greatest success as an ambassador to the emperor was in persuading Domitian to relax a ban on growing vines. In later life he was mocked for using depilatories made of pitch.

Dionysius of Miletus, whose memory-training techniques were famous, impressed Hadrian so much that he appointed him as an equestrian official and gave him the ultimate reward for cultural attainment – membership of the Museum at Alexandria, the sanctuary of the Muses set up by the Ptolemies, where an endowment supported professors in the various liberal arts and gave them access to what was left after several fires in the world's largest library.

Polemo of Laodicea, one of the most arrogant men in the empire, also taught at Smyrna, and played an important part in running the city; he persuaded Hadrian to give a gigantic benefaction to it (at least four million *sestertii*), as well as another to himself. Part of his empathy with Hadrian may have been his interest in hunting – he was criticised for travelling with a huge entourage including several varieties of dogs for different games. His most highly regarded speeches all revisited *causes célèbres* of the fourth century BC. He, too, received membership of the Museum, but his great moment of glory came when he was chosen to give the speech when Hadrian dedicated the Temple of Zeus in Athens.

In 132 Hadrian was back in that most famous of Greek cities. This time he effectively refounded it, building a whole new quarter. The gate between the new city and the old advises the traveller, 'This is no longer the city of Theseus but that of Hadrian!' The unfinished remains of a gigantic temple to Zeus of Olympus, started by Athens' absolute rulers 560 years before, stood in the new city. Hadrian completed it and presided at its dedication, succeeding where all his predecessors had failed. Zeus of Olympus could be seen as the Jupiter who had given the Romans their empire, and as the godlike Hadrian who ruled it. A splendid piece of theatre, and yet another astonishing architectural feat, it was the occasion for establishing Athens as the centre of a great League of All the Greeks, a Panhellenion, under the patronage of Olympian Zeus, but it was also a tremendous act of homage to history. Hadrian, 'the little Greek', has sometimes been thought self-indulgent in these gestures to ancient learning and the glories of the past. In this empire, though, expressing the solidarity of the world of civilised Greeks and Romans against threats to it from barbarians inside or outside its frontiers was a highly political act.

The age of Hadrian remained one in which civilisation, wherever it was found, involved copying the best achievements of olden times and the glories of the past.

This preoccupation with the heritage of ancient Greece and early Rome inhibited the writers of the time from the sort of innovation and creativity that generally appeals to our taste. It smacked of decadence for rich men to spend their time in the manner of Nestor of Laranda, who rewrote Homer's *Iliad*, in each book omitting a different letter of the alphabet. Satire and the lower-brow literary forms seem fresher to us than much of the stylised prose and artificial verse of the age. Where the past was the subject, however, works of the highest quality were produced by Greek-speaking Roman citizens – Plutarch's paired biographies of great Greeks and Romans, and from the century after Hadrian's reign, the very different, but highly ambitious, historical projects of Appian (from Egypt) and Cassius Dio (from north-western Asia Minor), from which important information about Hadrian's reign derives.

This backward-looking literary activity indeed regularly raised awkward questions about the relationship of Greek and Roman. The ruling power needed to be fitted into the picture. An inscription commemorates a typical literary figure in a provincial city, one Hermogenes of Smyrna whose output included *On Medicine* (77 books), *Origins of the Cities of Europe* (4 books), *On the History of Smyrna* (2 books), *Military Ruses* (2 books), *Origins of the Cities of Asia* (2 books), *On the Wisdom of Homer*, *On the Homeland of Homer*, and *Chronological Studies*. But he also compiled *A Comparative Table of Romans and Smyrnaeans*.

By and large, the Greek experts did not recognise the achievements of the Roman branch of the stream of classical literature. But at least some members of the oratorical and philosophical élite came from the Roman west. One of Hadrian's colourful quarrels was with one such, a philosopher called Favorinus, from the Roman city that is now Arles in Provence. Favorinus was a hermaphrodite, with a reedy voice like a eunuch, but had a reputation as a womaniser. Hadrian contented himself with promoting Favorinus' rivals (such as Polemo), and did him no other harm.

Hadrian's involvement in Greek culture was by no means unusual for a rich Roman. The leading figure in Roman public speaking under Trajan, Pliny, was certainly ambidextrous in the two cultures. One of his correspondents planned to celebrate

Trajan's invasion and subjugation of Dacia. Pliny was enthusiastic:

What a terrific idea – an epic about the Dacian war! Relevant, masses of material, inspiring – just the job for poetry, amazing stories and all of them true! You can deal with the diversion of new rivers across the land, new bridges over them, craggy mountains with brooding fortresses, with a king who never gave up, though expelled from his palace, and eventually from life. Lots of work, though, especially since the uncouth barbarian names – and the king's especially – won't go into Greek hexameters.

So, a Roman contemplating a loyalist and patriotic display reached for the language of Homer.

Pliny wrote to another friend:

What should you be doing on your long holiday break? Translation from Greek into Latin or the other way round. This is an exercise that gives you a sense of the nature and beauty of words, the richness of ways of putting something, and the power of demonstration. Rendering the best models enhances your literary inventiveness. Things that escape you as you read cannot hide when you are translating.

Literary taste was part of the complete way of life. Pliny wrote again:

Please find enclosed with this letter my hendecasyllables – cheering pastime of my idle hours, composed in the carriage, or the bathhouse, or during dinner. Here are jokes, games, love, grief, complaint and anger, low-key or more ambitious in tone, trying to offer something for every reader by sheer diversity.

In another letter, he speaks of inviting the equestrian Septicius Clarus, later to be commander of Hadrian's bodyguard, to a literary dinner: 'a lettuce each, 3 snails, 2 eggs, barley pasta and sweet wine chilled with snow, olives, beetroot, cucumbers, shallots, a comic sketch, a reader, a lyreplayer'. But Clarus has accepted an invitation to a quite different sort of evening – 'oysters, udders, sea-urchins and flamenco *danseuses*'. Pliny's own detachment from distractions and immersion in study was such that as a young man he had watched his uncle, who was in charge of a Roman naval base, go off to rescue people from the eruption of Mount Vesuvius, then return to reading Roman history, while the mushroom cloud and the ash fallout dominated the view across the bay.

Pliny helps us appreciate Hadrian's own literary and intellectual accomplishments. He loved to write, and was competent in many genres in both Latin and Greek. The fragments of his speeches that survive are straightforward and competent. Scraps of his poetry, including two epitaphs for his favourite horses, also survive. He was noted for his ripostes – rapid, and always intended to cap, and to outdo, what had just been said to him. His biographer quotes an exchange with a poet called Florus, which demonstrates that Hadrian had a sense of humour. Florus the poet, came up with a verse on how he wouldn't want to be the emperor, travelling to so many different places, where it gets too hot and too cold – and he particularly couldn't imagine putting up with British winters. Quick as a flash, Hadrian came up with a composition, in a similar metre, in which he said he wouldn't want to be a poet hanging around the cheap bars and the cookshops of Rome. We hear that Hadrian was also addicted to writing verse about the young men he loved, and eventually he wrote an autobiography, although nothing of that survives.

Education was a benefit that was available or not in much the same way as the other good things of the Roman world. In many towns, a basic education was one of the benefits that might be made available, at least to those who could pay, as a service to the community. Pliny helped provide teachers, and a library, in his family home, Como, in northern Italy. There is evidence that both boys and girls sometimes attended schools.

The very rich might employ freeborn teachers in their homes, and ensured that some of their slaves were literate enough to be able to help in educating their children. It seems that Hadrian's family were in this league, given the richness of his training at home. In these households girls could be educated in the same way as boys. Pliny praises the character of a girl who died at thirteen displaying 'the common sense of an old woman, the seriousness of a woman in middle life, the charm of a little girl, and a virginal modesty. How she loved her nurses, her teachers, her advisers, each according to his role.' If there were imperial children, it was a sign of special favour to be invited to join their lessons at the palace.

Schoolmasters, both inside and outside the house, had a reputation for brutality, as strict discipline was said to be good for children. Artemidorus thought it was good for the illiterate to dream of learning to read, but that benefit would only come with effort and fear because education involved both. Teachers sometimes had good relationships with their pupils: Lucius Verus, who ruled with Marcus Aurelius and had been educated by some prominent figures in the imperial palace, liked his teachers very much and was liked by them, even though, says his biographer, he was 'not gifted at literature. He liked poetry as a boy, and then oratory, and was better at the latter – or perhaps less bad would be the better way of putting it.' Later his more talented friends helped him compose.

One teacher in Hadrian's Rome who was proud and fond of his pupil, and very conscious of the historical setting, set up this tombstone – which also illustrates something beyond the basic numeracy of Roman schooling:

To the shades of Melior the calculator, who lived thirteen years. This boy had such prodigious memory and knowledge that he surpassed everyone's credentials from the record of ancient times to the day of his death. All the things he knew were better described in a book than on a gravestone. He left notes on his craft – all original, and which only he could have rivalled, if the Fates, unjust to human affairs, had not envied him. Sextus Aufustius Agreus, unhappiest of teachers, set this up for his own slave, on a plot two feet wide and six deep. He died in the 897th year since the foundation of Rome.

Literary sophistication was almost completely dependent on writing. The technology of writing determined who could read and write, and how they learned. Paper made from wood-pulp (a Chinese invention), which we take for granted, was unknown in the ancient Mediterranean. The nearest equivalent to paper was papyrus, a reed that grew in the Nile in Egypt. It was expensive, but exported all over the empire. An encyclopaedia from around the time of Hadrian's birth lists the types:

Grade 1: the Emperor Augustus' Own, the finest of all, favoured above all for letter-writing (13-inch sheets)

Grade 2: his wife Livia's Own (13-inch sheets)

Grade 3: priestly, reserved for Egyptian sacred texts (10-inch sheets)

Grade 4: amphitheatre papyrus, made at Rome in Fannius' workshop under the amphitheatre, and extremely thin (9-inch sheets)

Grade 5: Saite, named after an Egyptian town with low-quality papyrus-beds (less than 9 inches)

Grade 6: Taeneotic, named after another Egyptian town, sold by weight, not quality

Grade 7: traders', no good for writing on, used for wrapping bundles of finer-grade papyrus or other merchandise (less than 6-inch sheets)

In the Roman world publishing was simply a matter of having manuscript copies made: there was, of course, no printing.

Pliny had an enemy in the Senate who spoiled his son; when the boy died, he wrote a memoir of his life and had hundreds of copies made, which he sent to towns all over Italy and the provinces. The covering letter instructed the city council to choose the councillor with the best voice and have him read the eulogy to the assembled townsfolk.

Trained slaves made copies of a particular text. The most popular ancient high-grade literary works – Homer above all, at least in Egypt – were copied pretty accurately, partly because they were used for educational purposes, but also because they were read for pleasure. And there was much copying of 'middle-brow' material, apocalyptic prophecies, magical texts or cheap popular novels, many of which were mildly salacious. It was common among the rich and literate to borrow a book from a friend and have your own slaves make a copy.

The form that these 'books' took was almost universally the scroll. The codex, the shape of the book that we know, was used to bind documents, but it was only later that it became widely used for literature. The scroll held only a limited amount of text so longer works came in bundles of several scrolls. When ancient texts are divided into 'books', each was a separate scroll.

The copy might be fine or sloppy, either mounted on a fine handle of wood or ivory, of excellent quality papyrus, or in a much cheaper version. Given that everything was copied by hand, there was no control equivalent to 'being published', although if a work was housed in the world's great libraries it was a sign that it had been accepted as worthwhile. The Great Library in the Museum at Alexandria was still the most famous, but the Palatine Library in Rome had become important too. Being taken up by a bookseller, who had the staff to produce numerous copies quickly, was rather like being published.

Potsherds or plastered walls were good places to scribble with charcoal or a paintbrush. Notes could be made with any sharp point on wax tablets, which had the advantage of being reusable.

Wooden tablets without wax, if smoothly enough finished, could take a text written in ink.

Fewer than ten per cent of the population could read. But, like linguistic ability, literacy is a flexible concept: people might have functional literacy that wouldn't extend to reading long epic poems in Greek or Latin because writing was visible everywhere in a Roman city. The plastered walls of the fronts of houses were covered with graffiti, advertisements, election posters for the town council and slogans. One advertisement for a bath-house in a tiny town north of Rome read, 'Here you can wash in the style of the big city.'

It is easy to assume that the literate were from the élite, but graffiti sometimes tell a different story. A group of women spinning wool signed off on the wall of their workroom with their names and the numbers of baskets of wool they had processed in the course of each day, and jocular abuse – 'Amaryllis does cunnilingus.' Among slaves, literacy may have been unexpectedly high because of their proximity to the élite and access to informal education. The evidence for low-brow literature confirms that literacy of even a quite high level of complexity was not confined to the most highly educated. There were many unsophisticated romantic tales, involving separated lovers, miraculous escapes, improbable adventures, and happy endings, often with a good deal of sex. Some give shocking descriptions of everyday scenes. In a Latin romance, written around Hadrian's time, the narrator, Lucius, has been turned into a donkey by a magic spell, which was supposed to be a love-potion. He describes the 'unattractive' (his word) conditions in a countryside flour mill:

My God, what stunted specimens of humanity! Their skin was striped all over with livid scourge-scars. Ragged bits of old cloth shaded their wealed backs rather than covering them. Some just had a bit of a wrap round their genitals, but they all had such tattered clothing that nothing was really hidden. Letters were tattooed on their foreheads; their heads were half shaved; their feet were fettered. They were horribly sallow and the smoky gloom of the reeking overheated room had bleared and dulled their smarting eyes. Like boxers who fight befouled with the dust of the arena, they were smeared white with scurfy flour. But how can I describe the other animals, my comrades? I've never seen such decrepit mules and exhausted geldings! They drooped their heads around the manger as they munched the heaps of straw. Their necks were erupting with bleeding and putrefying sores. They coughed continuously and wheezed through feeble nostrils. Their chests were raw from the rubbing of the harness ropes and their sides were split by unending blows till their rib-bones showed. Their hoofs were crushed out broad and flat by their never-ending tramp in the mill-round. Their hides were scarified all over with mange and emaciation.

The slaves may well have been criminals, overworked as a punishment: the enormous stone flour-grinders would normally have been turned by the animals. The description is meant to appal, but not to surprise; and it is certainly no plea for reform.

Among the readers of this sort of literature, there was real interest in certain current affairs. A fragment of the libretto of a performance to celebrate Hadrian's accession survives. Versions of dialogues – trial scenes, accounts of embassies – between bold or rash local spokesmen and imperial authorities, governors or the emperor himself, were popular. Often these were connected with religious issues: this was how the first Christian martyrdom stories were composed. And the other spin-offs from high religious culture, which interested a wider audience, included horoscopes, magical prescriptions, and apocalyptic prophecies. The documents selected by Christian leaders during the second century as the New Testament originated in this milieu of 'middle-brow' writing and publishing in the eastern Mediterranean.

The nearest thing to a newspaper was a publication called the *Daily Acts*, which contained news of prominent events connected with the Roman state, minutes of Senate meetings, and so on. It was copied to all the military bases scattered across the empire.

Every regiment had a little sanctuary in the centre of the garrison, and it was there, alongside the standards, that the official record of what happened in Rome was displayed.

Another bulletin, the *Acts of the Roman People*, was livelier. It included details of condemnations, exiles and political crimes, as well as the birthdays of the Emperor's relatives and big public sacrifices. And it was racy, because it included society divorces, portents and extraordinary events. For example, it recorded a story about the killing of a crow that had become a pet of the tradespeople who had shops in the Roman forum. They had adopted this bird, which had learned a word or two and would greet the local stallholders every morning, until one got tired of its droppings on his shoe stall and killed it. The rest of the shop-keepers rioted and gave it a huge funeral, taking it to the cemetery on a bier.

By a happy coincidence, the place where papyrus was cheapest, Egypt, is also ideal for its preservation, thanks to the arid conditions of the desert. Our best evidence for literacy, and invaluable insights into much else, comes from the tens of thousands of papyrus scraps that have been excavated from ancient rubbish dumps of the Greek and Roman periods; they give us a cross-section of everything from administrative documents and tax returns to legal and literary texts. They preserve casual details, but like all human documents, they are brief and allusive, as well as fragmentary – rather tantalising.

All over the empire, the army required a certain level of education of all its members. Not everyone who was recruited, even if they were (genuinely) Roman citizens, found the necessary Latin easy. It was useful, given the levels of bureaucracy, to be able to read and write, and levels of literacy were notably higher in the military than among civilians. That is clear from the Egyptian papyri, but it is confirmed by the deposits of lime-bark tablets preserved by unusual soil conditions at the fort of Chesterholm, Vindolanda, behind Hadrian's Wall. Here, letters and jottings give vivid insights into the life of the garrison. Some of the soldiers could quote grand epic poetry, and there is evidence that some women could write – the wife of the fort commandant invites her friends to a birthday party.

The material from Egypt and Vindolanda shows that literature was the tip of the iceberg of written information, which helped ensure the cohesion and survival of the empire.

The specialised intellectual interests that were Hadrian's hallmark involve a different aspect of the world of teaching and literature: ideas, know-how, systematic enquiry.

Philosophy included what we would call science, and natural philosophy included meteorology, comets, movements of the heavenly bodies as well ('meteorology' means 'the science of things that happen high in the air'). The study of nature was part of the business of the philosopher, so what we would call geology and the description of the earth also fell under natural philosophy.

In general the ancients were less interested in the experimental or empirical method than in reasoning from first principles. They tended to discuss abstract ideas in preference to making deductions from observation, so the empirical method, which is so central to modern science, was relatively little practised.

Back in the fourth century BC, Aristotle, the greatest Greek philosopher, used observation of a meticulous kind as the basis for his principles as to why nature was as it was. Although people went on quoting him throughout antiquity, and indeed the Middle Ages, they did little to refine his observations of animals, plants and stones: they didn't want too much to do with the practical. For example, a learned, intelligent writer would say that menstruating women must be kept out of the cucumber fields or the cucumbers will die – and clearly never put the theory to the test.

Aristotle had said, 'Almost everything has been discovered, though it is sometimes not put together constructively: and sometimes people know things but do not make use of their knowledge.' The empirical method tended to be left to artisans, people who were not ashamed to call themselves craftsmen. That was how the Romans developed their skill in water technology, lifting devices and military hardware. A find in northern Iraq revealed that army smiths knew how to use metal torsion springs to fire a catapult bolt. The dryness of the desert has preserved a skill that is not mentioned in the literature. Some nameless craftsman worked out how to make the ballista out of metal instead of twisted hide, and found that its efficacy increased dramatically. He might have told his staff, but the discovery was probably never written down: composing literary works, even on technical topics, was the preserve of higher-status people. Nobody else in the Roman army found out about it, since it was only used on that particular campaign, and when those people eventually died, their knowledge died with them.

Some discoveries were written up in technical manuals and disseminated: how to lay out an aqueduct on the correct gradient, or lift massive columns weighing tens of tons. Another classical example is the automata invented by Greek scientists – for instance to make temple doors open automatically, with pulleys, weights and gearing. In Alexandria in the second century BC, one man even devised a kind of elementary steam engine, but it was never put to use. In a sense, the Romans came near to the know-how for railways, but self-opening doors and other such devices remained only a conjuring trick, never harnessed to any useful purpose. Water power was used more constructively. The watermill was becoming more widely known during the second century, and one of the forts on Hadrian's Wall had its own. In Germany water power was used in a sawmill.

Progress in mathematics was inhibited by the Greek and Roman numerical systems. Both were based on the letters of the alphabet, and did not encode multiples on a regular system. Because number theory was so poor, making calculations on the basis of figures was hard. Excellent results could be achieved with the abacus, but errors multiplied in copying the results. In inscriptions

many numbers were recorded wrongly. Trigonometry and geometry, on the other hand, were demonstrated diagrammatically
and were more sophisticated. It was only in the Middle Ages,
with the introduction, from India, of a sign for zero, that higher
mathematics became possible.

Medical knowledge is an eloquent example of the strengths
and weaknesses of intellectual life in the age of Hadrian. No
one could heal anything much before the drug revolution in the
first half of the twentieth century. Ancient therapies were at best
limited to palliative care, and at worst were spectacularly harmful.
Greek and Roman doctors were notorious for the damage they
did: the danger of medical advice was a comic stereotype. In
establishing what they claimed to be able to do, observation,
common sense, experience and skill shaded into a general cultural
education in which religion and philosophy might be more
prominent than anything clinically useful to the patient. Doctors
were expected to participate in competitive displays of their
healing prowess, just like learned professionals in the world of
international culture.

Medicine derived from two main sources: religion and philosophy. In illness, most people turned to the gods. Many deities
were invoked for healing, above all Asklepios, whom the Romans
called Aesculapius. We have some vivid glimpses of how devoted
people could be to his worship in the writings of Aelius Aristides,
a rich man in western Turkey during the reign of Hadrian's
successor, whose Roman citizenship had probably been a gift
from Hadrian. The priests of Aesculapius specialised in unusual
cures.

In January 149, Aristides had a dream from Aesculapius, who
was, he understood, also Apollo, in which he was told to swim
in the river at Smyrna:

> It was mid-winter, the north wind was strong, it was icy cold. The
> pebbles were fixed to each other by the frost. When the divine
> vision was announced, friends and various doctors escorted us.
> There was another great crowd, for some distribution happened

to be taking place outside the gates. Everything was visible from the bridge . . . Being still filled with warmth from the appearance of the god, I threw off my clothes and plunged in where the river was deepest . . . When I came out my skin was pink and my body was comfortable everywhere. And there was a great shout from those present 'Great is Aesculapius!'

Sanctuaries of Aesculapius acted as hospitals of a sort or, better, as convalescent centres, and there were some purpose-built infirmaries in the larger Roman military bases. In Rome itself the sanctuary of Aesculapius was on an island in the Tiber, where later a church dedicated to St Bartholomew took over the healing tradition. There is still a hospital there today, and others across Europe in his name.

Sixteen years later, in summer 165, Aristides was desperately ill with plague. His slaves and livestock all fell sick too. This time it was the goddess Athena who appeared to him and re-assured him that he would recover.

Then it occurred to me to take an enema of Attic honey, and there was a purge of the bile. Then some curatives and a little nour-ishment (first, as far as I recall, goose liver – after refusing all food). Then some sausage. Then they brought me into the city in a long, covered carriage. So little by little I recovered, but the disease did not leave me until the most valued of my ex-slaves died.

Alongside the purely religious approach, there were several philosophically based medical traditions, whose followers structured their treatments on theoretical ideas about how the body worked. Anatomy was studied attentively, there being plenty of opportunities to inspect corpses. In Egypt under the Ptolemys human vivisection had been briefly permitted, but imperial warfare now gave doctors their best opportunities. Even so, ignorance of physiology and pathology remained nearly total.

The most influential doctor of antiquity, Claudius Galen, practised in the Rome of Hadrian's successors, and left voluminous writings that shaped medical thought in both the Christian and the Islamic world throughout the Middle Ages. He was capable of experiment and made many thoughtful deductions: observing pulsation in the circulation of the blood, he attributed it to the artery walls, not the heart, which was, we might say, at least interestingly wrong. Alert, practical, and sensible, Galen made advances in pathology despite not understanding what was going on in human ill-health, and against the bitter and unrelenting competition of other professional healers – 'bandits of the city rather than the mountains', as he called them. As in other societies before the pharmacological revolution, the inability of doctors to heal did not prevent them from achieving great influence and wealth.

Galen endorsed a remedy invented by an imperial functionary based at Dover.

The mercury eye-salve of Axius, Commander of the British Fleet, for eyes sore at the corners, persistent eye-problems, serious itching, and long-standing conditions.

> 24 drams itching cream
> 24 drams calamine
> 16 drams saffron
> 16 drams white pepper
> 16 drams cinnabar
> 12 drams poppy-juice
> 24 drams gum
> rainwater as required.

Highly infectious eye-disease might have been a particular problem in barracks and other dense housing conditions. We can only guess at the results in Rome's English Channel fleet of widespread anointing of officers' bleary eyes with pepper, opium and mercury.

The different specialities of ancient medicine were sometimes combined by talented all-rounders. An ex-slave in Italy did well out of this, nearly making enough money to qualify as a senator, as his tombstone helpfully boasts in some detail:

Publius Decimius Eros Merula, former slave of Publius, clinical physician, surgeon, oculist; official of the Board of Six at Assisi. This man gave 50,000 *sestertii* for his freedom; for membership of the Board of Six he gave the town 2000; for statues for the Temple of Hercules he gave 30,000; for paving the streets he transferred 37,000 to the public treasury; and the day before he died he left 800,000 *sestertii*.

As ex-slaves, medically qualified or not, weren't allowed to be town councillors, membership of the Board of Six was a special honour they were given in return for generous benefactions to the community.

Dietetics and therapy, the main ingredients of clinical medicine, were usually highly imaginative and mostly unhelpful. Here is a fairly typical sample of discussion of medicinal ingredients:

Endive is very like lettuce. There are two kinds. The darker, summer variety is better than the paler winter one. Both are bitter and very good for the stomach. Taken as food, in vinegar, they cool it down nicely when it aches; and crushed and applied externally they drive it (and other aches) away completely. The roots of the wild kind are taken in barley-pottage for the stomach, and in case of heart trouble, smeared on the left nipple (sometimes with vinegar). All kinds are good for gout, coughing blood, and premature ejaculation – take every other day. Petronius Diodotus, in his *Selected Cures*, says endive is utterly worthless, and has a great many arguments to prove it. No one else agrees with him.

In its limited way, surgery was more of a success: specialists concentrated on specific techniques, such as removal of bladder stone (a common result of nutritional deficiencies). Equipment was designed to suit these procedures, and one example resembles modern lithotomy forceps. More complex mechanically was the vaginal speculum, which ingeniously widened the aperture to permit inspection and what passed for diagnosis of vaginal or uterine disorders. The most sophisticated medical equipment known is a highly crafted kit offered by an oculist to the goddess of a sacred spring in Gaul, a marvellous set of precision sliding hollow needles designed for cataract surgery, breaking up and removing the afflicted lens.

This was a world without gunpowder, printing, the stirrup, the windmill, the wheelbarrow, and the mariner's compass. Coal and mineral oil were not burned as fuel. Olive oil in lamps and animal fats or beeswax in candles provided the only night-time illumination. The only form of energy available, other than human or animal labour (with the exception of sailing), was water. On the positive side, water-lifting was sophisticated – the force pump was known – and equipment to haul, lift, and lower extraordinarily heavy blocks of stone was advanced. Pulleys and gearings were quite complex. There was no algebra, but surveying, including levelling, was highly developed. Military engines were often made to extremely high specifications. Shipbuilding was skilful and responsive to Mediterranean conditions.

Similarly, in agriculture, trial and error and the possibility of profit led to a steady improvement of crops and animals through selective breeding and the introduction of new strains. The vine was deliberately introduced into provinces where it had not grown before. Some major elements in modern Mediterranean cuisine not available to the Romans include the orange, banana, aubergine, tomato, potato, chilli, coffee, tea and maize. Pepper, cinnamon, silk, emeralds, amber, pearls and cloves, however, all reached the empire from distant sources, sometimes in large quantities. Sheep, pigs and cattle were much larger on average than at any time before the end of the eighteenth century. Grafting was practised, and manuring understood. Forests were managed by coppicing rather than being indiscriminately felled. Metalworking was advanced: steel was known, and iron widely used in building. The fallout from the scale of Roman metallurgy has left an unmistakable set of layers in the icecap of Greenland. Weaving and the manufacturing of cloth was, again, highly developed, but there was little incentive to industrialise. Economies of scale were achieved in mining, in the making of cheap pottery, and in some agricultural outputs, in all of which enormous volumes of material were often handled in a single locality.

There isn't much point in trying to praise the Romans for their discoveries or blame them for their ignorance. The balance-sheet has plenty of both. They were as eager to enquire as most people, but the enquiries, shaped by traditional literature, mythology and religion, often went in unhelpful directions. A typical figure of Hadrian's court was Phlegon, whose book of marvels survives. He was interested in superhuman skeletons and in abnormal births. He reports that a two-headed baby was born in Rome in 112, when Hadrian was magistrate at Athens; the priests instructed that it should be thrown into the Tiber. Someone sent a centaur to the governor of Egypt; when it died it was embalmed and sent to Rome. Phlegon had seen it in the emperor's storehouses: 'At first it was exhibited in the palace. Its face was fiercer than a human face. Its arms and fingers were hairy . . . it had the firm hoofs of a horse, and its mane was tawny. In size it did not match the usual depictions . . .'

With slaves cheaply available everywhere, the complacency that came from unquestioned superiority of wealth and status, and a deep-running conservatism, affected the dissemination and harnessing of ideas. In Hadrian, it is clear that the Roman empire had a superb opportunity: the absolute ruler was a skilled, unconventional, enquiring, brilliant intellectual. The only enduring product of this happy chance, typically, was the vault of the Pantheon.

The place of teaching and learning was ultimately unhelpful: so much of it concerned recreational and competitive position-taking in relation to other practitioners of the past and the present. This was a world in which scholarship was subordinate to other more transient goals, the library and the school to the theatre and the circus.

As Artemidorus the dream-interpreter said: 'Eating books is a favourable dream for teachers or rhetoricians, and anyone else who makes a living out of literature or books. For everyone else it means death, and soon.'

V

CIRCUS MAXIMUS

To celebrate his birthday in January 119, Hadrian gave a show free
to the people of Rome, and killed many wild beasts – in one round,
100 lions and 100 lionesses died. Then he organised a lottery in the
theatre and in the Circus, distributing small wooden balls as tokens
to men and to women separately.

DIO

If there was a representative type of public event in Hadrian's
empire, it was the religious festival. These were the key
moments in the all-important worship of the gods, and it was
on such occasions that the continuity and complexity of Greek
and Roman culture were most visible. Attendance at a festival,
in town or country, was one of the most effective ways of reassuring yourself about who you were and how you and your
community fitted into the world. And the festivals were enjoy-
able: they were an opportunity for handouts of pleasant treats,
and for the spectacles in city life: theatre performances, mimes,
gladiatorial contests, and games in the circus. Rome prided itself
on its religion, and there were a great many festival days in the
city – in Hadrian's time, something like half of the days in the
year.

Of the spectacles available at the festivals, the racing of chariots in the circus was Rome's favourite. The largest building for
public entertainment was the Circus Maximus, where chariots
had raced since the earliest days of the city. This, too, had been
rebuilt, on the most generous scale, by Trajan, and now had
seating, in raised tiers, for between 150,000 and 200,000 seated

spectators (how many actually crammed in is hard to tell). The circus filled a narrow valley between two of the Seven Hills, and was like a hairpin in plan, one and a half kilometres long. Chariots were released from pens along the open end, and competed for the lead as they converged on a circuit defined by a central bank, covered with monuments, obelisks, statues and shrines, running most of the length of the hairpin. They kept to the right, and rounded the end of the central bank, where the circus came to its curved end. In all they ran seven laps, the number being displayed to the audience by a contraption with eggs and dolphins on it, one of which fell at the end of each lap. The first convergence on the lane to the right of the bank, and the subsequent turning of the ends of the central spine were exciting moments: this was where mishaps occurred most often. But the best seats were beside and above the finishing line, midway along the left-hand side, and it was here that the massive imperial box was located. Once again, Trajan spent unstintingly on furnishing the seats in fine materials. Under the stands, though, there were storehouses, workshops, and bars with an unsavoury reputation. Occasionally part of the structure collapsed: in the reign of Hadrian's successor a supporting column gave way and 1112 people died; 150 years later a bigger disaster killed 13,000.

Four factions, Red, White, Green and Blue, competed, and the best charioteers became popular heroes. Green and Blue were the leading teams, and emperors and senators joined in as enthusiastic fans. People even put the team they supported on their tombstones: Crescens, 'slave of a woman, born by the mouth of the Danube, oil-dealer from the Portico of Pallas, Blues fan, supporter of the Lightweight shield-fighters', a typical outsider, brought to Rome from the Black Sea as a slave, defines himself by his heroes in the circus and the amphitheatre.

The more detached intellectuals took a predictably disdainful view – not of the sporting element but of the fan clubs. Here is Pliny:

The circus games interest me very little. Nothing original, nothing different, nothing which it isn't enough to have seen once. It really astonishes me that so many thousands of men at the same time can be so childish as to like watching horses running and men standing in chariots. It might be understandable if it was the speed of the horses or the skill of the charioteers that they liked, but it's the shirt they support. If in mid race the colours could be changed round, the fans would all change sides at once. A cheap shirt is far and away the most important thing, not just among the crowd, which is cheaper than the shirt anyhow, but even for serious people.

Pliny might have been expected to admire the theatre more: at least the spectacle was literary – sometimes. The great dramas of the Greek and Roman traditions were performed, but many other types of entertainment were provided on the stage: music and dancing, mime and acrobatics, clowning and singing.

Rome's three theatres were among its finest buildings. They were named after Pompey, Marcellus and Cornelius Balbus, and had all been established between 55 and 13 BC, but frequently embellished and reworked. Unlike modern theatres, they were not enclosed halls but huge, semi-circular auditoria open to the sky and facing a long, raised stage. Behind the stage a massive screen, decorated with precious marbles, statues and ornaments of every kind enclosed the theatres. They seated between 10,000 and 25,000, and were one of the key locations for imperial pageantry and spectacle.

These theatres were the traditional venue for spectacles in honour of the gods. A rigid pattern of seating was enforced by law, with public officials at the front, good seats for soldiers, women and slaves at the back. Theatres and circuses had roots in the Greek cities. For the third type of popular spectacle the Romans invented a new architectural form – they used a Greek term to describe it, *amphitheatrum*, which meant 'double theatre'. They built two theatres front to front and made a giant ellip-tical enclosure. The amphitheatre we call the Colosseum, the largest in the world, had been dedicated when Hadrian was a child. It held 50,000 people.

The point of the amphitheatre was to display two sorts of combat. The first, and original, was single combat between armed gladiators (the word means 'swordsman'). Violent and dangerous fighting had been linked with death for centuries in Italy, and in Rome, where the first gladiatorial spectacles had commemorated the deaths of prominent men. Their development from the grand funeral to pure entertainment must reflect the enthusiasm of those who watched, giving the incentive to provide more fights, and then to build special structures in which the maximum number of people could watch. Many gladiators were slaves. True, they were low in status; true, the chances of violent death were high. But there were winners as well as losers: public esteem brought honour; there was a place for skill and courage; and there was a way out at the end for the lucky few who lived long enough.

We can only make sense of the taste for watching hand-to-hand fighting to the death by skilled armed men (in so far as we can make sense of it at all) by recalling that this was the way in which real soldiers fought. When the practice of staging gladiatorial games was born, Rome's soldiers were conquering the world and, in the process, running huge risks: several wars of the second and first centuries BC caused widespread anxiety because all might be lost. As time went by, there were as many wars of Roman against Roman as of Roman against enemy, and fighting became still more fascinating. But all the time, in the development of the world Hadrian ruled, there was a real chance that a man might not experience the horrors of battle or the sacking of cities for himself. By Hadrian's time, fewer than one adult male in fifty across the empire had served in an army. So, military combat in the arena came to be further removed from reality. It also gave the observer a chance to take the general's-eye view, to share in the excitement and glory of war without the risk.

Gladiatorial games brought war home, in an exciting but fundamentally reassuring way. As the fights became more and more elaborate, in this profoundly historically conscious society, they re-created the great battles of history. Spartans fought Athenians, Greeks fought Persians. When the Colosseum and the Baths of Titus were dedicated, the arena was flooded, and naval combats from the history of Thucydides were revised, with the Athenians capturing Syracuse. Sometimes the combatants were more unusual kinds of underdog: Domitian set up battles between women and dwarfs. The re-creation of historical wars invited identification of the 'us' and the 'them', and fostered the expectation that there would be losers who deserved something nasty to happen to them. That could be arranged too – with staged fights in which some or all of the participants were convicted criminals.

In these penal gladiatorial games criminals were armed and forced to fight for their lives in front of jeering crowds. This was popular in Rome's Circus Maximus, but disapproved of in Athens where Apollonius, the holy man, persuaded the Athenians to stop holding them in the theatre of Dionysus – 'They paid high prices to buy up convicted adulterers, male prostitutes, burglars [the word means 'people who dig holes through walls'], cutpurses, and kidnapping slavers, armed them, and told them to fight.'

Similar adaptation of well-known stories to the world of public order and punishment happened in the theatres, such as the execution of the bandit leader Laureolus: a real criminal was immobilised on the stage in the posture of crucifixion and savaged by wild animals. A contemporary of Hadrian described simple-minded spectators who gawped at criminals in these lethal pageants, watching them dance, and admiring the gold and purple in which they were dressed, not understanding that they were to be killed 'until they are seen goaded and whipped and with flames bursting out of that brightly-coloured and costly clothing'.

The second basic form of display in the amphitheatre was the hunt. Trained huntsmen displayed their skills on a variety of captured wildlife. The crowd thrilled to the spectacle of larger, fiercer and more exotic animals – the first giraffe, the first rhinoceros, the first tiger – being killed. At the Colosseum opening, nine thousand animals, domestic and wild, were slaughtered, some by women.

The hunt was another aristocratic privilege made available to a mass urban audience in the arena. The macho nobleman had always demonstrated his virility by crashing through bushes in pursuit of wild beasts. There had been lions in Greece until the fifth century BC, but bears, boar and deer were now the commonest prey. Hadrian was much keener on the hunt than most of the Roman upper class: more typical was Pliny, who wrote of how his idea of hunting was to sit in deep woodland, reading a book, at one end of a net into which his beaters drove wild animals . . .

The essential point of the staged hunt was that these savage creatures (and they could be made savage by cruel treatment, if they seemed to lack ferocity) were a threat to humanity, and stood for the opposite of the civilised life of the cities. Their destruction was ultimately reassuring. This, too, was often made into an allusive pageant, with tableaux of imagined exotic locations, appropriate huntsmen and hunting methods. Audiences in the capital of the empire were shown images of its distant and unpleasant margins.

Hence the punishment of 'condemnation to the beasts'. There are descriptions, and even pictures: this was a subject that the rich liked to commission in mosaic for the floors of public buildings or the dining rooms of their houses. The human victims of many such slaughters could be considered to have sunk to an even lower level of civilisation than that shared by good slaves because they had practised criminal activities such as brigandage. If you lived outside the world of order that went with Roman power, in the untamed wilds on the edge of the empire, or in underdeveloped zones within it, on mountains or in swamps where the lawless fled, you deserved all you got. Under Augustus, a Sicilian bandit was killed in the heart of Roman order, at Rome in the forum: he was dropped into a cage of aggressive wild animals. The message could hardly have been clearer: this was 'keeping the violent in constant fear', seen as an essential part of the Roman emperor's job description.

The element of chance was not always missing. Sometimes the victims were given an opportunity to run or resist. And folk-tales told of wonderful escapes. The story of Androclus, spared by the lion he had helped, is well known; similar tales occur in popular literature about Christians who were condemned to die in this way.

It is hard today to imagine the audience reaction. It is often said that the excitement, suspense and horror combined to produce intoxication, and accounts by philosophically minded writers suggest you could be carried away. But how easy was it to watch prisoners being eaten by wild beasts, and how exciting was that compared to the competitive element in the combats of the gladiatorial arena? How much of the agony and shame did you want to see, and why? The popular stories of escapes suggest that some felt a little sympathy or compassion – even for the animals. Cicero (whose own attitude is studiedly philo-sophical) described an unusual occasion in the wild-beast spec-tacles:

> The rest of the hunts took place twice a day for five days; they were magnificent, nobody denies it. But what pleasure can there be for a civilised man when either some powerless man is ripped to shreds by a powerful beast or some magnificent animal is trans-fixed by a spear? But if this kind of show must be viewed, you have seen the same thing often in the past. We who were present at these spectacles saw nothing new. The last day belonged to the elephants. The common crowd found much to admire in this event, but did not really enjoy it. On the contrary, a certain pity was aroused in them and they came to the opinion that this beast shared a certain affinity with the human race.

The audience could not be relied on to take the official line on criminals either. Even bandits could earn celebrity status. A century after Hadrian, a brigand chief in Italy became a popular hero, famous for his lucky escapes and challenges to the authorities. When he was finally caught he was interrogated by the commander of the praetorian guard himself: 'Why are you a bandit?' Coolly, the prisoner replied, 'Why are you a commander of the praetorians?'

The spectacle was intended to make onlookers glad that it was not happening to them, and to reflect on whether, and in what circumstances, it might. It was an effective control on slave disorder: the unfree knew that this could happen to them if they stepped out of line. If you were a rich man, though, you knew that it was illegal for you to be put to death in this way, no matter what you did. And if that didn't remind you of the usefulness of rank, it is hard to imagine what might have done.

The difference between our world and the pleasures of Roman spectacle seem immense, so it is salutary to recall that it is only two centuries since women were burned as witches at the stake in London, and only three since the luckier English political dissidents from Somerset or Dorset, who had supported Monmouth's bid for the throne, were sold as slaves for the Jamaica plantations. As for participation in the regime of punishment, the last public hanging in Britain took place as recently as 1868.

The key point in making death and pain a spectacle was that you could tell who was scoring most points. Prestige was on show: it was *visible*. You could not escape the demonstrations of status, and some were extremely impressive. But what was added here was an element of luck. The uncertainty of fortune, the threat hanging over all the city-dwellers, especially in Rome, was a vital part of the spectacle. Hadrian played to that when he made the games the occasion for a lottery, involving the audience directly in the excitement of the show of the revealing of what chance had in store.

* * *

In Hadrian's time the competition between cities to give the best prizes to artists and sportsmen, through holding grander and more prestigious festivals, narrowed the empire's horizons. There were hundreds of such competitions, ranging from the Olympic Games, the Pythian Games of Delphi, the Nemean and Isthmian Games (these four were known as the Circuit), to local events in remote backwaters such as the one in Lycia, for which Hadrian gave his personal permission. A tide of competitors made its way from city to city around the empire, attracting hordes of spectators and providing a lucrative commercial opportunity for opportunists.

Just after Hadrian's death, the athlete Publius Aelius Nicomachus received an honorific statue in his home town of Magnesia-and-Maeander in western Turkey, with the inscription:

> victor of the Circuit, manager of the training-ground, the first and only, in all time, to have won all of –
>
> 1. The boys' *pankration* in the 224th Olympic Games
> 2. immediately after, the Capitoline games at Rome
> 3. the Augustan games at Naples
> 4. the Actian games
> 5. the Pan-Athenian games, given in their upgraded form for the first time by the God Hadrian
> 6. in Smyrna, the Common Games of Asia
> 7. the Isthmian games
> 8. the Nemean games
> 9. the Heavenly Games at Sparta
> 10. the Isthmian games again, in the *pankration* of the beardless
>
> – with never a draw, never a stalemate. He was honoured by the god Hadrian with Roman citizenships for himself, his father, his mother and his brothers, and put in charge of the training-ground at Cyzicus; he frequently served as ambassador to the emperors, going both to Rome and to Pannonia.

The *pankration* was a violent form of all-in wrestling. Nicomachus' experience shows how useful it could be to a community to produce a hero of this kind, who would bother the emperor with petitions on behalf of his city – perhaps even get a hearing.

The spectacles produced celebrities: gladiators were popular with ladies of high birth, some of whom developed the taste to fight. That an edict was drawn up prohibiting them from doing so suggests that the possibility existed.

Charioteers might become just as distinguished. Here is the record of one of the heroes of the Circus Maximus:

Crescens, driver for the Blues, from Morocco, aged 22. He won the four-horse chariot race for the first time on 8 November 113, at the Games in honour of the Birthday of the Divine Nerva, starting in 24th place, with the horses West Wind, Hawk, Refinement and Wild Olive. Between 113 and the Games in honour of the Birthday of the Divine Claudius, 1 August 124, he drove in 686 races, of which he won 47–19 in the four-chariot race, 23 in the eight-chariot, 5 in the twelve-chariot. In one he won by default, in 8 he had the lead throughout, 38 he won at the finishing line. He won 130 second prizes, and 111 third prizes. The profit he took home: 1,558,346 *sestertii*.

The property qualification for a senator was a million *sestertii*. Crescens could never have aspired to rise so high (he was probably born a slave) but in spending power he was in that league.

The greatest celebrity in the circus, theatre or amphitheatre was, of course, the emperor. The games were intended to glorify him and his family. Many of the occasions for the best festivals were the birthdays and other anniversaries of the ruling house. After the death and deification of his wife's mother Matidia, Hadrian concluded a programme of the most colossal entertainment by giving out free perfume to the people in her honour, and by making balsam and saffron flow down the auditorium of the theatre in honour of his adoptive father Trajan. The record of the achievements of the emperors in presiding over the unparalleled holiday life of their capital was part of the official history. A fragmentary list of events in a year of Hadrian's reign includes:

14 days before the Kalends of May were held with . . . games and a show of 38 days, and [ ]28 pairs of gladiators, and 2,246 beasts killed. 7 days before the Kalends of June the emperor gave the first game of the festival for Venus. There were fights for [ ]3 days, with 195 pairs of gladiators, and 443 beasts were killed.'

This was business as usual in Rome. The emperor was covered with glory for the imagination, organisation and expense that went into the spectacles. But he had a more direct function too. The crowd was watching how he behaved and how he communicated with them. They played to him, and he responded spontaneously. There was a dialogue between him and the people: the emperor addressed them through heralds or with placards. In the theatres it was a three-way exchange, as it involved the actors too. 'Bye-bye, Dad, bye-bye, Mum,' sang a performer in front of Nero. No one in the audience missed the eating and swimming gestures: the emperor was believed to have poisoned his father and attempted to drown his mother. Nero didn't dare punish the satirist. It was in exchanges like this that rumour and gossip about the emperors originated.

VI

THE TRAVELLING EMPEROR

He will travel the empire with unclean foot . . .

SIBYLLINE ORACLE

No other Roman emperor travelled anything like as much as Hadrian, and it is startling to reflect that no one else has ever travelled between Seville and Belgrade, York and Cairo, Frankfurt, Aleppo and Tunis as the unquestioned absolute ruler of all the lands around them. Hadrian was famed for his endless journeys around the empire, which became a defining characteristic of his reign.

The Roman empire was vast. Every inch of the Mediterranean coast was Roman, and all the lands with easy access to it: Spain, Portugal, Italy, Croatia, Montenegro, Albania, Greece and almost all of Turkey, with all the islands, great and small. In Africa, Roman rule extended down the Atlantic coast of Morocco, and inland to the Atlas Mountains and the edge of the Sahara. The north of Tunisia was a rich and populous part of the empire, as was Egypt: the annual flood of the Nile renewed the minerals in the soil, which made for reliable harvests in most years. Roads led hundreds of kilometres across the Eastern Desert to the quarries of rare building stone at Claudian Mountain, the ports on the Red Sea, White Harbour and Mouse Harbour, at which traders in spice or jewels from south India put in.

To the east, Roman rule during Hadrian's reign stopped where an ancient bridge called The Link crossed the Euphrates. Beyond, prosperous Mesopotamia was subject to the king of Parthia, but all the fertile country of Syria, Jordan, and Palestine and Israel as far as the desert was also Roman and Trajan had built a great road down to the Red Sea at the Gulf of Aqaba. The mountains of eastern Turkey and the plains of Georgia were mostly Roman. Roman fleets controlled the Black Sea, and the empire controlled the flourishing cities of the Crimea and its region, markets for the trade of the great rivers that flow into the Black Sea out of the steppe.

The settled Mediterranean coastlands had always suffered from raids through the passes that gave access to the north – the Carcassonne and Rhône corridors, the Alpine passes, the saddle where Zagreb commands the route into Italy from the middle Danube, and the Vardar gateway from Serbia, Macedonia and Bulgaria, which comes out at Thessaloniki. The Romans had set up provinces as bulwarks and barriers beyond the ends of all these routes, linking them with an intricate 1800-kilometre frontier system along the Rhine and the Danube, and all of today's France and Hungary with a good chunk of Austria and Germany. Finally, imperial adventuring had added two substantial provinces still further from the Mediterranean heartland: the mountainous centre of today's Romania, and most of the island of Britain.

Southern Spain, Catalonia, Provence, northern and central Italy, central Dalmatia, the east coast of the Aegean, north Syria and Lebanon, Egypt and Tunisia with Sicily and Cyprus were among the most urbanised and densely inhabited regions of the empire. Morocco, north-western Spain, northern France and Belgium, much of northern Britain and the strip of provinces along the Rhine and Danube were the main military zone.

By any standard it amounted to a vast territory. It seemed to its people to be the greatest and most important part of the inhabited world *and* the known world. Inside, it was the familiar zone described in literature, and united by the common cultures of Greece and Rome. Outside, civilisation fell away, and the systematic knowledge of observers and writers tailed off.

Hadrian's first imperial journey across this world was his progress towards Rome, by way of the Danube, from Antioch, where he had been hailed as emperor, in 117–18. He spent less than three years in Rome before he set off on an ambitious tour of the western provinces. The furthest destination, and very likely the main objective of the expedition, was the province of Britain, where he spent several months in 122. In 123 he was in Spain, and responded to news of danger in the east with a voyage the length of the Mediterranean. In 124 he made two significant stops: in central Turkey he met the love of his life, the young Antinous, and a return visit to Athens gave him the opportunity to demonstrate his great fondness for the city with a massive building programme. In 125 he returned to Rome.

In spring 128 he set sail for the African provinces, came back to Rome briefly in the autumn, then headed east again. He spent the winter in Greece, and moved on to the eastern frontier. In 130 he passed through Judaea on his way to Egypt, and refounded the ruined city of Jerusalem as a chartered Roman town. In Egypt, Antinous died. Hadrian returned to Athens for the winter of 131.

In 132 the Jewish war demanded his personal attention, and he was back in Rome, never to travel again, by spring 134. He had spent half of his reign away from the capital, and had visited nearly every province in the empire.

Transporting and supplying the emperor and his entourage was a major operation. It deserved its reputation as the pinnacle of meticulous planning. Except on long sea voyages the aim was to move him, his wife, their companions and most intimate slave attendants to a city where they could be reasonably comfortable. They would stay as guests of the richest men in the community, who had their own houses or country estates. Most considered it an honour to play host to the emperor, however much it cost, because it was seen as a benefaction to their city, which would otherwise have had to foot the bill. The soldiers, with other dependants and functionaries, were either billeted on the townspeople or found lodgings, as did the crowds of petitioners and sightseers who arrived with the imperial party. Hadrian usually stayed for a few weeks in a comfortable place. His trips were not hurried.

The emperor and the other VIPs travelled at a reasonable pace. Hadrian and his companions might ride their horses, but the ladies of the court always used carriages. To dream that you are travelling in a chariot or by four-wheeled wagon with a company of men, says Artemidorus, tellingly, means acquiring great authority, or the birth of useful children. But it isn't of great help if you are planning long journeys – the dream guarantees safety, but also extreme slowness.

Between cities, public posting-stations were maintained for officials and state messengers. In military zones, Hadrian and his officers would stay with the commander of each base, who invariably had a stylish and well-appointed house that went with the job. Occasionally the travelling court took equipment for a bivouac, with luxurious tents, portable furniture and cooking equipment, but there was always a huge amount of baggage, including clothes and home comforts, and also to service the imperial administration, which followed the emperor wherever he went.

The emperor did not usually travel in imperially owned ships and vehicles, but relied on local resources, hired or requisitioned for the occasion. Sometimes there were spin-offs for those lucky enough to get involved: Hadrian was once ferried across the Aegean by a captain called Erastus, and wrote on his behalf afterwards to the city council of Ephesus suggesting that they might consider the man for membership – a high honour for someone in his walk of life. Typically, Hadrian remembered to suggest to the Ephesians that they should make their usual checks on eligibility and background – he did not wish to impose someone on them who wasn't suitable . . . The council probably didn't hesitate for long: someone had Hadrian's letter of recommendation cut into a slab of marble, which speaks for itself.

Sea travel was far quicker and cheaper than inching along the imperial highways, but it was unsafe. Except in the height of summer, and sometimes even then, storms make the Mediterranean dangerous and shipwreck was common. In storms, the terrified passengers were advised to put on their gold ornaments: if the person who found their corpse got a reward, he might be more likely to give it at least a perfunctory funeral.

Seafaring was mainly the preserve of traders. The movement of goods by sea was essential for the survival of ancient cities, and could be hugely profitable, but it was seen as a gamble. Nevertheless it happened on a huge scale, and sophisticated infrastructures developed. There was a traders' centre in Rome's port city, Ostia, where thirty or forty cities from up and down the empire each maintained an office, floored with mosaic pavement depicting their own symbols. The largest vessels carried the wheat provided out of tribute for the basic needs of the population of Rome. The run from Alexandria to Italy with each year's harvest was glamorous: the arrival of the fleet was a great event, and the captains 'drove the ships on like race-horses'. Vessels carrying 340 tons were standard, but some giants carried more than a thousand. Many trading ships were much smaller, though, and tramped heroically from port to port, exchanging small, mixed cargoes.

The trade ships also carried hundreds of passengers – St Paul found passage towards Italy on a grain-freighter. Emperors did not travel in that way, of course, and were generally unwilling to entrust their persons, entourages and valuable equipment to the weather. They tended to limit their seafaring to short ferry-like journeys, which saved huge detours: between Italy and Greece, for instance, or the crossing to Africa, or the hop across the Aegean, which Erastus provided for Hadrian. The emperors maintained fine ships for themselves and could make use of the fast vessels of the fleet, which was maintained to protect trade links from the threat of piracy.

The public post – the official message-relay system used by provincial governors and other officials to communicate with Rome – relied on posting-stations at regular intervals of fifteen to twenty miles along the highways. These were inns, with overnight accommodation, stabling, store-rooms and other facilities. Like other instruments of the Roman state, they were run by local people with labour and materials provided by the communities as part of their taxes. Official travellers carried documents that entitled them to service at these establishments. As usual, the problem was the grey areas. Soldiers implied or made use of intimidation and violence. Documents were forged or issued to too many people as a result of corruption in the bureaucracy or special cases – Pliny persuaded Trajan to let him use them for his wife's journey from his province back to Rome to console her aunt on a bereavement, and Trajan also gave the privilege to his favourite orator-philosopher Polemo. Those supervising the exaction of services or food, animals or materials, took too much. Before Hadrian's arrival in Egypt in 130, a document attests to huge demands levied on a pair of insignificant villages in the Nile valley, including 372 suckling pigs.

The public post depended on the road network, and Roman roads deserve their reputation. They provided a reliable, dense net of transport and communication covering the whole empire: they crossed waterlogged areas on embankments, reduced gradients with cuttings and tunnels, and bridged streams or deep valleys. Their stone or gravel surface could be kept reasonably clear of mud or other obstructions. Even more important, distances and routes became predictable: milestones were set up and itineraries published. Officials and soldiers, traders and tax-collectors knew where they were going. Roads, bridges, milestones and posting-stations were also a visible demonstration of power, ruthlessly cutting across settlement patterns or landscapes with minimum deviation from the surveyed line.

To the Roman observer, the roads had a military feel. They had been developed for strategic needs, and were often built by soldiers. The vigour with which they were maintained derived from their security value, which lay in the use of the road to deploy troops and supplies, and in the awe that the ability to construct it instilled in a region's inhabitants. When Trajan invaded Dacia, he bridged the Danube – accomplishing the impossible: he inverted the order of nature, turning wet into dry, and brought together Roman and barbarian. At the wondrous bridge there was a tax office. The manager, a slave of the emperor, put up a religious dedication to three deities: 'To Jupiter, Best and Greatest, of the Land of Dacia and to the Genius of the Roman People and of Commerce, Felix, slave of our Emperor, manager of the office at Imperial Bridge, former acting manager of the office at Micia.'

Hadrian's wandering helped to promote the precarious integration of the Roman empire. A king's progress through his dominion had been a familiar feature of monarchies in ancient Persia; and Roman governors had borrowed it, combining it with the administration of justice under Roman law on assize tours around their often sprawling areas of responsibility. Inspection was the best way to make sure that people were doing things according to the blueprint.

The presence of the emperor was electrifying. As self-advertisement it was way ahead of publishing correspondence with governors, useful as that was for the literate strata of society from which imperial administrators were drawn. Under Hadrian, far more of the empire's subjects set eyes on their ruler than ever had before, and Hadrian was the subject of numerous anecdotes.

He was once petitioned by a woman at the roadside. 'I do not have the leisure,' he replied, to which she responded, 'Then stop being emperor!' Hadrian turned back and allowed her to present her case.

Bothering the emperor was a principal activity of the age. As he moved, so did the petitioners. In 115 an earthquake devastated Antioch. Many people were killed because the city was tightly packed with densely inhabited high apartment blocks. The emperor, Trajan, was in residence at the time, which ensured that the disaster's effects were all the greater. As the historian Dio puts it, 'Many soldiers and many private citizens had come together there from all over the world, for lawsuits, or petitions, or because of the commercial opportunity, or just out of curiosity, so that there was no community or city-population which was left undamaged by the catastrophe, and in a certain sense the whole inhabited world ruled by Rome was smitten in Antioch.'

Wherever Hadrian went, people from all over his dominions followed him. The documents that record routine replies to queries or petitions track his movements. Hadrian was reported to be magnanimous, generous, kingly, and he liked to extend his reputation by reaching as large a public as possible. He initiated grants and benefactions, renamed, rebuilt, reorganised, inserted 'Aelius' and 'Hadrianus' into titles and names across the world, ensuring that his reign was woven into the fabric of local memory – Aelia Augusta, Aelia Capitolina, Hadriane, Hadrianeia, Hadrianopolis, Hadrian's Harbour, even Hadrian's Hunt, the new name of a town in the mountains of Turkey where he had a particularly satisfying hunting expedition.

As usual, imitating the blueprint was the key. The empire's cities were kept going by the prodigal expenditure of local bigwigs, whose power depended on prestige that in turn depended on displays of loyalty and gratitude for services rendered. This spending – on buildings, shows, services, handouts, improvements – could easily be moulded and patterned according to imperial priorities. Local benefactors everywhere rushed to show that they were on-message, equipping their cities with monuments to keep Hadrian's visit fresh in people's memories.

Hadrian, the travelling benefactor, fitted perfectly into the world of competing cities, setting the trend, then regulating the taste and the tone of hundreds of other benefactors. Competing aristocrats in the cities were all soaked in the history and literature of the glorious Greek past, and Hadrian lapped up the flattering oratory, criticised the poetry, commented knowledgeably on the honorific architecture. His way of ruling the cultured élites was to travel among them as one of them, as Roman notables had done for two hundred years. This was an intellectual on the move: 'He was a glutton for travelling: so much that he wanted to learn more in person about all the places in the whole world which he had read about in books,' according to an ancient biographer.

That explains the hunting as well as the high culture. Hadrian might give a city baths, a gateway, or a water supply – or the skin of a she-bear he had killed with his own hands. The heroic huntsman was a persona adopted by many an ancient aristo-crat, and dated back, like so much else, to Homer. It enabled Hadrian to explore the fringes as well as the urban heartlands. What may appear as a touristic element in Hadrian's journeying is an element of his self-image as the intellectuals' intellectual. So with his mountain-climbing: he ascended Etna and – just before his death – a high, holy mountain in Syria where his sacri-fice at the summit was disturbed by the terrible omen of thun-derbolts. But it is most vividly seen in the graffiti left by the imperial party on their Egyptian trip.

The site is the ancient colossal statues of Pharaoh Amenhotep IV in the plain on the west bank of the Nile at Luxor. The account given to wealthy travellers was that these statues repre-sented Memnon, the son of the goddess of the dawn. This inter-pretation was neat, because there was a strange acoustic accident in the stones that produced a weird noise most mornings when the already hot sun warmed up the stones after the night's chill. It was said to be the son's morning greeting to his mother. Traditionally this sight featured on a tour itinerary of the area, and the excited visitor carved on the lower limbs of one statue a record of their visit. Hadrian's party was no exception. The oddity in this case is that the record took the form of a self-consciously learned poem, composed in the archaic Greek in which Sappho had written. These verses were also by a woman, Balbilla, who came from one of the richest milieux in the eastern provinces, in which the descendants of local kings, rich Roman entrepreneurs, officials of proud ancient cities and recently appointed career senators mingled. Hadrian's cultured entourage was part of the network through which the empire was run.

Hadrian took pride in reaching remote destinations on the map of the world, however difficult the terrain. Trajan had also been where no Roman emperor had been before, and had shown off his power by building roads, bridges, canals. In the Parthian wars he had fought his way past what is now Baghdad, to the ancient capital Babylon, where he visited the house in which Alexander the Great had died. Then he went on to where Basra now stands, in southern Iraq, to reach the shore of the Persian Gulf. As he looked out across its shallow waters, he envisaged India beyond, and lamented that, unlike Alexander, he would never be able to extend his wars of conquest so far. Hadrian was not interested in conquest, but he was keen to reach the edges of the known world as an observer. He took pride in getting into the mountains on the edge of what is now Georgia because it was where a famous Greek commander, persevering against all the odds, brought his army down to the Black Sea half a millennium before. He was also in a place that no Roman emperor had been before . . . out towards the extreme east of the empire.

Something similar, no doubt, led to his early journey to Britain: intellectual and historical excitement combined with practical military needs. One of the largest Roman armies in the empire was stationed there, and emperors were expected to review their troops, and fight wars; they had always derived much of their prestige from their victories. New emperors undertook aggressive military action. It was one reason why the post of emperor had come into being: he was *imperator*, wielder of the power that Romans called *imperium*.

VII

IMPERIUM

Both in public addresses to the People in Rome, and in the Senate, he often said that he would run the state as if it belonged to the People and not to himself.

HISTORIA AUGUSTA

In many of his surviving portrait-statues, Hadrian appears arrayed as a general, with a breastplate of gold and silver, finely decorated with images of gods and auspicious symbols, a purple cloak and military boots. Wherever he went he was accompanied by his official entourage of twenty-four bodyguards, called *lictors*, who carried the *fasces* – the bundle of rods and an axe tied with crimson ribbon. ('*Lictor*' means someone who ties up a bundle.) The rods were for beating and the axes for decapitation: they stood for the official's power to give orders, with the sanction of capital punishment if he was disobeyed.

The *lictors* and the *fasces* were the outward sign of the highest authority that the Roman people could bestow. It was called *imperium*, and it was essentially the power of command over Rome's citizens as soldiers. The idea was so central to them that the Romans used the same word to refer to their empire across the world: the power given to Rome's commanders and the power of Rome were the same thing. The commander was called *imperator*, and Augustus used it to emphasise his domination of the armies of the Roman people, the Roman state and the empire ruled by Rome.

But military command, though central, was only part of the story. The power of the commander was traditional and constitutional: with it came a wider set of governmental associations. They, too, were reflected in Hadrian's appearance. There were many formal public occasions when military attire was inappropriate. Then he would wear the heavy woollen wrap of a Roman citizen, the toga. This was part of the elaborate charade through which the emperors played along with Augustus' old idea that he was the successor of the legally appointed officials of the old Roman constitution, and was what Hadrian meant when he said he would 'run the state as if it belonged to the People and not to himself'.

Whether military or civilian, punctilious about tradition or not, an emperor could not do without help, and he was surrounded by concentric circles of senior men who helped to run the empire.

The smallest and most intimate group contained the few people with whom he spent most of his time. Much of an emperor's day was spent on the activities of an ordinary wealthy man: religious rites, bathing, exercising, reading, dining and social life. Family members might be included in this group, with intimate friends and favoured slaves or ex-slaves. Hadrian's inner circle was composed of Antinous and a few almost unknown freedmen. His wife does not seem to have been an intimate.

The élite members of the inner circle usually belonged to the more formal body called the Emperor's Council: a flexible gathering of a dozen of the most senior senators, ex-governors and other officials, such as the prefects of the praetorian guard. It met at the emperor's convenience, wherever he was. Although emperors picked new members when they came to power, senior figures served for long periods and helped provide continuity between reigns. The emperor decided the agenda, which meant that the subjects discussed might sometimes be frivolous. The satirist Juvenal wrote a sketch of a council meeting in Domitian's fortress-like country estate and its discussion of the best way to cook a giant turbot that had been presented to the emperor.

Hadrian, however, made a point of including the foremost legal experts of the time, and became pedantically interested in the working of Roman law and justice.

On Hadrian's journeys, his inner circle and many of the council moved with him, but he needed reliable deputies in the metropolis. For the emperor to be away from Rome so much was popular neither with Senate nor people, for whom the emperor was a vital source of handouts and spectacles. One figure of authority was Hadrian's close relative Julius Servianus, but the two men who seem to have been trusted most were socially and, by their military rank, significantly junior – less of a political risk to an absent emperor. They were energetic, disciplined, competent and far from pushy. Marcius Turbo and Sulpicius Similis had both held the vital job of commander of the praetorian guard. Anecdotes about their toughness and straightforwardness were constantly repeated.

Another circle around the emperor was formed by the provincial governors, some twenty men of varying importance according to the size and status of their province. But they were, of course, based a long way from him. They were almost all members of the Senate.

When Romulus founded the city in 753 BC, the senior heads of households were said to have formed a hereditary aristocratic élite known as the patricians. Up to Hadrian's time and far beyond, a group of them believed they had the most venerable ancestry and highest status in Roman society. Everyone else was a plebeian, but since some plebeian families had won access in the mid-fourth century to senior positions, such as consulship, power and success, they became just as aristocratic as authentic patricians. They included some of the grandest families in Rome and were indistinguishable from the true blue-bloods.

Some offices of the state were reserved for patricians, others for plebeians, which perpetuated the élite. At the end of his year in office the former holder retained for life a seat in the Council of Office Holders – the Senate. A man became eligible for the Senate at the age of thirty, and could remain a member for as long as he chose, providing he could show he owned property worth one million *sestertii* (most had much more: Pliny is estimated to have had a property worth altogether at least thirteen million).

It was these ancient offices that the assembly of Roman citizens had traditionally filled by voting, in a unique first-past-the-post election in which the better-off voted first. The Roman citizenry was divided into thirty-five named voting units, each of which had a corridor marked out in the Enclosure outside the city, between ropes and posts. The voters filed along it in order of wealth, dropping their token into the urn bearing their favoured candidate's name. When a sufficient number of votes had been cast, they were counted. It wasn't democracy as we know it, but the outcome was uncertain, and there was both bribery and electoral violence. By Hadrian's time it had ceased, and all public appointments were ratified by the emperor, who thereby controlled the career of everyone in the Senate. Every citizen continued to be assigned to one of the old units, however – Hadrian's family was in the one named Sergia.

Many ancient public appointments were open to senators. There were posts in charge of the public treasury, and supervising buildings and festivals in Rome. There were judicial offices, and various specialised functions administering the sewers, the banks and bed of the Tiber and the aqueducts. There were military offices too. An important and unusual position involved responsibility for the political well-being of the people. The Tribunes of the People held a veto on the actions of the office-holders and the Senate, designed to help them protect any citizen who was being threatened unjustly. Augustus had annexed the symbolism of the tribunate and although the Tribunes of the People still existed under Hadrian, it was a largely ceremonial function – as were many evocations of the old Roman state, including the senatorial offices Hadrian had held as a young man.

The Senate still met regularly: it had 600 or so members, of whom 250 to 400 attended. The atmosphere was sometimes less than dignified: Pliny records how the tablets in a secret ballot were found to have been scribbled on with facetious or obscene messages. Hadrian's absences from Rome accelerated the decline of the Senate's importance except as an emblem of the past and the aristocracy, although he treated it with respect.

Other official functions were performed by members of the equestrian order, who had to have assets worth at least four hundred thousand *sestertii*. In the dim and distant past, they had been the cavalry of the citizen army (horses cost a lot to keep), but now every Roman citizen in the empire with assets that met the means test was seen as a member. They filled particular officers' jobs in the army, in charge of the non-Roman regiments, while senators commanded the legions, the citizen regiments. It was a logical system.

The emperors often recruited to the Senate promising men from the equestrian order (seldom from further down the social scale), including people from rich provincial backgrounds like Trajan and Hadrian. However, most senators inherited their position and many came from the upper classes of towns in Italy. It didn't take many generations for senators to adopt the airs of the ancient Roman aristocracy, and periodically the emperors promoted the grandest (and most loyal) families to the patriciate, so that Romulus' institution didn't die out.

So much for the top and the centre. But the grandees of the senatorial and equestrian offices were not the people who ran the empire on the ground. The Roman empire was divided up into jurisdictions, each of which had a city at its heart. Everyone was subject to their local city, which ran most of its own affairs, saw to its own finances, often struck its own currency (coins of the Roman state were everywhere, but there were local currencies too). Roman governors ruled the cities, which ruled the people, who gave orders to their slaves.

In some places autonomous cities were only a few miles apart; in others they were widely scattered. Most cities contained only a few thousand people, but some were larger. Jurisdictions often included several villages dependent on the city.

In the past, cities had been more or less independent: they had trained their young men as soldiers and gone to war against each other. Under Roman rule this did not happen – any trained young men joined the Roman army – but cities still competed with each other, for honour, tax breaks, status and disputed territory. The only way to win was to gain the favour of a regional governor or, even better, the emperor, and the best way to do this was through petitions or long, formal speeches, backed up by lavish spectacles and sometimes even bribes.

The rich families in each community managed the competition between cities. In most, a handful of families owned most of the land and provided the town councillors and officials. Public institutions varied, but the same basic structure was to be found everywhere: officials who served for a year, a council, composed of former office-holders, and a nominal assembly of the people, usually a few hundred of the freeborn inhabitants. In larger cities there might be as many as a hundred town councillors. Former slaves could not become councillors, but there was often a sort of parallel council and offices for them. Everyone in public life was expected to spend handsomely on handouts, shows, buildings, subsidies and embassies to the emperor or governor. In return they received acclaim – literally, since the main function of a public meeting was to chant approving slogans about popular officials. Many dignitaries did not like having to spend their money in this way, especially when times were hard, and constantly devised ways to raise new sources of income – hence the special public offices for ex-slaves, who were sometimes quite rich. Some cities even appointed wealthy women to official posts.

The system resulted in some curiously skewed priorities. Cities were filled with huge buildings, performance and entertainment flourished, while literature and art received a major boost through ostentatious expenditure by city élites. But the money to pay for it all was screwed out of the tenants, slaves and casual labourers of the élite, who sold the food these people grew at maximum profit to themselves. The holy man Apollonius came across a place where the people ate vetch and other famine foods because the élite had hidden the corn in their barns for export at a higher price than the local community could pay. The people there were so desperate that they were threatening to burn the governor alive. Apollonius was sworn to silence, but wrote down a terrifying prediction of doom and showed it to the hoarders, who hastily gave up the food. This city was lucky, but it was a common predicament.

The autonomous city-states fell under the jurisdiction of a provincial governor, usually a senator, appointed by the emperor: the empire was too big and communications not nearly good enough for centralisation to have been an effective way to manage them. Provinces were allowed to retain their own traditions, languages, religions, customs, and even, to some extent, laws. The governor received detailed instructions before making his formal departure from the capital, then had to be relatively independent of Rome and the emperor during his term of office, which was usually short, sometimes just a year.

Most Roman officials were amateurs. They had passed no tests, and were rarely selected for their ability in running the Roman world. Loyalty, birth, wealth, political skill, experience, probity and intelligence were criteria for appointment, in roughly descending order of importance: provincial government was often careless and decisions arbitrary. On top of that, governors were often eager to enrich themselves by fair means or foul. Between competence and greed, some provinces had a terrible time: during the first century AD, Judaea was one of the least fortunate jurisdictions.

In the days when the empire was newly won, governors had had extensive opportunities to plunder their provinces. It was a tradition that was slow to die: Pliny recounted in a letter his lead role in prosecuting for corruption a governor of the province that was Hadrian's family home. The governor had been foolish enough to keep accounts 'in his own hand, of his takings from each transaction and each legal hearing. He had even sent cocky and self-important letters to one of his mistresses in Rome – "Yippee! I'm on my way – got away with it completely – I sold off a good chunk of the provincials and made four million . . .'"

Maladministration was a convenient charge for a hostile emperor to level against political enemies, so governors did not have *carte blanche*. During Hadrian's reign, and for long before, higher standards were often discussed, but practice was a different matter.

For a generation before Hadrian, government documents show decision-makers increasingly keen to tell us they are getting it right. A 'culture of good practice' developed, in which it was 'the glory of the times we live in' to do things in exactly the way that the handbooks prescribed. Indeed, the display of good order also took the form of composing them, such as the aqueduct-commissioner Frontinus' *On the Waters of Rome*.

Central to the Roman idea of good order was the law, on which the Romans had long prided themselves. They had four monosyllabic words that meant 'law', and each illustrates something important about how Rome worked. The obvious one was *lex*, statute law, the big documents in which how to do things, what you could do and couldn't do were set down. Then there was *jus*, the law of the courts. The third, *mos*, related to custom: what had always been done in good practice in the Roman state and social order. It was similar to the unwritten British constitution: 'Well, it doesn't say in any statute that we have to do this, but it's always been done like this . . .' The fourth, *fas*, was divine propriety: the Romans believed their success lay in their ability to work their relationships with the gods.

In this period, people talked about professionalism, swallowing hard: 'I spend my time writing the least literary of letters,' says Pliny, then director of one of Rome's most prominent treasuries, in a very literary letter. A conscientious equestrian lamented that the unending mounds of business generated by administration and, above all, by the stream of petitions pouring into Rome meant that no one could enjoy the unrivalled accumulation of great art. But in the end the limitations – of capacity, interest, energy and time – of the few hundred people who held official posts put the brakes on the efficiency of the system.

Pliny, as governor of an important province in the area east of modern Istanbul, shows us in action the contemporary fashion for being seen to take your duties seriously. Fifty or so of his letters to Trajan survive, written over a couple of years just before Hadrian became emperor. The emperor's replies to most are attached. They are a mixture of information and requests for advice and guidance, and in the exchange a reassuring portrait of the process of imperial decision-making is skilfully painted. How much the governor knows! How careful he has been to find precedents! How splendid that he gets on so well with the emperor, and what fun to see the emperor being tolerantly wearied by Pliny's endless correspondence! How unfailingly wise, practical, benevolent and enlightened are the emperor's suggestions! It all adds up to what Pliny calls the 'lustre of our age'.

Arrian, provincial governor in charge of the eastern part of Turkey, wrote a literary official letter to Hadrian, carefully displaying how thoroughly he was doing his job.

We came to Trebizond, a Greek city, as the famous Xenophon says, founded on the seashore . . . and we saw the view of the sea far below from the same point as Xenophon, just as you did. The altars are already standing, too, but are made of a coarse stone, which means that the letters carved on them are not easy to read: and the Greek inscription has errors, being written by barbarians. So I decided to have marble altars set up, and to have the inscriptions carved on them in good legible script. Your statue is nicely posed, with a gesture toward the sea, but the workmanship is generally poor, and it doesn't look like you. So I have sent for one which is worthy to have your name on it, in the same pose – this is a place extremely well suited for a commemoration which will last for ever.

He has revealed the nature of Roman professionalism and the key to the 'lustre of the age'. When he says he stood where the Greek general Xenophon stood, at the famous moment when his exhausted men came out of their long wanderings in the mountainous and alien interior of eastern Turkey, and saw the coast, he might have been wrong about the spot, but he had read Xenophon's text, written 520 years before. Hundreds of other authors, Greek and more recently Latin, were faithfully preserved in the same way. There were mistakes, occasional additions, careless updatings of phraseology: but millions of words of literature had been preserved by manual copying.

This was how Romans and Greeks of this period thought about law: laws were originals, to be copied, and to which comments could be added. Then the comments became part of the original, gaining authority. Precedent was regularly cited. Each new decision was added to the accumulating store, which could be preserved on papyrus or parchment and kept in archives, or on the multiple copies sold or despatched to individuals. 'Fixing' the fleeting spoken or written word was intensely popular. These texts, called inscriptions, were sometimes painted on boards, and have almost all disappeared. The best material was bronze, as metal was considered the most enduring substance, but thanks to its scrap value in later periods, only a sprinkling of bronze inscriptions has survived. But hundreds of thousands of short and long texts were inscribed on every kind of stone, and it's a text of this kind that Arrian is talking about improving at Trebizond.

This was how uniformity was managed in the empire: cities looked to what governors and emperors had said to their forebears. Army commanders checked how camps had been built or battles won in earlier periods. Emperors looked at the collected actions of earlier emperors, conscious of their own place in a gallery of imperial portraits. And lawyers studied the accumulating mound of precedent, in every sort of law, reaching way back into the distant Roman past. It was like writing a history or a speech: the context was new, and you might have some new ideas, but you started with a look at Thucydides, Demosthenes or Xenophon.

Arrian's report from Trebizond, like Pliny's letters, is meant to convey to the reader reassuring messages about how the empire worked. The spirit of the age is embodied in the pursuit of correct evocation: Greek history and decent architecture, a realistic and aesthetically adequate statue, a text in accurate Greek that was easy to read. But the point of the exercise was the emperor, Hadrian, who had been to Trebizond, and whose visit was to be commemorated by the altars and the statue. Hadrian's tour was a rerun of the great history of the distant past, and combined with it to be the subject of everlasting commemoration.

The lustre of the age was promoted effectively by Hadrian's travels. His career before he became Trajan's heir had been shaped by the mode of good practice, and he reflected his experience in many ways when he took *imperium*. His energy and attention to detail fitted well with what was thought desirable: Apollonius, the holy man, had called at dawn on the soon-to-be-emperor Vespasian during his bid for power and was told that he had been up for some time answering his mail. 'This man will be emperor,' he said. Hadrian would have qualified too.

Hadrian's involved, sensible decision-making is clearly on record. The *Digest*, the great compendium of classical Roman law, quotes Hadrian's words to governors in furtherance of high judicial standards:

> To Vibius Varus, governor of Cilicia: you are [as the judge] in a position to find out how reliable the witnesses are, what their position in society and reputation is, and who have seemed straightforward in what they say – assessing whether they've all brought along a single prepared speech, or are making plausible replies to your questions without pre-meditation.

Hadrian had a real impact on Roman law: it was he who began, in accord with the mood of the time, the spirit of codification that eventually led to completion of the *Digest*.

Hadrian's interest in the fine detail of government fitted with the still-important myth that the emperor was a senator like all the others. Hadrian was scrupulously polite to the consuls, and was conscious of the artificiality of his relations with other people. Time-honoured custom led the admirers, dependants, flatterers and friends of important Romans to pay them court, walking them home from public occasions and making friendly visits to them in the morning. Hadrian preferred to dodge them: he went home in a litter, cut off from other people, and on the days when he had to stay at home because the calendar said public business was unlucky, visitors were kept out. This appears to have gone down well, rather than being taken amiss. Another piece of good domestic management strikes a chord: it was claimed that none of the imperial household could be prevailed upon to leak details of what Hadrian said or did 'as the entourages of rulers normally do', says the historian.

He was an emperor whom the writers describing his reign have acknowledged to be unusually well equipped with the intellectual gifts needed for the job. As the biographer puts it:

> He had a gigantic memory, and immeasurable talent. He could match names to most people without the help of an announcer, even when he had heard them just once and in no particular order, so that he regularly corrected announcers' mistakes. He could recite the names of the veterans he had discharged at some point. He had a tenacious memory for books he had just read, often ones that most people hadn't heard of. He could give his attention in a single session to writing, dictation, hearing petitions, and conversing with his friends. He understood the public accounts so intimately that by comparison the most conscientious citizen's knowledge of his domestic affairs would seem skimpy.

Ancient governments did little of what we would call governing.

The Latin word *gubernare*, which gives us 'government', is a version of a Greek seafaring term for piloting a ship: government was keeping the ship of state (a popular ancient metaphor) on course.

The ancient approach was responsive and minimal: wait until an issue came up and leave it where possible for a local solution. Hence the practice of bothering the emperor, which may have engaged the ruler of the world with a few lucky individuals but wasted his time in the most unsystematic manner. Administrative jobs and specialised positions were kept to a minimum: people might otherwise think that a public job made them important when prestige was better derived from birth and wealth. So, a good deal was done by deference to status: just ask a great man for a decision.

Governing according to nine hundred years of accumulated historical, philosophical and literary precedent committed the Roman emperor to persuasion, providing information, dispensing justice, practising diplomacy, maintaining social discipline and regulating the structures of honour and status across the world he ruled. It could hardly be put better than by Fronto, a young contemporary of Hadrian:

> The job of the Caesars is to persuade the senate of what is most expedient in any issue, to expound many important matters to the people in public meetings, to emend unjust law, to send letters constantly throughout the world, to control the kings of peoples outside the empire, to improve the bad behaviour of our allies by issuing edicts, to praise benefactors, crush rebels, and keep the violent in constant fear.

The potency of the unifying culture must be part of the explanation for how all this local diversity added up to a coherent entity called the Roman empire. But the iron hand of *imperium* and the armies that made it possible to complete Fronto's vision were also instrumental in preserving this sprawling, unwieldy organism for nearly half a millennium.

VIII

WAR AND PEACE

In his fifteenth year he made a return visit to his homeland, and immediately started his life as a soldier.

HADRIAN'S BIOGRAPHER

Hadrian's title *imperator* meant 'general', and it was his principal job as emperor to be the commander-in-chief of the three hundred thousand or so Roman soldiers who were dotted around the empire. When the philosopher Favorinus disagreed with Hadrian, then gave way in the heated argument that followed, his friends were surprised: 'How can you argue against someone who has thirty legions?' he replied.

Imperium, the emperor's military command, was, like so much with Rome, a sacred thing. It was intensely personal to the commander, whose independence was carefully established: for *imperator* the Greeks used the word *autokrator* (from which our 'autocrat'), which means someone answerable to no one else, making their own decisions about command. The *imperator* took his own auspices – made ritual observations of the signs the gods offered through the flight of birds and other heaven-sent events.

But it was recognised that the general couldn't be everywhere at once, and that it was possible to delegate large or small chunks of command. This was the theory on which the military hierarchy worked. The governors who looked after individual garrisoned provinces for the emperor were one, rather senior, sort of delegate. If they were senators, and had been consul, they were grade one; senators who had not been consul, grade

153

two; equestrians, grade three. The Romans could not manage without strict hierarchies. The younger senators who commanded individual legions were another kind of delegate, still drawing on the fountainhead of the emperor's command. Still more junior officers drew their more limited authority from them. Each legion (a body of 6000 infantry) also had six junior officers called 'military tribune' attached to it, of whom one was a young member of a senatorial family, often related to the legionary commander, gaining early military training. Trajan had served as tribune under his father's command; this was the post that Hadrian (unusually) held three times in his twenties. The other five were equestrians, men of wider experience in commanding auxiliary regiments.

The whole system was confirmed as a religious bond by the Soldier's Oath, swearing fidelity to the *imperator*, and cemented by ongoing devotion to the symbols of loyalty, the standards, which were kept in a shrine in the middle of military camps. Surrendering enemies of Rome were compelled to make obeisance to them.

Like all ancient officials, the officers of the army were amateurs, members of the upper classes, educated in the traditional literary mainstream. They learned about war from ancient history; they trained their bodies and minds through the manly pursuits that the Greek and Roman élite had practised for a millennium. Their time in military camps, though often substantial, was broken up into short postings, and alternated with civilian duties in state or civic employment, so that all officers had some experience of judicial and financial authority outside the military world.

Continuity in the armies was provided by the soldiers who served, if they survived, for twenty-five years or more; and by the junior tier of really professional officers, above all centurions, senior and junior. Sometimes men of middling status joined up as centurions; more often they rose from the ranks. They were hugely influential in the army. This was the secret of its military effectiveness. A century after Hadrian's time, the old system of drawing senior officers from the empire-wide élite gave way to one in which they were more specialised and professional, and entered the élite from the army, rather than the other way round. But that revolution could not have been imagined in Hadrian's lifetime.

The army was a mirror of society. There were three principal tiers, demarcated by pay, conditions of service and prestige. Following ancient tradition, which had made citizens the protectors of their city, the highest tier in the army consisted of those soldiers who were Roman citizens. They joined the legions. There were about 150,000 citizen soldiers, distributed in thirty legions among the provinces, units of 5000 men if they were up to strength, each commanded by a senator. The legions were more or less equal in prestige, but Roman citizens from privileged backgrounds, and especially from Italy, the empire's heartland, had a better chance of the highest-grade military service, in the units that acted as the emperor's bodyguard, the praetorian guard, and in the cohorts which maintained order in Rome. Three legions were stationed in Britain at the end of Hadrian's reign, based at York, Chester and Caerleon, near Newport in south Wales.

Rome's loyal allies and subjects had always provided troops, and they formed the second tier, usually called the auxiliaries. The theory was that those conquered by Rome, if they had not resisted too strenuously, should provide contingents of soldiery for the empire's purposes. In return for loyal service, surviving soldiers of this kind were given full Roman citizenship on discharge, which would, of course, be inherited by their children. This category included around 150,000 men. There were thirteen cavalry and thirty-seven infantry regiments of auxiliaries in Britain in 122 when Hadrian arrived.

Only freedmen could be soldiers. Sometimes, in dire emergencies, slaves had been armed, but normally there was a complete split between the world of the slave and that of the soldier. Ex-slaves were recruited, but only to the third tier, the fleets, the nightwatchmen and firemen of Rome and one or two other cities.

The Romans regarded the achievements of their land armies as more honourable, largely because the sea was associated with the risky and sordid pursuit of commercial gain. But Roman control of the sea – and this goes for the Atlantic coasts, and the Narrow Seas too – was an essential part of the security of the infrastructure of the empire (the Narrow Seas are the Channel, the Straits of Dover and the southern North Sea). The fleets kept the seas largely clear of pirates, an achievement that was not managed again until the nineteenth century. The navy, still known as Classis Populi Romani, the Roman People's Navy, had two principal fleets, one based at Ravenna on the Adriatic, the other at Misenum near Naples. Apart from freedmen, recruits often came from barbarian areas where wetlands and lagoons made them familiar with boats. The captains were Roman citizens. The ships were relatively small, fast, oared warships, the sort we call triremes, although in fact a trireme has three banks of oars where most of the warships of the imperial period had only one, and they combined oars and sails. Fleets were also a vital arm of the military in frontier zones such as the Black Sea, or the Danube and Rhine. Britain would hardly have been viable as a province without the one in the English Channel, which was called the Classis Britannica, and had its headquarters at Dover.

This framework formed a strict hierarchy even before we take into account differences between officers and men and the different grades of officer, mirroring society right up to the equestrian and senatorial élites. Continuity and experience were provided by the officers below the rank of equestrian, who could rise from the ranks as a reward for merit, and, above all, the centurions.

Centurions were often recruited from the better-off citizenry far outside the income range of the equestrian or senatorial ranks.

They were in charge, as the name implies, of the smaller units of 100 men into which regiments were divided. The legion also had ten intermediate-sized sub-divisions called cohorts, with a senior centurion in charge of each. Unlike the aristocratic officers, centurions joined up, like ordinary soldiers, expecting to serve for twenty-five years. Sometimes there were vacancies in the centurionate, which might be filled by merit from the ranks, and sometimes the soldiers were consulted as to who most deserved promotion in a kind of quasi-democratic election. There was enough chance of promotion to encourage competition but, as in civilian society, connections, influence and patronage played a part alongside merit.

The Roman soldier lived in a kind of parallel universe, imitating ordinary social life but at a carefully prescribed distance. Unlike his officers, he was not allowed to marry. Military bases were like towns: within the walls men lived in barracks, with facilities like baths, amphitheatres and other such luxuries – which Hadrian is supposed to have suppressed. They formed relationships with women in the informal townships that grew up around the camp. Prostitution was rife, but many soldiers, based for decades in one place, formed families in all but legal status. No doubt frequent service away from base, some of it dangerous, caused difficulties, but the soldiers of the second century spent relatively little time at war.

The army was an attractive career for the poor, and could bring promotion and success. But many features of soldiers' lives were potentially problematic, and had to be offset with special privileges. The rules were waived to keep them happy. Soldiers' children were not allowed to inherit in the ordinary way, and it was Hadrian, in a remarkably personal letter to the prefect of Egypt, who set up loopholes, concerning himself with making sure that news of the reform reached the men: 'I am looking for ways of making the rather tough system of earlier emperors more humane . . . Make sure my gift is publicised among my soldiers and veterans, not so that they have a higher opinion of me but so that people who at present don't know about this can have a chance to make use of it.' Hadrian the modest citizen, soldier among soldiers, was careful to appear not to seek praise. Evidently he knew that it was one thing to change the rules and quite another to ensure that all who were entitled to benefit knew about it . . . and in this case he showed the insincerity and addiction to spin of the consummate natural politician.

In Hadrian's time, no war meant no booty to add to the accumulating salary on which a better life might be based after discharge. It also meant boredom and drudgery: were these soldiers an imperial élite, honoured and important, or indispensable but dangerous dogsbodies? There were plentiful signs of honour and favour, messages from the emperor, decorations, the cult of the standards, ceremonies and rites, but routine, bureaucracy and rules ordered their lives. In this segment of society, written documents seem to have been used seriously and, no doubt, the disciplinary regime reflected in the paperwork was unpopular. There was desertion: it was by no means unknown for Roman soldiers to join the other side, even those they considered barbarians. There was suicide, and Hadrian's rulings on this subject paint a sombre picture of army life. A soldier who had tried to kill himself because he could no longer endure pain, shame or illness, and was weary of life or insane, was to be dishonourably discharged. If none of those applied, he should be executed.

Soldiers' status was resented and feared by civilians, who were ever conscious of the abuses they practised and the unlikelihood of seeing redress through the courts or official complaint. Indeed, soldiers succeeded in keeping order largely because only they were supposed to be armed. At the same time they appear not to have welcomed their lot, and that seems to be confirmed by difficulties with recruitment in Hadrian's reign.

On the other hand, the lime-bark tablets that have survived, because of the unique chemistry of the soil, from the fort at Vindolanda, Chesterholm in Northumberland, give a less unhappy picture. An extensive range of documents – bills, letters, lists, accounts – was found at this base of an auxiliary regiment in northern Britain during Hadrian's lifetime.

On 18 May, in a year early in the second century, the regiment at Vindolanda was from the area around Tongres in Belgium. Its commander was Modest Julian – Verecundus – and 752 men were on the books, including six centurions. A startling 456, and five of the centurions, were absent in York to collect pay, and on various duties around the frontier zone. Thirty-one were listed as unfit – fifteen sick, six wounded, ten suffering from inflamed eyes. The detail of this snapshot is typical of the fanatical record-keeping of the army. Military organisation was incredibly regular and systematic: it was, more than anything else, the similarities of equipment, camps, titles across the whole vast empire that gave the Romans such a reputation for efficiency and order. That it was achieved in an age without the printing-press made it even more impressive.

The tablets show us how wide the horizons of the garrison were: even a little of the lives of the officers' womenfolk – the birthday-party invitation, mentioned earlier, is a rare example of a Latin text written by a woman. They betray ordinary preoccupations, with hunting, illness, provisions ('My fellow-soldiers have no beer'), and the variety of jobs undertaken by the army.

A roster list of this period, preserved in Egypt, refers to a military unit in the central Balkans, and gives a series of explanations for not being present on parade: transferred to the army in Hungary; died in the water; killed by bandits; requisitioning clothing in France; in Bulgaria on mine-police duty; on the governor's staff, in the provincial finance department; across the Danube on an expedition; at headquarters with the clerks; in the mountains to catch wild horses . . .

It was in the army that technical innovation flourished most in Hadrian's world. Architects, surveyors and engineers were necessary to the military, which was plant-heavy – not just in weapons and body-armour, which needed replacing and repairing, but in barracks and fortifications. Twenty tons of iron nails were excavated by archaeologists from where the army was based in the Scottish lowlands during Hadrian's youth. This sort of thing reinforced the superiority of the military presence, as well as providing it with an awe-inspiring appearance. But there was cutting-edge military technology of more innovatory kinds. From the second century BC the Romans had specialised in developing weapons that were particularly efficacious against fortified positions, stone-throwers and mechanised bows called *ballistae*. These complex machines were difficult to build and required expert maintenance, but were a huge advantage to those who could deploy them. With gifts of equipment and artisans, emperors built up the power of local rulers whom they favoured as pro-Roman strongpoints in difficult regions.

Experts were in short supply. Pliny asked Trajan for surveyors, but none could be spared. Around this period a city in Africa got into trouble when it bored a tunnel for an aqueduct through the mountain nearby. They started at both sides: each tunnel had gone more than half-way and they hadn't met. Eventually help arrived in the shape of an expert in levelling and surveying – who nearly didn't make it because on the way he was beaten by brigands and left naked by the roadside. He soon convinced the tunnellers of who he was by solving their problem, and received appropriate honours. Characteristically, Hadrian tried to resolve the predicament with organisation: he enrolled all the most significant experts, the 'builders, levellers, architects and anyone involved in the building or ornamenting of city-walls', in special regiments.

Once upon a time Roman legionaries had been adult male citizens of Rome, and other towns in central Italy, who wielded a certain economic clout – they had to contribute to their own equipment. Now there were millions of Roman citizens, scattered across the provinces, as well as the whole free population of Italy. In this loose, dispersed community, it is hardly surprising that the notion of what it was to be Roman became fluid and adaptable. But the Romans did not care much about the variations in Roman-ness across the provinces: this citizen body was still the one from which soldiers had to be drawn. The army was one of the few institutions in which a serious attempt at achieving uniformity was made – and one of the most effective. From Iraq to Scotland, archaeology and the documents show that the soldier's lot was consistent.

In one way, recruitment was easier than it had been in the old days. The status rule had been relaxed and then abolished, so that very poor citizens could now join up. But now soldiering, though better than destitution, was not the attractive prospect it had once been. The wars of conquest were mostly over, and soldiers now spent most of their time in (somewhat) safer but less lucrative employment. Roman citizens, though, had a tendency, encouraged by the Roman state, to think themselves a cut above anyone else. They might have oddly mixed customs and social frameworks, but they still had citizenship of the power that had conquered the world.

In Italy especially, people felt they had a special relationship with the metropolis, and aspired to share with the people of the city some of the perks that marked out the heirs of the successful empire-builders. They did not want to join the regular army: instead they attached themselves to special units, grand enough to reflect their superiority to the citizens of the provinces. But those citizens, too, felt a degree of one-upmanship. The folk they looked down on were closer to hand, the sense of social gradient that much more vivid: around them were the majority of the people of their province, free, sometimes rich, but not Roman citizens. And in these mixed communities, Roman citizens had often had the chance to better themselves, the rules being regularly interpreted in their favour by Roman officials. However, despite widespread poverty, they were surprisingly unwilling to sign up for a long spell in the army.

Recruitment should have been a routine matter, but here

Hadrian's empire was on the knife-edge. In an empire of fifty million people, with frontier zones covering thousands of square miles, 300,000 soldiers were not very many. And soldiering was ambiguous in its appeal: even when populations were buoyant, it was difficult to persuade enough people to join up.

Joining up entailed a decisive leaving-home as there was no regular furlough. Soldiers who had few ties to home often remained permanently in the province of their service. Becoming a soldier was therefore a prominent example of the mobility and deracination that was such a feature of the age. Like the Jews before them, scattered by mercenary service around the eastern Mediterranean, Roman citizens were dispersed by military service through the provinces. The rootlessness fuelled mutiny, desertion and political troublemaking, which became chronic a century after Hadrian's reign. It was natural to counter it, and the pattern by which veterans were settled near where they had served, and their children were later recruited to the fathers' legions nearby, was something of a remedy. But this encouraged the separation of a global empire into regional loyalties.

Recruitment to the higher-status units, such as the praetorian guard, was brisker. The pay was the highest in the army, the prestige was enormous, fighting was minimal, and a certain level of comfort and all sorts of lucrative opportunities were more or less guaranteed. More than once the praetorians, as the only substantial body of trained and armed soldiers on the spot, were in a position to accept or reject would-be emperors, who rewarded them appropriately. So uppity had they become by the end of the second century that they were disbanded. The consequence was a disaster for a whole generation of Italian youth, which had relied on the prospect of this service for advancement and financial survival. They became so desperate that many ran off to join brigand gangs.

A Hadrianic army scene turns up, of all places, in a school-book for Greek speakers learning Latin:

> If, though, we want to speak Latin or Greek without mistakes, let's begin like this: someone was petitioning for military service.

Hadrian said, 'Where do you want to serve?' He said, 'In the Praetorians.' Hadrian asked him what was his height. 'Five feet and a half.' Hadrian said, 'For the time being, serve in the City cohorts, and if you're a good soldier, in your third year of service, you'll be able to transfer to the Praetorians.'

One might think that the criterion for selection as a bodyguard would have been toughness: a bullet-headed, broad-shouldered, truculent image springs to mind – and the dialogue between Hadrian and the petitioner shows that height mattered. But the tombstone of a lad from Rome who had gone straight into the praetorians offers a different impression: 'Lucius Marius Vitalis: I lived seventeen years and 55 days. I was completely obsessed with literature, and I persuaded my parents that I should learn the art properly. I left the City in the bodyguard of the emperor Hadrian. While I was pursuing my studies there, the Fates grew jealous, snatched me away from my art, and left me in this spot. Maria Malchis, unhappiest of mothers, to her most special son.'

For all the religion of loyalty that pervaded military life, emperors who didn't form a good rapport with the armed forces lived dangerously. Their soldiers and other commanders could depose them, especially if the men who commanded the armies of the more heavily garrisoned provinces were more popular than they were, or more ambitious. No one could have been more ambitious than Hadrian, and he made sure that he was esteemed throughout the army.

Normally that was best done through a lucrative, exciting and not-too-dangerous war. Hadrian, apparently, took a different route. 'There were no serious wars of aggression in his reign,' says his biographer. 'Wars went on more or less in silence. But he was greatly loved by the soldiers, because of his excessive attention to the army, and because he was extremely generous to them.'

The expectation of conquest in Hadrian's world grew out of

a different psychology from anything familiar today. This was an empire that constantly proclaimed its military might, and soldiers had a taste for the excitement and glory of victory. An unusual dedication in a sanctuary at a hot spring in Africa takes the form of a wish-list from a happy veteran of Trajan's wars – all fulfilled.

I wanted – slaughtered Dacians – got it.
I wanted – to sit back in the chair of peace – have done.
I wanted – to walk in a famed triumphal procession – did it.
I wanted – the perks of being chief centurion in the cohort – got them.
I wanted – to see the Nymphs naked – saw them.

Rome was no beleaguered island of stability and civilisation in a sea of wild destructive outsiders: its wars had always been aggressive. Trajan's were no exception: the wealth of the Balkans, the glory of conquest in the east, the image of the conquering Roman general had all been instrumental in shaping the three great wars that patterned his reign. In the middle of the second century another member of the extended imperial family network couldn't resist the lure of heading east, like Alexander the Great, with disastrous consequences.

Hadrian himself was at the top end of the scale of military experience. The three stints he undertook in his twenties with different legions are hard to parallel; and they were followed by a legionary command, and the governorship of a pretty tough province.

But his soldiering, like that of the centurion at the sanctuary of the Nymphs, had been dominated by service with Trajan, in both Dacian wars, and in Parthia. The scenes on Trajan's Column in Rome, the victors' monument, are uncompromising about the horrors of the Dacian campaigns: they show abuse and mass execution of prisoners, the systematic destruction of Dacian villages, the selling of captured women and children into slavery. Roman soldiers captured by the Dacians are tortured. Others display strings of Dacian heads proudly to the emperor.

Hadrian's pedantry and obsessiveness about detail fitted as well with his military leanings as his physical fitness and energy with the hunt. 'He simply looked into everything himself. That meant all the usual military paraphernalia, weapons, engines, ditches, fortifications, palisades. But it also meant the personal business of each soldier, the rankers as much as the officers. He investigated their daily life, their quarters, and their habits,' says the historian Dio. This must have been disconcerting, but ultimately made him popular.

The *imperator* was commander of all the armies in all the provinces, and might be expected to see to their welfare. Hadrian's knowledge of the army suited him to this aspect of his job. Much of his journeying was connected with visiting the places where there were most soldiers, and in the spirit of tradition and precedent-making, these things were recorded in detail. We have some paragraphs of the addresses that Hadrian made to the citizen-soldiers of the Third Legion in what is now Algeria in July 128. He was impressed with the manoeuvres that were put on for him, and so generous in his remarks that someone went to the expense of having the text carved on stone, so that the record of the units' achievements would never be lost.

To the First Regiment of Pannonians

You did everything in orderly fashion. You covered the whole field with your manoeuvres. Your javelin-throwing was not without grace, although you used short, stiff javelins. Many of you hurled your lances equally well. And your mounting was athletic today and very quick yesterday. If there were anything lacking I should notice it; if any fault had stood out, I should point it out. But you pleased me evenly throughout the whole exercise. My legate, the senator Catullinus, clearly gives equal care to all the areas in which he commands . . . Your prefect evidently looks after you carefully. Receive a bonus!

And again:

Address to the cavalry unit

Fortifications which others take several days to construct you have completed in a single day. You have built a wall entailing sustained work, such as is customarily made for permanent winter quarters, in a time not much longer than it require to build one of turf. In this kind, the turf is cut to standard size and is easy to carry and to handle, and the laying is not troublesome, as the turf is naturally soft and level. But yours was built of large heavy stones of all sizes; and no one can carry or lift or lay these without their irregularities making themselves felt. You have cut a trench straight through hard, coarse gravel and have made it even by smoothing it.

The emperor's language is direct, with lots of brisk military terminology suited to his audience. A culture of emulation and pride developed in the army across the empire as a result of this kind of interest. On the northern frontier Hadrian watched a different kind of display: a non-citizen cavalryman from the mouth of the Rhine swam the Danube in full armour and put on a virtuoso performance in shooting an arrow, then shooting again to hit the first arrow while it was still in mid-air – a feat, as the soldier said in epic verse on his tombstone, that no Roman or barbarian had been known to achieve before.

Arrian's tour of inspection in the Black Sea shows us a governor imitating the emperor's concern for military order: 'And before midday we came more than thirty miles to Apsaros, where the five cohorts are stationed. I gave the army its pay and inspected the weapons, the walls, the trench, the sick and the supplies. My opinion on the last subject is included in the Latin report.' This base was Rome's substantial military headquarters in what is now Georgia, commanding the eastern end of the Black Sea. Elsewhere Arrian regularly inspected the same things, and also – like Hadrian in Africa – praised the agility of the cavalrymen in leaping on to their mounts.

On this showing, Hadrian appears to have been one of the more military emperors. But this is not the whole story. Trajan had made Going to War with a major Enemy his signature; Hadrian dropped it, abandoning Trajan's conquests in Iraq, and considering evacuating Dacia too. Trajan had thirteen salutations as *imperator*; Hadrian had two. He even boasted that he had made more gains through peace than other emperors had through fighting. The Latin word for 'peace' here is an oddity: it really means 'leisure', 'cultured ease', the pleasurable, scholarly private life of the wealthy of the ancient world. Looking back from the viewpoint of difficult wars in 165, one opinion of Hadrian's attention to the soldiers was scathing: he was fine at talking to the troops but gave them nothing to do so that they became demoralised. He entertained and amused them more than training them.

It looks at first sight as if Hadrian was lucky. Was he spared major conflict, allowed to be the role-model civilian, aesthetic, philosophical emperor in an age of temporary breathing space between wars? Did the jealous, restless, needy enemies of Rome beyond the frontier happen to be in disarray during those twenty years, only to return with ever more devastating results to their onslaughts on the peaceful Greco-Roman Mediterranean? It isn't as simple as that.

First, Hadrian's reign was no miracle of golden peace. Constant preoccupation with the behaviour of peoples and communities outside the empire had its monument in Hadrian's most famous building, the Wall that bears his name. His reign was remembered for Roman losses in Britain. Still less in tune with the pacific and civilised images is the fact that this period saw the most violent revolt against Rome of any of its subjects, the Second Jewish Revolt, and its bloody suppression. The cultured ruler, the pacifist who abandoned his predecessor's conquests, the enlightened diplomat who preferred treaties to war, then, turns into a rather different figure.

The definition of the emperor's job, that he should crush opposition by force, elides the difference between enemies inside and outside the frontiers. *Imperium* was about subduing both threats. The most pacific of all the emperors, Hadrian's successor Antoninus Pius, faced significant disturbances in Britain, Morocco, Germany, Romania, Judaea, Greece and Egypt. 'Through his governors and commanders,' says his biographer, 'he smashed these uprisings down.'

Expeditions against exotic foes were a special predilection of Trajan and the – relatively few – emperors like him. It added, no doubt, to Hadrian's credibility that he had participated in this kind of activity. But most soldiers led a quieter life: based in well-built fortified camps, they policed the dangerous parts of the empire, waging war more on brigands and tax-evaders than on external enemies. Their jobs were after the style of what we would call civil service but exercised here with characteristic military brutality. When collecting taxes on behalf of the empire, for example, Roman soldiers were known for their heavy-handed tactics: they often used force and threats to extort extra money from citizens. Soldiers, their commanders and the emperor at the top were all part of a system in which *imperium* was enforced in the civilian as well as the military world, inside the empire as well as beyond its borders, and in which military activities complemented the arts of peace.

At one time, all the young men of an ancient community went through a coming-of-age ceremony to celebrate their arrival at manhood. The Greeks enrolled them in a sort of youth-training-scheme-cum-boot-camp. They were called ephebes, and they trained their bodies and minds in the gymnasium, exercising naked, and forming liaisons with wiser, older men who took on the combined role of tutor and lover. When the time came for the rite of passage, they were sent out into the wilder parts of the city's territories to live rough on their own resources, at the same time guarding the boundaries and keeping down wild beasts, brigands or outsiders. Restored to the city, they were welcomed back as full warriors, ready to undertake the defence of the community as regular citizen soldiers; it was now that they took up full political rights. This tough regimen was not just a memory of the hardihood of distant antiquity: like so much else in the Greek mainstream, it had suffused the cultures of the Roman empire (it was a major strand in the make-up of public bathing in Roman towns). Many cities had training grounds, gymnasia and associations of young men who shared hunting, sporting or military exercise – it was to this that Hadrian devoted himself so completely when he went back to Italica at fourteen. He is likely to have seen himself as an ephebe of the old kind, and probably saw his sexual preferences through the lens of the institutions of male homosexuality as they had been described in the literature and art of classical Greece. Certainly, when he went to Claudiopolis in northwest Turkey in 124, it was in the gymnasium that he found the most beautiful of all ephebes, the young Antinous.

The men of this age read both soldiers and philosophers in the language of Plato and Xenophon. Education, in all its parts, was about producing a single rounded type of manhood, whose purpose and gauge was success at war. There was, after all, nothing so strange about Vitalis, the literary recruit to Hadrian's praetorian guard. When the biographer wrote the words that opened this chapter, he saw no difficulty about making the experiences of the young Hadrian in the dusty hills of Italica, or the wetlands at the mouth of the Guadalquivir, the beginning of his life as a young officer in the legion, and eventually the dutiful commander-in-chief of all the armies of Rome. Hadrian got a thrill out of treading in the steps of Xenophon above Trebizond. 'Nature's philologist', the reader of Greek literature, was the hero of the second Dacian war and the builder of the Wall, because architecture, and the technical skills in which Hadrian rejoiced, also spanned the divide we see so clearly between the arts of peace and war. Hadrian's beard was the beard of a soldier as well as a philosopher. But there was not so much difference between the two.

IX

HADRIAN'S BRITAIN

I don't want to be Emperor, ambling round among the British,
putting up with the frosts of the North.

ATTRIBUTED TO HADRIAN'S FRIEND, THE POET FLORUS

Each year during much of Hadrian's early childhood, news
came in of dramatic Roman military success in one of the
most remote and colourful parts of the empire. The energetic
and capable governor Sextus Julius Agricola, one of the practitioners of the new professionalism in Roman public life – until
he aroused the emperor's jealousy – fought his way as far north
as the Scottish lowlands, and briefly set up Roman military bases
in what is now Fife.

The mood of the 80s was captured by the poet Statius, specu-
lating as to the parts of the empire where a young senator, son
of a former governor of Britain, might find himself posted:

Where in Caesar's world will you go? Will you swim in the broken
ice of the northern Rhine? Will you sweat in the torrid fields of
Libya? Will you scare the hills of Pannonia or the nomads of the
seven-mouthed Danube? Or will you visit the cinders of Jerusalem,
and the conquered palm-groves of the Jews, who are planting
orchards for the gain of others? Perhaps the land bridled by your
great father will receive you. What a proud moment, when an aged
cultivator of that foul land tells you, 'Here your father was judge
– here he used to address the cavalry – these are the forts he built,
the walls he surrounded with ditches – here (look at the inscriptions!) are the weapons he dedicated to the gods, his own breastplate, and one of which he despoiled a British king.'

Compared with the other places where Rome had conquered or was still fighting, the point about Britain was how horrible, and truly distant, it was. Since Homer, people had thought of the known world as surrounded by a 'river' of deep, rough sea called Ocean. It was exciting and noteworthy to reach it, but if you could venture out on it and get somewhere, public opinion offered big rewards.

This was why Julius Caesar had made two expeditions to Britain in 55 and 54 BC. He was engaged at the time in an ambitious programme of conquest and self-advertisement in Gaul, and made the sensible decision to be his own reporter: he described his exploits in *On the Gallic War*. He built a bridge across the Rhine, received the homage of a German king, astonished his opponents with a series of virtuoso military flourishes, especially highly technical sieges, and demonstrated that he could defeat even the seaborne peoples of the Atlantic coast, although their boats and seas were unfamiliar to the Romans. He would gain even more prestige if he crossed the Narrow Seas to the huge and mysterious island of Britain.

His two visits were not failures, but that was partly because he had never intended to do more than a spot of looting and tribute-collecting, and receive submission from the communities of Kent, who were closely linked to the people he was busy subduing on the other side of the Channel.

Like Gaul, Britain was divided up into dozens of independent communities, ruled by chiefs and sharing similar culture, language, religion and values from one end of the island to the other. These peoples were classified by Greek and Roman observers using all the stereotypes of barbarism they could find. The Greek philosopher Strabo, who visited Rome during Augustus' reign, was struck by the appearance of some British adolescents ('little more than boys'): they were as much as half a foot taller than the tallest of the Roman population, loose-limbed, bow-legged and lacked grace. He estimated that the British were taller and less blond than the Gauls of the mainland, as well as less sophisticated in producing food – despite abundant milk, he claimed that the art of cheese-making was unknown among them. Later, after the Roman occupation, the historian Tacitus distinguished the darker faces and curly hair of the southern Welsh, the red hair and large limbs of the Scots highlanders. The predominant feature of the British climate for all ancient observers was not so much cold as wet – perpetual fog and vast marshes. The wilder inhabitants were supposed to spend considerable amounts of time literally immersed in the swamps, and to prefer to be unclothed, so as to display the tattoos with which their bodies were covered, except for certain iron ornaments around neck and waist, indicators of status. They also had a fearsome reputation for their fierceness and violence at war. Like the suggestion that there were no proper communities or that women were shared by all the men and the children brought up communally, much of this is the standard evocation of barbarians unwilling to submit docilely to the rule of Rome.

The result of Julius Caesar's visits and the final subjugation of Gaul was inevitably much more contact between southeastern Britain and the now Roman territories on the other side of the Channel. But it was nearly a century before the Roman armies returned. Augustus didn't need the glory: his advisers calculated that it would take a legion permanently based in Britain to make it a province, and that the revenue from tribute and tax would be less than its maintenance costs. He received homage from southern British leaders and left it at that. Wisely.

When Claudius saw Britain as the obvious place to achieve the military success that would make up for his unprepossessing appearance and lack of experience, and turned it into a province, it took four legions to keep it in order. Why did Rome bother to keep it when withdrawal was a real option? It may be that Augustus' advisers had miscalculated the returns: the metal ores of the island (especially lead) were exploited rapidly after Claudius's conquest, and the agriculture of the south-east was soon supplying the Rhine army with cereals. It looks, too, as if the British upper classes were a soft touch when it came to the webs of money-lending and patronage in which Rome specialised. By the end of the Roman occupation three hundred years later Britain had become a wealthy province.

In AD 43 Chichester and the area around it were particularly supportive to the Romans. The local ruler, a man called Cogidubnus, welcomed them, and made his region one of the bases for invasion. The huge villa of Fishbourne, just outside Chichester, paid for at Roman expense and built according to the latest Italian design, was part of the pay-off for his loyalty. He also took the title of king of his own area within the new Roman province. Elsewhere, there was determined opposition. The British leader Caratacus defied Rome in the Welsh Marshes until 51; in 60 the devastating revolt of Boudicca, queen of the Iceni, destroyed the nascent Roman towns at Colchester, London and St Albans; ten years later, in Yorkshire, Roman troops found themselves rescuing a British queen, who supported them and had even handed over Caratacus to the Romans, when her spurned husband and subjects decided that resistance was preferable to Roman rule. When Agricola arrived, around the time Hadrian was born, Roman control in Britain had been systematically expanded from the south-east, with expeditions from the heart-land of the province along the north and south coasts of Wales and the east and west coasts of northern England, and consolidation behind.

Agricola's fleet had circumnavigated the whole island, and he recommended the conquest of Ireland. Nothing was done, and the view of the Hebrides his sailors must have had could hardly have been inspiring. He had beaten the inhabitants of the Scottish lowlands, but there was nothing in the highlands for Rome – nothing, that is, to tax.

In the southern part of the province, with a view to those crucial revenues, the British communities had been reorganised as units in a Roman local-government system. Each now had a territorial jurisdiction, and a small city at its core, which was beginning to do quite nicely – such as Winchester, Canterbury, Cirencester and Leicester.

The historian Tacitus wrote an account of the governor Agricola, who was his wife's father. He explained how Agricola encouraged the chiefs of the British peoples to take up the competition for honour which was normal in the cities of the empire:

> He put pressure on them in private to build temples, forums, and Roman-style houses, and gave state assistance. He lavished praise on those who co-operated, and criticised the slow-moving. One-upmanship worked better than compulsion. He saw to it that the sons of the chiefs got a classical education: the intelligence of the Britons got them further than the willingness of the Gauls. The same people who had rejected Latin now started to hanker after learning rhetoric. They came to esteem our clothing, and the toga became widespread. But they slowly slipped into the attractions of depravity – promenades, bath-houses, and fashionable dinner-parties. They called this civilisation, but it was actually a sign of enslavement.

The remains of the houses, temples and baths can be traced today. For the toga and the Latin oratory, we have to take Tacitus' word.

The legions had steadily moved on from the south-east to the hilly fringes, and their earlier bases were now chartered towns of Roman citizens, the veterans of the legions, whose sons joined up in their fathers' regiments – so, Lincoln in relation to York, or Gloucester in relation to Caerleon near Newport. The original heart of the Roman province had been Colchester, but by Hadrian's time it had been overtaken by London, base of the provincial governor and an increasingly prosperous trading centre. Its forum had a basilica that was by some way the largest in any of the north-western provinces: its remains are beneath Leadenhall Street. Colchester, as we have just discovered, enjoyed its very own version of the Circus Maximus of Rome, a purpose-built chariot-racing track on a monumental scale.

The core of the province, then, began to look a little like the landscapes of other parts of the empire. Around it three citizen legions had their bases: the Second Legion (Augustus') in south Wales near Newport; the Sixth Legion (Victorious, Dutiful, Faithful), at York, and the Twentieth Legion (Valerius', Victorious) at Chester. Soldiers from other provinces are commemorated on tombstones at these places – Gaius Lovesius Cadarus, from Mérida in Spain, soldier of the Twentieth died at Chester aged twenty-five after eight years' service; Gaius Valerius Victor, from Lyon in Gaul, standard-bearer of the Second, died at Caerleon aged forty-five after seventeen years' service.

Beyond these great military bases, Wales and northern Britain were heavily garrisoned, with a secure network of roads cordoning off difficult country, forts at their junctions and at strategic command points, and soldiers in watchtowers and outposts. It was in this zone that the British people continued to seem wild outsiders to Roman onlookers, and it was here that major unrest continued at intervals into Hadrian's time and well beyond.

In 121, Hadrian set out, as befitted the *imperator*, to visit some of his most heavily garrisoned provinces. His first destination was the Rhine frontier, but then he went on to Britain, where he arrived in 122. There were heavy Roman casualties in the province during his reign: this was no peacetime tour of inspection. On 17 July, he discharged soldiers from all the forty-seven auxiliary regiments of the province who had served their full twenty-five years, then pushed on northwards, as far as the river Tyne. Spanning the estuary at Newcastle, Hadrian's Bridge, Pons Aelius, marked his visit, a wonder of Roman engineering in a remote place.

But there was a more impressive monument to Hadrian's journey. The journey to the Tyne also, no doubt, served to conduct a ceremonial inauguration of the building of the Wall, the symbolic destination of the imperial journey to Britain.

Hadrian's concept was daring: a fortification from shore to shore, joining two great river estuaries, cordoning off a whole segment of the island. It was, indeed, building on a gigantic scale: with its own towers and large and small fortresses, it spread a garrison in and on a construction across some wild terrain, the barren glaciated moorlands, as high as four hundred metres above sea-level, the crags and cliffs of the Whin Sill, and the remote lakes to its north where the Tyne rises.

Like Roman roads, the Wall was surveyed where possible to run with geometric precision. It was some four metres in height, and built of stone where that was available (the western section was built of clods of earth at first, and only later in the century replaced with stone). The Wall faced outward from the province, and was fronted by a deep defensive trench; behind, at varying distance, it was paralleled with another large earthwork, marking off a military zone that extended the breadth of the island. There were sixteen large forts, where there was a main way through the Wall, and between them, at every Roman mile, a fortified outpost with a postern. Between each of these outposts two turrets dominated the walkway along the top of the Wall behind a crenellated parapet. Roads to supply the garrison completed the work. This vast enterprise caught the imagination of the province: the battlemented Wall, and the forts with their names, formed the decoration on drinking cups.

The garrison was mainly auxiliaries, with some legionaries. There were Belgians at Vindolanda, but the regiments came from other parts of Gaul, and from Spain, with some from the Danube; later units named for Hadrian – of Dacians and marines – are attested too. The most exotic of all must have been the troop of boatmen from the Tigris in Mesopotamia, who were stationed at the breezy fort of Arbeia, where the promontory of South Shields separates the Tyne estuary from the North Sea.

Hadrian had given up Trajan's conquests in the east, and was said to have thought about abandoning Dacia too. In Germany, on his way to Britain, he had seen to the reinforcing of the frontier defences that had been built beyond the Rhine, with great timber palisades and earthworks running even further than the Wall in Britain. Many saw his military strategy as an abandonment of the glorious expansionism of the Roman past, embodied so spectacularly by his predecessor. His investment of so many hundreds of thousands of man-hours, so much money and planning in building the great barrier of the Wall across Britain, seems to confirm this. But Hadrian was not trying to produce a U-turn in Roman policy, turning his back on four centuries of aggression for pacifistic or even practical reasons. There is much more to the Wall than the advertisement of a new, less aggressive, attitude to frontiers.

Hadrian's western journey was that of an emperor wielding *imperium* like a proconsul of the old school (in fact, like Trajan, he used 'proconsul' in his official titulature). Trajan's war had begun with spectacular engineering. Invading Dacia, he diverted the Danube at the gorge of the Iron Gates, and bridged the huge river, following the direct precedent of the Persian king Darius six hundred years before. In Parthia, he planned to build a canal from the Euphrates to the Tigris so that he could move his fleet from one river to the other. He celebrated the conquest of nature and geography: despite the failure of the Parthian war, he had reached the Persian Gulf. Building a bridge across the huge river Danube echoed the engineering tour-de-force of Julius Caesar, who had thrown a bridge across the Rhine 150 years before. Julius had come to Britain not to conquer but simply to achieve the impossible. Claudius had joined his invading armies across the Channel to attract a good press for his military achievements.

No other emperor had been anywhere in Britain during his reign, so Hadrian had the perfect opportunity to make his mark. He came to the Tyne, and both bridge and Wall were fully in the magnificent tradition of Roman conqueror-engineers changing previously untamed landscapes for ever. His bravado in employing river-sailors from central Iraq, as far as conceivably possible from their origin, fits the rhetoric perfectly. The

Wall also followed traditional Roman practice in dominating inaccessible provincial territory where violence threatened. The messages were unchanged.

The sea – even the rough seas off Britain – was the easiest medium of communication. The Romans were, of course, seaborne invaders, like the Anglo-Saxons, Danes and Normans who came later, and it was by sea that they explored and surveyed Britain; all the great roads of the province were laid out as lines joining the estuaries that mark out the coast – Thames to Dee, Exe to Humber. The rivers gave important access to the interior, and gave their native names to Roman centres. The lowlands along the coasts and river valleys were the places where agriculture could be developed and its profits taxed: a proportion of what was grown was taken for the occupying Roman army – and, in all probability, used also for the provisioning of other Roman units stationed across the Narrow Seas, and especially on the lower Rhine. The highland core of north Britain, then, offered a zone that was triply dangerous: away from the easily understood coastlands, unpromising for growing cereals, and offering in its own inaccessible way a set of routeways by which potentially disruptive elements could travel unchallenged and unobserved deep into the heart of the province. The Roman technique with inaccessible uplands had been developed centuries before in the forested mountains of Italy: it involved roads to cordon off blocks of high ground, and more roads to split them up, running right through the heart of the dangerous area, along routes carefully chosen to be, where possible, somewhat higher than the surrounding terrain; a criss-cross military logic. The roads were called 'limits' after the pathways that divided vineyards in the distant south.

A 'limit' of this kind did not have to involve a wall: built by soldiers for soldiers to march along, it took a route that was easily defensible, giving the advantage to those who had possession of it. Agricola had penetrated north Britain with corridors of this kind. Two routes foreshadowed Hadrian's wall: one crossed the moors between Barnard Castle and the Eden Valley, beside Cross Fell; and one ran only a mile or two behind the line of the Wall, where a road was built to join Tyne and Solway. It was remembered into the Middle Ages as the Stanegate, the stone-built pathway. It was along this route that the fortress Vindolanda was built, from which we have gained so much illumination of Roman Britain.

The tablets from Vindolanda help make sense of how Rome managed to keep a hold on such difficult zones as the bleak fells where the Stanegate led across from coast to coast. They illustrate how, rather than shutting up permanent garrisons in strongholds where they might become demoralised, or vulnerable to marauders, the units of the British garrison were constantly being posted to new duties, in new combinations with detachments from other units. The flexibility and efficiency of the deployments were of an order of magnitude greater than anything else known at the time, and gave the Romans a crucial organisational advantage.

The edge provided by controlled mobility and flexible mastery of resources depended on bureaucracy and training, but also on physical infrastructure. Without roads, and signalling, the communications net on which it depended would not have existed. So the Roman occupation of an area was always based on roads, with strongpoints commanding them and especially their junctions, and on signal stations providing a further network alongside. Roads, forts and towers were seen as a system, joined by the road and linked with it. The lines and networks defined the Roman presence and were how the Romans thought about the area they were dealing with: a new frontier zone usually involved the establishment of a linear system like this along a protected main road. It was an easy step from that to a fortification, linking the strongpoints in a single barrier structure – a wall. And that is what Hadrian's Wall was.

This interpretation fits well with the wider picture of Hadrian's Britain. At this date there was no major cultural or ethnic difference between the peoples of the subdued parts of the province and those in what is now Scotland. The area controlled by Roman forts and roads extended, even after the Wall was built, far to the north into the Cheviots. The Wall itself, and its earthworks, looked both ways. It controlled movement, and it announced that the Romans could seal off movement of any kind, at any time. There are modern parallels: walls intended to promote security by advertising coercive power as chillingly as possible have been constructed in Berlin and, more recently, Israel. Hadrian's application of time-honoured Roman cordon-policing in the turmoil of north Britain was intended to awe, and to increase the advantages of his constantly alert and aggressive garrisons. It was certainly not intended to proclaim an abandonment of Roman military expansion.

Emperors' wars were dynamic, their monuments transient. Hadrian dismantled Trajan's Danube bridge and gave up his territories in Iraq. And Hadrian's successor, Antoninus the Dutiful, built a new cordon across the Scottish lowlands, through the hills between the Forth and the Clyde, on a much shorter line than Hadrian's Wall. Before long that, too, was abandoned and Hadrian's barrier revivified. Permanent and uncompromising as these structures seemed, they were part of the imperial military and administrative repertoire, and that went on for generations combining aggression and containment, responding dynamically to the changing problems of the different parts of the empire.

Although the Wall was not so startling an innovation, it eventually brought about a change in attitudes. By the end of the Roman empire, when Hadrian's biography was written, it seemed plausible that Hadrian had been trying to separate a civilised empire from a barbarian wilderness. Structures like the Wall helped bring that about. But when Hadrian travelled the empire, and invested in works of this kind, the homeland security argument was not terribly strong. No outside enemy had been in Italy for more than two hundred years; and it was to be another two generations before that level of insecurity was to be repeated.

It was two years after the death of Hadrian's successor Antoninus that people were reminded of the danger: a roving band of men from outside the empire wandered deep into Greece and sacked the ancient sanctuary of the Two Goddesses near Athens, the religious centre where Hadrian had been initiated into the holy mysteries. But the rulers were happy to encourage a sense of peril from outside enemies, and the building of huge barrier walls played well with this. It helped distract from the horrors of the conflicts that caused the deaths of scores of thousands well within the imperial perimeter, while paradoxically helping – by heightening the mood of insecurity – to justify repression.

These were unusual times in which to live. But people's sense of the state that ruled them and the community of which they formed part was subtly shifting, and whatever it now involved it had come to have edges.

X

DINNER AT TIVOLI

Hadrian developed his villa at Tivoli in the most amazing way, giving it the most famous names of provinces and localities, and so as to leave nothing whatsoever out, he even built a pretend Underworld.

HISTORIA AUGUSTA

The Roman upper class had long outgrown the city of Rome. Conquering Italy and the world had given them wide horizons, the ultimate origin of the globetrotting habit that was such a feature of Hadrian's imperial style. They needed a base in the ancient city, but there were more spacious locations for better-appointed living especially in the suburban belt that surrounded the metropolis. It had long been the practice of the very rich to have a town-house, an inner-suburb residence and a set of country properties, for when Rome became too hot, or when festivals closed down the world of public life.

The élite had long bought and developed agricultural estates in all the best parts of Italy. Plan A was to make money out of them – but they could be agreeable places to visit. There was no harm in watching the slaves, tenants and wage-earners getting in the harvest or the vintage, and it was quite fun sometimes to join in – 'We worked up a nice bit of sweat in the pressing-room', says one affluent Roman and 'We had a good laugh watching the yokels getting cross with each other', while another writer speaks of the 'show of people decently labouring'.

Even better than the spectacle of money coming in, was the recreation to be had. Some estates were high in the hills, where the hunting was excellent. Some were on the coast, where superb seafood was to be had. Many of the richest proprietors built intricate fish-ponds with channels to let sea-water in and out, controlled with sluices and weirs. But it wasn't all greed. The Romans came to appreciate the beauty of the countryside, and a quality they called *amoenitas*, which meant 'pleasantness', and gives us the word 'amenity'. Shady groves, beautiful trees, water trickling, cascading or in still pools, flowers, moss and turf – the sensibility was shaped by charming poetry and expressed in numerous artful arrangements of the Italian landscape. Country estates, including Hadrian's at Tivoli, were designed with this in mind. The word used for estates of this kind was *villa*. Originally it meant a working farm, but it came to denote also the height of luxurious contrivance.

The coast was especially attractive, above all where it was diversified with cliffs, crags and islands. Villas were built around caves, which were adapted as dining rooms, or high on promontories, with views along miles of coast, or perched on remote island cliffs. The volcanic rocks of the area around Vesuvius produced one of the most striking coastlines in Italy, and the igneous nature of the region offered another overwhelming advantage – hot springs. Throw in an ancient Greek past, the attractions of Italy's most successful port, Puteoli, and a hinterland that was the most productive region of Italy (it was here that the most famous Roman wine, Falernian, was made), and it is hardly surprising that the Bay of Naples became the single most frequented region for luxury second homes. They even called the bay the Mixing Bowl, so continuous was the banquet that went on around its shores.

The focus of this heartland of cultured relaxation was the place where the hot springs were best. It was called Baiae, and the biggest coastal villas of all the best people were here. Richly fitted public baths were constructed, using the thermal springs. There were lagoons on which sailed pleasure-boats crewed by musicians, and myrtle groves sacred to the goddess of love. Best of all it was nearly two hundred kilometres from Rome, and

almost everyone there who belonged to the Roman upper classes
was on holiday. As in eighteenth-century Bath, normal standards
could be relaxed. Baiae became proverbial for adultery and sexual
frolics. But it was also a place where healing was available, as
the waters were thought to be powerfully medicinal; and it was
esteemed as extremely beautiful in its own right. It was here that
Hadrian came to die.

The emperors found it useful to adopt the villa habit. Augustus
and his successor Tiberius had been fond of escape to the island
of Capri in the Bay of Naples. Tiberius spent most of the last
thirteen years of his long reign there, never returning to Rome.
Lurid stories circulated about his cruelty and debauchery – the
cliffs over which he pushed victims, the pools in which he liked
to swim naked with children – but Capri's remoteness was incon-
venient. In the cooler hill-country, within an easy day's journey
of Rome, an emperor could relax without too much scrutiny yet
was close at hand in case of trouble.

Hadrian easily exceeded his predecessors' villas in scale and
lavishness. He chose a quite different location, the slopes below
Tivoli, twenty miles east of Rome. His retreat was far and away
the largest villa complex ever built in the Roman period. And
he did not escape the criticism and the rumours that went with
setting up your base well outside the city of Rome.

His biographer sums up the criticism well:

Later he did the normal thing when there are no crises: he relaxed,
left the city in the hands of Lucius [his heir apparent], and took
himself off to his own country estate at Tivoli. There, as is the
habit of the untroubled rich, he built palaces and specialised in
dining, and collecting sculpture and paintings. In the end he got
quite obsessive in his hunt for anything extravagant or titillating.
Nasty stories started to circulate about debauchery with young
boys, and his excessive passion for what Antinous offered: why
else should he have founded a city with his name or paid for so
many statues?

The villa was a sprawling mass of pavilions and courtyards, loosely joined by colonnades and larger garden spaces on the surface and underground by a network of corridors large enough to take wheeled vehicles. There was a wonderful reflecting pool, again flanked by colonnades, with green marble crocodiles, and a high belvedere tower with a pavilion from which Hadrian could look out across twenty miles of gently sloping terrain and catch a glimpse of the towers and pinnacles of Rome, with the morning sun glinting on the golden roof of the Capitoline temple or the colossal statue of Jupiter beside it. The heart of the villa was a circular courtyard in which was a ring-shaped pool with a circular island in the middle, and on the island an exquisite suite of rooms and tiny garden courtyards. There was a mile-long portico, whose colonnades were large enough to drive a chariot through, with extra space at each end so that the horses had room to turn without going out into the open. And there was a complex of halls and courtyards with curvilinear vaulting and roofing that looked as if they might be the product of the emperor's architectural doodles on wax converted by huge ingenuity into permanent built form. Everywhere there was water and greenery with views across the countryside and especially the picturesque valley to the city of Tivoli on the first crags of the Apennines.

Hadrian's biographer also tells us that the emperor named the different sections of his villa after famous buildings or places he had seen on his travels. Even when he was settled in Rome, he wanted to evoke the wider world. Athens, of course, was there, with the philosophical schools of the Lyceum and the Academy, and the Painted Portico from the marketplace, an evocation of the gorge at Tempe in Macedonia, a famous beauty-spot, and a replica of Canopus, a suburb of Alexandria notorious for festivals and hedonism. There was also an attempt to represent the underworld.

Hadrian's fondness for hunting gives us a glimpse of the villa at the time it was built. To be Hadrian's horse was a risky business. A favourite steed called Samis was badly injured – indeed, nearly killed – when Hadrian was hunting boar in Etruria. Nothing but the best would do for the emperor's companion and friend: Samis was brought (perhaps carried by slaves) to the healing sulphurous waters of the springs below Tivoli, and his damaged leg healed. Hadrian himself (it seems) wrote a poem in thanks to the nymph of the hot springs, in the horse's name:

> In his sickness, Samis rested at the outflow of Albula, to relax his limbs in the healing waters. His leg had been wounded in Etruria, at Russellae, by the tusk of a wild boar, had swollen up, and he had nearly died. Now his stiff tendons are easier, the scar has lightened, and the swift steed has started to run with a rider once again. Samis presents himself in marble effigy in return for what you've done, where the lord of Tivoli oversees the place where you emerge beside the highroad, and the Aelian villa, with its coloured façades, looks on.

The lord of Tivoli was the hero-god Hercules, whose gigantic temple platform still looms over the plain beneath, but it was also Hadrian, who used his family name to lay claim to the villa, and who here told himself one thing that we can never know from the remains: how the amazing complex looked to passers-by. Crowning the low hill above the road, the villa was clearly intended to impress those passing with opulently painted and imposing elevations. Like the ancient temple of Hercules further up the hill, this, too, was the home of a divinity: Hadrian himself.

The layout of Hadrian's unsurpassable fantasy home sums up an important aspect of Roman society. It was largely devoted to one social activity: dinner, the most important shared occupation that marked out the Greco-Roman culture of this period. A millennium before, Homer had set the pace: his heroes bathe, anoint themselves, cook the meat, pour the wine, and share the meal while some form of entertainment takes place. The pattern survived throughout the ancient world.

Bathing was the precursor to the meal, and resembled ritual ablution: for the Romans, as for other ancient peoples, eating in company was a solemn act that involved acknowledgement of the gods. But the meal was also when the pleasures and privileges of the aristocratic life came together, and preparation of the body symbolised it.

When and how did this preparation break out of the confines of the private house and become a public institution? The answer must lie to some extent in the natural world. Mediterranean winters are cold and wet. Hot water was a treat, and in some places it was miraculously available to all comers: Italy is particularly well endowed with natural hot springs – like the Whitish Waters just below Hadrian's villa. The most abundant occur in the Bay of Naples, the volcanic zone around Mount Vesuvius. This area became the favourite leisure destination of the Roman rich, and Rome's first bath complexes were built in an attempt to transplant for the benefit of all the pleasures and indulgences that had developed on the Bay of Naples and at the luxurious centre of Baiae. Long before the emperors had built the major bathing establishments of Rome, though, the rich had equipped their private properties with arrangements for hot bathing, heating the water by burning wood.

The baths were the origin of another famous amenity of the Roman élite: central heating. Comfort in low winter temperatures was a prominent aim of bath-house design. Glazed windows were oriented to catch the winter sun. The water was heated in boilers. Voids beneath the floors, and terracotta ducting built into the walls, were heated with the smoke and hot air from large fires in furnace rooms below the building. Vents at the top made the system draw, and if the fire was maintained for some hours, the whole structure became very warm. The technique survives in the traditional hammam of Muslim cities. It was called *hypocaustum*, 'burned underneath' in Greek.

The system was extended to provide background heating in certain special rooms in private houses and villas, especially the winter dining room, and has traditionally been a much admired hallmark of Roman civilisation. Like so much else, it would scarcely have been possible without slaves, as the effort of maintaining the necessary fires in the furnace rooms was great, especially in collecting sufficient fuel. But ingenuity helped protect forests: like hammams, Roman baths could work on chaff and straw from the harvest, and all sorts of combustible materials were used – so much so that we hear of the need to regulate against accidentally drugging bathers by burning plants that produce poisonous fumes.

It was easy to run your own bath in deep countryside, on large villa estates. In towns, people of middling wealth lived much closer together and pooled resources to provide central facilities, especially if they involved heavy fuel consumption. The bakery oven was a commercial enterprise to which, for a small consideration, families could bring their dough, and baths worked in a similar way. Benefactors decorated and extended them, and provided the necessary water and fuel. (The holy man Apollonius took only cold baths: hot baths were a sign of 'society's senility'.) What had begun as a convenience for the reasonably wealthy grew so that all could use and enjoy it – and honour those who had paid for it all.

Ancient towns were miniature states, which had traditionally been in charge of their own defence. Young adult males needed to train to fight, which meant keeping fit in gymnasia – then washing off the sweat of exertion at the nearby baths. The provision of good facilities for this section of the community was an attractive way to support public service.

As the public baths became increasingly popular, the place of bath-time in the shape of the day changed. Bathing could no longer be seen as so closely dependent on mealtimes. Hadrian forbade the non-medical use of public baths before mid-afternoon, thus reinforcing the tie with the last mealtime of the day. No doubt the fashion continued to shift: the emperors were powerless to effect social change. The bath-houses allotted different periods to men and women. At the same time, the practice of bathing was extended to include a time-consuming variety of other pastimes. Social interaction was a natural part of this, with cultural, intellectual, athletic and other activities. 'Baths, wine and sex are physically bad for us', went the saying, 'but what makes life is baths, wine and sex!' And at Pompeii two slaves of the emperor scribbled a graffito on the wall of a bath-house to record how much they had enjoyed the nice lunch and sex they had there.

The use of water in bathing was more limited and less salubrious than might be thought. Dry or steamy heat were an important part of the process: the immersion pools, cold or (especially) hot, became filthy, as the water was seldom changed. A doctor wrote that anyone suffering from purulent sores should bathe early in the day . . . For all the dirt, the premises, as rich archaeological evidence shows, became more and more spectacular to match the ostentation of the water-supply. But there were always dank corners full of cockroaches. The baths were a place of some anxiety, and that was reflected in people's dreams. Artemidorus finds dreams of fine bath-houses, well lit and at the right temperature, generally good. But going into a hot bath dressed, or not being able to sweat, or finding the roof gone and the bath open to the sky, was worrying. He relates the story of a competitor in the Sacred Games, which Hadrian founded at Smyrna in western Turkey, who dreamed that he was in the baths, but all the plunge-pools were dry. This foretold that he would be accused of attempting to bribe the judges at the games, fined and excluded from competing.

From the first bath-houses built at the beginning of the imperial period, the complexes funded by the emperors became larger and more magnificent, housing more and more facilities, and capable of providing services to thousands of people at a time. Hadrian equipped his villa with baths comparable to those of the capital, if not quite on the same scale. There, he and his family mingled with whoever was admitted to the villa, just as in Rome the baths offered a real social mix, rich and powerful beside those of much lower status. It made for a kind of social levelling. This did not mean egalitarianism; rather, it provided a wonderful opportunity for one-upmanship. And, no doubt, access was carefully controlled: there was usually an admission charge. The services offered by the baths depended on human labour, not just the technical sophistication in heating systems and water-piping. The hypocausts and boiler-rooms were kept going by slaves, and working conditions would have been appalling.

There were hazards for the bathers too. Hot water was such an unusual luxury that it was considered a bit frightening, especially if it was natural, and in that jumpy society, people suspected bath-houses of harbouring demons. They were, therefore, good places to invoke your curses:

> Hand over to death Praeseticius son of Apelle, the bakery manager, who resides in the Ninth Region where he pretends to carry on his trade, and give him to Pluto guardian of the dead, and if he escapes this fate let him suffer fever, chill, cramp, pallor, sweats, convulsions by day, every day, in the evening, at night, from this day and this hour and this night, and disturb him so that he can take no remedy and if an opportunity offers roast him Praeseticius the son of Apelle, in the Imperial baths or the local bath-house, or in whatever place you wish, break him . . .

Someone else left a tablet at a bath-house cursing whoever had stolen their clothes while they were splashing in the hot springs.

Hadrian, the ostentatiously good citizen, made a point of shared bathing in public baths when they were filled with 'everyone'. One anecdote is telling. In the baths, Hadrian met a man whom he had known during his military service, rubbing off the oil against a wall because he could not afford a slave to scrape him down. This was unusual: almost everyone who came to the baths had a slave attendant. Magnanimously, Hadrian gave him a supply of slaves and an endowment. Predictably, the next time the emperor came to the baths, the place was full of old men rubbing themselves against the walls; the emperor suggested drily that they should help each other scrape down . . .

With bathing so luxurious and such a central part of the

cultivated life, it is easy to see why the Roman word for 'smart', 'chic', 'spruced-up' also meant 'recently washed' (*lautus*). It was especially applied to fashionable young men.

The baths, then, were an opportunity for self-display of a rather different kind from obvious expenditure on vaults or statues, plumbing, heating and marble veneers. They offered the chance to be seen dressed for private life and, still more so, to be seen dressing and undressing, relishing the process of adornment.

Roman clothing was essentially simple. It was believed that in early days men and women had both worn a basic version of the toga. In Hadrian's time there had been an official outfit for citizen men and women – for men the toga, for women the stola. This pattern was unique to the Romans. In the more or less Greek parts of the empire, dress was much more flexible.

The toga was a large sheet of woollen cloth, wrapped round the body in an intricate fashion, which could be done more or less carefully according to taste. The stola was a long dress, belted at the waist.

Men had once worn a loincloth under the toga, but the normal undergarment was now the tunic and, in informal settings, this was the standard clothing of the Roman male. For elaborate private occasions, such as formal dinners, more heavily decorated and ample clothes might be worn. Women wore a light tunic beneath the stola, and might support their breasts with a band of cloth worn under that.

The toga, which served as a kind of uniform, reducing social distinctions and levelling the wearers to a single citizen status, had become a major symbol, but it was difficult to put on and uncomfortable to wear. Only properly appointed officials had the right to wear one with purple stripes, indicating their status. In Rome sacrifices and shows were formal public occasions, so the rules and conventions controlled what people wore at these events too. The governor of Egypt under Trajan put a spectator to death because he had come into the theatre without the proper white festival garment. This was an abuse, but it shows that such things were taken seriously.

Hadrian wanted to perpetuate Roman tradition. Like other emperors, he therefore enacted that the toga should be worn in public by all senators and equestrians; and he always stuck to his rule in Italy. (Even so, the toga disappeared during the next century.) He allowed one interesting exception: the return from dinner-parties. This was, it seems, a public occasion but one on which the relaxed domesticity of the dinner-party held sway so that, as in the baths, the rigidity of official decorum might be dropped. His own costume at dinner was the philosopher's cloak or the informal version of the toga, which tells us something of how he saw the dining in which he specialised. Even though people might want to avoid the toga, it mattered to be neatly and conventionally dressed. Artemidorus again: 'Dreaming that you are incorrectly dressed, or in some ludicrous or inelegant way, is a bad sign for everyone except professional comics, as it is exactly how they normally dress.'

In ancient Rome there was a real distinction between the formality of public life, with its rhythms, rules and routines, and the much greater freedom of the household and its extensions. Wealth was easier to display at home, and that was why the baths, offering a compromise between public and private, were so useful for showing off taste and riches. Baiae and other resorts were better again than the baths, since their facilities were even more extensive, and holiday licence applied constantly and everywhere, making private display and domestic indulgence possible on a far larger scale.

Hadrian made a legal ruling that gives a glimpse of everyday attire:

The clothes people stand up in are not to be included in the property of the condemned (which is forfeit to the state): if someone has a belt on, no one is to seize it for himself. Likewise the tunic he is wearing, the small change in his money-belt, which he has about him for daily sustenance, or light rings (up to a value of 5 gold pieces). If the condemned man has a sardonyx on his finger, or another gem of great value, or if he has a bond for a large sum under his clothing, those can by no means be counted as 'day-clothes' in this sense.

'Dreaming of your usual clothes is good for everyone, and so is dreaming of the right clothes for the season – in summer linen, and comfortably worn-in, in winter, wool and nice and new,' says Artemidorus, in his *Dream Book*. He goes on to distinguish between Greeks and Romans and their slaves. Greek slaves who dream of white clothes will be freed because only free men wear white. At home, Roman masters and slaves dressed similarly, so there was no advantage for a Roman slave in having such a dream. White clothes meant holiday, so it was a bad dream for manual labourers as they would lose money through idleness. White was also worn at funerals.

Artemidorus saw purple, red and other-coloured clothes as normal for priests, musicians, actors and some very rich men. His audience dreamed of barbarian clothing and the Roman toga, and his response was identical in both cases: this was a good dream if you were travelling to places where people dressed like this, otherwise not.

For extra covering, when the tunic was not enough, there was a variety of cloaks, some with hoods. Those, and sunhats, were the only headgear worn by Romans, except ceremonial wreaths and some religious caps. A full shoe was worn by citizens on similar occasions to the toga; thonged sandals were thought informal, but were very common. Men's and women's shoes do not appear to have differed.

In public, women were circumscribed by certain conventions of modesty and inconspicuousness. But although luxury and ostentation in clothing and adornment were frowned on in both sexes, it was generally expected that women who could afford it would display wealth and taste in these ways. For Artemidorus, elaborate clothing, hairdressing and rich jewellery were good dreams for women, especially rich ones and courtesans. A story of the flamboyant and controversial only child of Augustus, the founder of the empire, had him rebuking her for appearing in more showy clothes than usual: 'Yesterday I was dressed for you,' Julia replied, 'today for my husband.' Men normally wore only rings as jewellery, but women who could afford it had a huge range of opulent ornaments. There was little variation in hair-styling for men, but rich women displayed the skills and labour of their slave hairdressers with complex treatments of their long hair; women never wore it short. The ladies of the imperial court set a fashion that was widely followed: what was new was on view in the portrait busts that circulated so widely in the empire. Emulation of the imperial family suggested powerful connec-tions: there is little evidence of commercial exploitation of fashion, let alone of fashion being driven by and for commercial ends.

There was, of course, a culinary norm and, inevitably, it dated back to Homer's epic heroes, which meant roast meat and plenty of wine. Most people in the ancient world ate meat rarely, usually after public sacrifices. The normal diet consisted of nutri-tious stodge and something to make it tasty. It was a mix of different cereals and legumes, processed as flour, groats, biscuit or cake, then made into porridges, soups, breads and so on, diversified with a repertoire of condiments, of which the most basic were salt and olive oil. From this more elaborate foods had developed, which were consumed at an élite dinner and at imita-tions thereof further down the social scale.

Variety had increased since Homer's day. More plants and animals were domesticated. Selection had produced new vari-eties. As the economic and political horizons of the ancient world had expanded, so new foodstuffs and new ways to prepare and cook them were introduced. Some, like peacock, were always exclusive to the élite; others gradually became more accessible to a somewhat wider market, such as pepper. Increasingly, global trade made variety cheaper.

There had also been a real change in the way food was trans-formed for the table: cooking had become the business of specialised artisans, with serious expertise. Cooks held a relatively low status so their world was marginal, and suffered also from the disapproval of indulgence, excess and extravagance. But that did not prevent some members of the élite becoming associated with food, of whom the most famous Roman was the celebrated gourmet Marcus Apicius, who had lived a century before Hadrian's reign. He became a byword for refined taste and conspicuous expenditure – so much so that later celebrity *bon viveurs* appropriated his name. The most recent had been famous under Trajan, and devised a way of fattening geese on figs to make their livers more delicious. The one Roman cookery book to survive goes under his name. Although it contains dishes named after him, it is certainly a later compilation. It was Apicius who was said to have committed suicide because with only ten million *sestertii* left he could hardly put on another decent dinner-party. Aelius Caesar, Hadrian's intended successor, was said to have interesting tastes in reading: the sexy love-poetry of Ovid, the obscene and witty epigrams of Martial, and Apicius' culinary treatises.

Cooking was a skill that appealed to Hadrian, and he was interested enough in fine food to have a favourite dish recorded (not all that common for Roman emperors), the Four-Drug, the *tetrapharmakon*. It appears to have been a blend of fowl and pork delicacies, composed of pheasant, peacock, sow's udder (*sumen*), wild boar and breaded ham. We only have the ingredients; the artistry with which the dish was prepared is lost.

With variety, subtle cooking, fine wine, more money, the Romans moved towards the reputation for greed and excess that has stuck with them. Entertaining at dinner became absurdly expensive, and fantastically elaborate. It is true that the Romans made themselves sick during dinner so that they could eat and drink more, but not that they did so in a *vomitorium* – which was the exit from a theatre. Here is a paraphrased description to illustrate the practice:

When Caesar came to stay at Philippus' on the second day of the Saturnalia festival, 19 December 45 BC, the house was so full of

soldiers – at least 2000 of them! – that there was hardly room to
set an arrangement of 3 couches for Caesar's own dinner. But an
officer arrived and they pitched camp outside. The next day Caesar
worked until 1 p.m., strolled on the beach, at 2 bathed, was
anointed, reclined for dinner, and because he was following a course
of emetics, ate and drank to his heart's content. His inner circle
dined equally heartily on three sets of three couches nearby; the
smarter dependants got a very good meal, and the 'less smart ex-
slaves and the slaves had no shortage'.

But drunkenness made the ancient world go round. The
psychotropic properties of ethanol were at the heart of what
Greeks and Romans shared in their communal meals. Access to
the stimulus and analgesic of alcohol was a key social issue in a
society that needed both. Who could drink, in what company, on
what occasion, how much, and what happened when they were
drunk were issues that marked out links and boundaries across
society. Slaves drinking, women drinking, children drinking: all
needed careful regulation and control, which was managed by
turning drinking into a social ritual. The Greeks had led the way,
inventing the formal dinner called 'drinking together', *symposion*. A person *was* what they drank: in uncouth parts of the
world, people fermented grain or honey and drank beer or mead,
but that was as barbaric as wearing trousers. The only drink for
the *symposion*, or its Roman successor the *convivium* ('sharing
life'), was wine. The soldiers at Vindolanda behind Hadrian's
Wall liked a regular supply of beer – but they were Belgians.

The *symposion* was a stylised social ritual. Traditionally, nine
men took part, reclining on three large couches, often beautifully
carved and decorated. In the Greek tradition, no respectable
women were present; the Romans were more inclusive. Food was
put on small tables in front of each couch. The diners were
served wine mixed with water from a huge decorated bowl called
a *krater*, which stood prominently in the room. The mixing of
the wine with water was the central formality of the occasion.
Drinking neat wine was thought unhealthy, and considered a

sign of serious debauchery or uncultured ignorance – this was another thing that only barbarians did. Somebody was appointed at a dinner to make the decision about how strong the wine would be at each round, and rounds were counted carefully.

The meal began with a libation to the gods: each diner poured a little wine out of his first cup on to the ground. Then a brief prayer for prosperity was said and people drank more toasts, and gradually the evening became rowdier. Singing and spontaneous composition of poetry were common diversions, and other entertainers might be present, such as flute-girls, whose sexual favours were available. The food was originally rather marginal. By Hadrian's time it had become much more important; and there was also now a taste for adding water, heated in special samovar-like vessels, to the wine.

The young Hadrian had made his mark with Trajan as a heavy-drinking companion on campaign in the wars in what is now Romania. Trajan liked to drink to excess, and Hadrian cannot have been the only courtier to join in just to please him. At some upper-class banquets, the effort was made to maintain the old tradition of discussion on learned and demanding themes, but this was now an antiquarian foible – although vital in the topmost intellectual circles. Otherwise, dinners often became boisterous. In one of the many legal rulings recorded from the hours he spent as a judge, Hadrian judged an extreme case of horseplay. Some dinner guests had tossed one of the party in a blanket and dropped him, to his permanent physical damage.

Wine had become an important commodity because of universal demand for it. If ever there was a consumable that trickled down from the exclusively privileged wealthy, this was it. There was a constant market for the cheaper varieties in the cities where more people had some disposable money. This, too, graded individuals: the wine you could afford located you precisely in social terms. The most prestigious vineyards were in Tuscany, the area around Rome itself and in the Naples region. A number of Greek islands were noted for their wine too, particularly Cos and Rhodes, but one of the most important came from Gaza, on the coast of Palestine.

Ancient wine was red. The finest was made with great care, and aged lovingly. In the time of Augustus people could still drink, and apparently enjoy, wine of a famous vintage then 120 years old. It must have been a strong sweet wine, like an old Malmsey or Madeira. Distillation was unknown, so there was no way to increase the proportion of alcohol beyond the levels naturally produced by fermentation.

Wine from all corners of the Mediterranean was available on the Italian market, shipped by sea for the most part in earthenware transport jars, but also increasingly in the barrels that took over in northern Europe in the Middle Ages. The availability of more and cheaper wine, and a greater variety of it was a sign of the success of a city, and the empire's capital, of course, had the most developed wine-shop culture.

Water is best, a great Greek poet had announced. But no one knew how important it was to keep it clean. In preventing the waterborne diseases that made ancient towns so dangerous, the aqueducts must have made some difference. But disinfecting the water with wine was another possibility. In ancient times, armies were vulnerable to polluted water – the poisoning of wells and the deliberate infection of water supplies were early forms of biological warfare. One of the reasons for the Roman army's success was its wine-drinking: it was significantly less vulnerable than its opponents to typhoid and the other diseases carried by polluted water. In taverns wine was also mixed with water and flavourings, and Roman families adopted the practice at ordinary mealtimes.

The machinery of social superiority went into motion as soon as guests arrived for dinner, a precision instrument for expressing status, for subtle promotion and demotion. Don't grab the best position and be humiliatingly downgraded: take an inferior one so that you move up. Who will be on the same couch as you and who on those nearby? How far away from the host will you be?

In settings like the Tivoli villa, the answer to the last question was usually, a very long way indeed. The porticos and halls of the villa could accommodate hundreds of groups of couches, and although they were usually arranged so that it was possible to see the emperor and his privileged entourage, it was often from a distance. But those huge feasts were one of the main interactions the emperor had with his subjects. The largest and finest hall of the Palace on the Palatine, which Hadrian inherited from his predecessors, was not a throne room or an audience hall but a gigantic dining room.

Another way in which Hadrian tried to show a becoming citizen egalitarianism was in being there to welcome some of the guests and in the case of senators, it was noted with in-drawn breath, *standing up*. Standing and sitting arrangements were as fraught with significance in ancient cultures as dress. Citizens were supposed to stand to greet one another.

Departure at the end of the evening was another matter for careful thought. How should one get home? Attendants were needed as the streets were rough after dark. One triumphant general was given a special reward: the right to return home by elephant.

Breakfast, taken very early, could be a substantial meal, but lunch was usually only a snack. If dinner was going to be formal, it took place around the ninth hour of the day (three p.m. in autumn and spring, but as late as five in summer). The traditional order was a first course of lighter dishes, followed by the main offerings. As in many cuisines other than the 'Western' today, the idea was to serve a large number of tempting dishes from which the diners could make selections. After the main business of eating, delicacies were served as the serious drinking began. During this stage the various entertainments were provided.

Who was invited to Hadrian's villa, and where did they stay, since Rome was too far away to go back for the night? It is hard to be sure, but earlier emperors had entertained all six hundred senators with their families and the 1800-strong inner circle of the equestrian class. The imperial ladies entertained the wives of senators and other prominent citizens. Sometimes the emperors gave banquets for thousands of the citizen population of Rome. Domitian had put on dinners for all of the spectators at shows in the theatre, and all-night feasts for the public when the fountains flowed with wine. Imperial triumphs prompted entertaining on this scale. We think of a triumph mainly as a parade, but the people of the city probably saw it as a chance for a slap-up meal and plenty of free drink, with especially good games thrown in. These gigantic junketings always remained versions of the *symposion*, with couches provided for the hundreds of guests.

In Hadrian's villa several areas were laid out for these mass *symposia*. In the biggest, colonnades flanked a pool several hundred feet long. The emperor and a couple of his most favoured companions could dine at one end in private but in the public eye. All along the colonnades, set after set of couches in threes made it possible for hundreds more on each occasion to say that they had dined with the emperor, even though he was safe from contact with any except a carefully chosen few.

This elaborate, stylised, sharing of life at the top is one of the secrets of how the empire worked. Just as the emperor shared his ultra-luxurious life with a few thousand people, so it went on down the social hierarchy. City populations came to expect perks of this kind in proportion to the pretensions of each community and its leaders. The army, based in camps that were like small cities, also expected signs of favour. All this kept the trickle-down effect working, to spread the values and some of the rewards of élite culture through the layers of ancient society.

A visit to a museum often reveals a routine collection of familiar Roman objects to illustrate 'daily life'. Pins and brooches, glassware and moulded pottery, small fittings of iron and statuettes of bronze survive in thousands from all over the empire. This daily detritus is important because there is so much of it. It shows that many thousands of households had reached a certain level of spending power. They were not expensive items, but they were bought, and most are more than merely functional.

They show their owner's investment in the paraphernalia of culture, taste and high living. The production of millions of decorated pots and hundreds of thousands of bronze figurines was a major economic fact. It shows a serious level of production and advanced networks of distribution. Detailed study of the artefacts helps us to map the networks, which covered vast swathes of the empire. There was a living to be made in supplying the market but, numerous as the consumers were, this trade was not big enough to kick-start an industrial revolution. When new provinces settled into a stable relationship with the rest of the empire, for example, there was a surge in demand for domestic hardware, and some thought must have been given to producing more, better and quicker. But the effect didn't last long. It was a significant if occasional ingredient in local prosperity but not part of a systematic change in the economy.

Much more important was the effect that this consumption had on society. It marked out a huge group of haves from the have-nots. Museum visits confirm the number of families who joined in. How many of the original total of six-inch-high statuettes of Hercules, or glass scent-bottles or bone hair-pins survive? One per cent? Less? This was hardly luxury. But it was a social marker: thousands of households, millions of individuals, did not have these things. The artefacts delineate two worlds. Outside the empire, especially to the north, use of such items dropped off rapidly.

Some of the forms and symbols of this cultural hardware were specifically linked to the Roman state. Imperial emblems, Roman deities, Latin words or phrases, activities that were strongly associated with Rome, such as the arena or the circus, turn up. People linked prosperity and security with the maintenance of the state, and they knew that the state was Roman. But it was precisely to prosperity and security that this material belonged. Like consumer goods in poor societies today, these small extras might communicate a message about the place where they were invented, made or first used, but they are more important as markers of success and social promotion.

XI

LIFE AND LOVE

Nasty rumours started that Hadrian had forced sex on underage boys, and that he had openly enjoyed the attentions of Antinous. That was why he founded a city in his name, and contracted for statues of the young man.

AURELIUS VICTOR

Hadrian's imperial wanderings display him and his empire in a panorama that stretches from the eastern outposts of Rome on the Black Sea and the July heat of the Saharan fringes to the turf of the cool Northumberland hills. His travelling was also the scene of an encounter that lasted for the central six or seven years of his reign and did far more for his reputation and place in history than his diligence in answering petitions or encouraging regimental manoeuvres – more, perhaps, even than the Pantheon or the Wall.

In north-west Turkey the mountains are wooded and remote. They were still more so in 123 when Hadrian headed this way for the hunting. He had a good time. The local town was upgraded to a city, and renamed Hadrian's Hunts. As was usual, the community organisations had been proudly involved in preparations for the imperial visit and were probably aware that the youths in training for their coming-of-age, the ephebes, would make a congenial part of the welcoming committee. Hadrian had enjoyed his youth with the teenagers of Italica, when he had joined his peers, as the scion of a prominent local family should, at the ceremony by which they became adults. Anyway, at a city on the main road through the region, Hadrian had been smitten by the exceptional good looks of a young man called Antinous. He shared Hadrian's enthusiasm for hunting and was invited to join the imperial entourage. Although more than thirty years the emperor's junior, for the next seven years he was Hadrian's intimate. This was extremely unusual.

Emperors' love-lives were a favourite topic for gossip and speculation on what the most powerful man in the world might like to do, and how far he might go. (The young emperors (usually the Bad ones) explored these possibilities most enterprisingly.) People were also interested in what imperial married couples said to each other – whether they quarrelled, what they had in common. Some emperors had had high-profile wives – Augustus' devoted but ambitious consort Livia, with whom he lived for more than fifty years, or Claudius' Messalina and Agrippina. Some had had more-or-less glamorous mistresses: Titus, destroyer of Jerusalem, was notorious for his affair with the Jewish princess Berenice; his father Vespasian's lover was an ex-slave of the imperial household called Antonia Caenis – when he became emperor Vespasian remained loyal to her, bringing her to live at the palace. The wives of impulsive young rulers were renowned for the intensity of the passion they could elicit – for a while – from their imperial partners; Caligula's wife was supposed to have given him a love-potion – unreliable as any other ancient medicament, it sent him insane.

It was not unusual for emperors to have sexual partners or relationships inside or outside marriage appropriate to their time of life. What was unusual was that Hadrian found a long-term partner who fitted his preference and his age. No other emperor ever became known for such a public romantic attachment to a male partner, rather than indulging a passion for an especially decorative slave.

Salvius Zosimus the freedman is buried here. His advice is what he did himself: anoint yourself, love, drink, enjoy, use up – know yourself, unhappy man, for what you are – be greedy, and live off the nest-egg of your heir. His wife Sexy put up this memorial.

In the cities of Hadrian's empire, people liked talking, writing, reading about and seeing pictures of sex. Erotic literature, from scenes in Homer to Greek comedy, love poetry, the erotic epigram and the romantic novels of the Roman empire might have been accessible only to the literate, but through stage enactments, recitation, word-of-mouth and, above all, pictures as widespread as images of the emperor, sexual narrative was everywhere in ancient urban life.

A mock-tombstone describes (with a rough picture) the conversation between the implausibly named Mr Hotly Sexy (Lucius Calidius Eroticus) and an innkeeper:

– Landlord, let's have the bill.
– You've had a pot of wine and some bread, a quarter *sestertius*; pottage, half a *sestertius*.
– OK.
– And a girl, two *sestertii*.
– OK again.
– And hay for the mule, half a *sestertius*.
– That mule will be the end of me!

That was a one-off, but everywhere there were graffiti, daubed paintings, images stamped on cheap pottery lamps showing athletic coupling (*symplegmata*, as the archaeological literature calls them coyly, using the Greek word for 'embrace').

The Roman world offered a wide range of relatively unproblematic sexual opportunities to most sections of society below the élite, who developed rococo sexual indulgences. Colourful harems are two-a-penny in world history. In the cities of the Roman empire, though, an enthusiastic and spirited participation in a lively and varied sexuality, enriched by performance, word and image, was experienced by hundreds of thousands of men. Admitted to the pleasures of the baths and the hunt, favoured with access to cheap intoxication and subsidised food, entertained and cushioned – at least to an extent – against some of the risks of the world, Roman urban society participated in a life that in most other places has only been accessible to tiny élites. 'Baths, wine, sex, all rot our bodies,' ran the popular saying, 'but what is life, except baths, wine and sex?'

That the men of the towns remained vulnerable to poverty, disease, violence and crime does not change the reality of their pleasures. The relaxed attitude to sex, and its depiction, may seem precociously modern, but we should perhaps recall that it would have been unthinkable without omnipresent slavery and the systematic oppression of women.

What the townsmen of the Roman empire were given in baths or at the circus was a sign of power, of the empire and its leaders, their community and its benefactors. Their sexual opportunities were another sign of power. Sexual relations in the ancient world were inseparable from status and authority. Penetration was the issue. Active and invasive was superior; passive and recipient was subordinate. Artemidorus, the dream-interpreter, thought, as we have seen, that it was normal to have sex with slaves. He went on, 'On the other hand, to dream of being penetrated by one of your household is *not* good. It means damage and loss from the slave in question.' The male and female roles in traditional heterosexual intercourse were the norm, and they were seen to reflect the normal and reasonable superiority of men over women. Through sexual acts this hierarchy was transferred into other relationships.

Sexual morality policed what was appropriate between people of similarly high status: a man committed adultery by sleeping with another citizen's wife; sex with his slave did not count. The expectation that slaves of either sex would be available for sexual acts of any kind was a principal sign of their subjugation. It was pointed up by the use of degrading names that – every time they were used – emphasised their sexual accessibility.

SOME SLAVE NAMES

It should be made clear that this is a substantial minority of names. Most are less offensive, though condescending, such as the names of gods, goddesses or heroes and heroines of Greek mythology, or kings and queens from Greek history, or famous places in the Greek world.

Laughter
Hope (women, very common)
Lucky (both sexes, extremely common)
Pleasure (women, very common)
Desire (women)
Drunkenness (women, quite common)
Kiss (women, quite common)
Perfumed (women, occurs in various forms)
Lock [as in hair], curl, tress (both sexes)
Beloved (both sexes, very common)
Sweetie, darling (both sexes, occur in various forms)
Sexy (both sexes, quite common)

The abuses suffered by slaves as a result of their sexual vulnerability were unlimited – until the spirit of the law changed to improve it – at least a little, in theory. Hadrian took a strong line on deliberate castration: slaves who castrated other slaves were condemned to death, and so were doctors, even when they were approached by men wishing to be eunuchs. He extended the law to a further kind of genital mutilation, the making of people into *thlibiae*, a genital mutilation whose nature we can only guess (the Greek word has overtones of crushing).

Anal rape or forced oral sex were standard forms of humiliating violence threatened or practised in male competition and aggression – even in the carefully crafted poetry of upper-class men such as Catullus. And your status depended crucially on how old you were. Older men trumped younger ones. In homosexual encounters, therefore, men of similar social standing might have a relationship with little blame, but only if the penetrating partner was considerably older. In élite society in classical Greece, male homosexual love had been a central social institution – the classic wooing, as the theory had it, of the loveliest (and best) boys in the athletic training-ground by the wisest, most influential (and best) men in their prime, as we see it on the painted pottery of the time, and in the dialogues of Plato. For two older men to continue such a relationship was irregular and objectionable.

Age, then, was central to ancient views of sex and there were three stages: before, during and after sex; the middle one was shaped by procreation and parenthood.

Children were second-class citizens. Once, Romans had used the same word (*puer*) for 'child' and 'slave'. Slaves never lost the stigma of being assimilated with children, and were referred to as 'boy' or 'girl' whatever their age. Roman parents entrusted most aspects of child-rearing to others, to slaves if they had them – first to wet-nurses, then to a team of male pedagogues, who were responsible for education, manners, morals, feeding and safety. They also inculcated a sense of decorum, and taught – often with strict discipline – demeanour and manners: 'to walk in the street with lowered head, to touch salt-fish with only one finger, and fresh fish, bread and meat with two; to sit in the appropriate position, and to wear a cloak in the correct way'. The child was brought up in the slave world, but he or she retained a strong place in the visual imagination of the parent. Children were thought picturesque.

The biographer Suetonius, who was Hadrian's first – and very learned – chief secretary, collected Greek insults and children's games, including dicing, ball-games, riddles, and Blind Man's Buff, which was called the Bronze Fly. He includes a little girls' dancing game, enacted to a suitably obscure chant:

> Torto-to-tortoise, what's going on?
> 'I'm weaving Milesian yellow and yarn.'
> How did your father happen to die?
> 'Jumped off his white horses into the sea.'

Children, we hear in passing from Artemidorus, liked to parade around mad people in the streets, as a mock entourage. That meant it was good for teachers to dream they were insane . . .

A letter written a few years after Hadrian's death by a senator describes his pleasure in his baby grandson, just at the age of feeding himself grapes. The writer notes how the little boy keeps saying, '*Da*,' which means 'give' in Latin, and how he gives him little writing tablets and scraps of papyrus to encourage him as early as possible into literary interests, but chicks and other little birds are what the child really likes. The affinity between children, small animals and birds fascinated the Romans. Pliny's old enemy the senator Regulus was so grief-stricken at the death of his little son that he killed all his pets around the funeral pyre – 'all his Gallic ponies for driving or riding, his dogs, large and small, his nightingales, parrots and blackbirds'. Gardens were decorated with marble statues of chubby children, usually naked, often with birds.

The chubby children also appear as the mythological creatures we call putti, cupids or erotes – versions of Cupid, the mischievous infant son of Venus, the goddess of sex. They were depicted in wall-paintings, charmingly performing the menial tasks that workshop slaves might have done. And in big households they were evoked more literally. Hadrian's intended successor, Aelius Caesar, gave his slave messenger-boys cupids' wings and often called them by the names of the winds. He made them run up and down ceaselessly, without pity for their increasing exhaustion. A more common, though still highly specialised, slave role was 'the Whisperers – little boys whom the ladies keep around them for fun, usually naked'. It was a Whisperer who stole a wax tablet from under the emperor Domitian's pillow during siesta-time on an afternoon in late summer 96. On it had been jotted the names of some members of his staff he suspected of plotting. The child couldn't read – but the empress could, and told the conspirators, who hurried ahead with the hated emperor's assassination.

At the age of fourteen or so, a child came of age. A citizen boy at Rome would be taken to the Capitol, and there would dedicate to Jupiter the pendant he wore round his neck. Then he put on the citizen's toga for the first time. It was a solemn occasion, and marked by a family celebration; the ceremony of first shaving was another turning-point. A girl of similar age might dedicate her toys to a goddess. But what happened next widened the gap between the sexes. For a young man, these were the years of the ephebate, of training for fighting and first military service. Marriage was postponed and homosexual encounters with other youths or older men might be expected. For a young woman, the menarche meant that marriage was not far away. Meanwhile, there was a brief moment of licence: this was known to be the age of young love, teenage passion, a picturesque spectacle looked at by older people with a fond imagination a bit like the way they saw children. Religion provided opportunities. As Artemidorus remarked, 'You can't go to an all-night festival unless you are feeling good. Dreaming about it also indicates boys and girls making love without fear of punishment, as this is normal on these occasions, and even if it goes beyond ordinary decency, those who go to such festivals expect it, and there's a certain sense in which it is thought acceptable.'

Typically, men married at around twenty-five to thirty; women averaged around fifteen. This made for an automatic generation gap between a father and his teenage children. There was an ancient arrangement in which a woman was transferred by formal marriage from the power and family of her father to the family of her husband, remembered in a ritual called 'the sharing of the spelt cake'. The tradition was nearly dead in Hadrian's reign, and if practised at all, was preserved only among patricians because it was needed for appointment to certain priesthoods. This, and other forms of a woman's transfer 'from hand to hand', had been obsolete for centuries. There had always been a surprisingly informal arrangement by which a marriage might be tried 'on approval' for a year before it became permanent. Apart from a few patricians, Roman men and women lived together as husband and wife by an arrangement that left the woman a high degree of legal independence.

There was still a ceremony of inauguration of a marriage, with picturesque traditions, and it included a number of invocations to the gods for the well-being of the couple, but it was not a religious act as such. A sumptuous wedding dinner was arranged, and presents were given to the bridal couple. The bride was dressed and adorned by her mother and other female relatives, in a style particular to the wedding day – with the hair parted, traditionally by spear point, into six plaits, and her head then covered with a saffron-coloured veil. The legal aspect of the wedding related to the handing-over of a dowry: witnesses placed their seal on the tablets that recorded the event. It was traditional and auspicious for the procession that accompanied a bride to her new home to be as lively as possible, with all kinds of obscene banter, songs and festive ribaldry.

Legal regulations governed the dissolution of properly agreed marriages, and there were expectations as to a couple's behaviour. Not surprisingly, these were asymmetrical: efficient household management and woolworking were seen as the preserves of a good wife; sleeping around was less indefensible for a husband than for a wife. But there was a widespread sense of partnership and that harmony and affection should be normal in marriage – combined with a high incidence of domestic violence. The wife's honour, and the legitimacy of the children that depended on it, were vigorously defended. A surviving record concerns a case of the birth to a virtuous mother in the eleventh month after the death of the father. Hadrian ruled that the child might be considered legitimate – and perhaps he was right. In another case, a young man seduced his stepmother; the father went hunting with him and killed him. Hadrian banished him to an island, on the grounds that he had gone far beyond the rights of a father and behaved more like a brigand.

This letter was written in Greek in Egypt in 'the 29th year of Caesar Augustus', 1 BC:

Hilarion to his sister Alis, very many greetings . . . know that we are still at Alexandria. I beg and entreat you, take care of the little one, and as soon as we receive our pay, I'll send it up [the Nile] to you. If you bring your child to term, if it is a boy, let it be; if it is a girl, throw it out. You said, 'Don't forget me.' How can I forget you? So I beg you, don't worry!

It is only unusual in that the loving couple are brother and sister, a common enough basis for marriage in ancient Egypt, even among Hellenised folk. In other ancient societies incest was taboo, as it is today.

With contraception unreliable, and abortion dangerous, the exposure of unwanted children was normal. No doubt it was most common where parents like Alis and Hilarion could not afford more girl-children, whose labour might bring in less to the household, and who would eventually be a burden to them in needing a dowry. But handicapped or ailing children were exposed even by better-off parents. Romantic fiction told of exposed children who survived and came into their own – like Romulus and Remus. Did Hilarion and Alis expect their daughter to die? It might have been common for the exposed to be collected and reared as slaves. An exposed child was refered to as *koprios*, the dunghill child, derived from the place where it would traditionally have been abandoned.

For all that, procreation was promoted vigorously by the Roman state. In Hadrian's time, foundations were set up in Italian towns to support orphans. At one small town, a foundation supported 246 boys (including a bastard) at sixteen *sestertii* each per year, and thirty-five girls at twelve *sestertii* – the girls, of course, were thought to need less food than the boys. There were incentives to have three or more children, including important tax-breaks and accelerated promotion. The implication must be that, whatever the illegitimate procreativity of masters having sex with their slaves, citizen households tended not to produce many children. The last Roman word on marriage should go to Hadrian's intended heir, Aelius Caesar. When he was ticked off by his wife for taking his pleasures elsewhere he is said to have replied, '"Wife" is the name of a social status, not a type of enjoyment.'

Old age meant an end to sex: it was thought revolting for the elderly, especially women, to be sexually active. The philosophical claimed that emancipation from the tyranny of sex was a release. But there was no emancipation from the ties of family that sex had created, even in death. Status mattered in death as it had in life. The poorest were carried out with no ceremony and interred in mass graves. Infants were stashed in old wine-jars and buried. Those who could afford it had tombs like small houses, containing a chamber with a door. The slaves and freedmen of the rich were cremated and their ashes placed in small pots in niches in huge communal tombs. The rows and rows of niches reminded the Romans of dovecots, the name used for these tombs; with similar jocularity, the pots of ashes were called 'saucepans'. Disused quarries made cheap cemeteries, and were soon extended with maze-like tunnels, lined with dozens of spaces for the ashes or burials of poorer people – the origin of the Christian catacombs. Richer people had separate tombs, but often in shared lots, or in serried rows along the streets outside cities. Roman law rigorously forbade disposing of the dead within the city limits.

The last journey, from the house to the tomb, was a formal and ritualised occasion for those who had means. Cities were surrounded by cemeteries, often huge, complex areas like those outside Islamic cities today. It was not only when deaths happened that they were used: there were feast-days when the dead were honoured, and anniversaries were celebrated. The rite involved a meal for family and friends at the tomb (and for the dead too – sometimes wine was poured through a tube into the tomb), which was sometimes made into an attractive place to spend a day, with couches and a dining room. Many tombs were in gardens, which symbolised the well-being of the deceased, made a pleasant setting and might produce flowers, fruit and vegetables, for which the nearby town made an excellent market.

Until the time of Hadrian, cremation was the normal Roman funeral rite. Burial became more popular in the second century. For the very wealthy, this was an excuse for further display, especially in the design and size of the sarcophagus. The great marble bath-like tomb structure that we see so often in museums became a much more prominent feature of Roman funerary archaeology at this time.

Another type of tomb was the circular burial-mound that the ancient Etruscans had used – Augustus and his family had been buried in an elaborate version. Trajan's ashes were lodged at the base of his column – by special permission, since this was within the city. Hadrian, interestingly, built a new version of Augustus' mausoleum, an enormous drum of stone originally topped with a mound and on top of that a statue of himself in a four-horse chariot. It was so huge that a large man could get through the pupil of the eye of each horse. The building was fortified in the Middle Ages, and is now the Castel Sant'Angelo.

Funerals of emperors were an opportunity for grand pageantry, carried out with tremendous pomp portraying the divinisation of the emperor. They were commemorated on coins that were circulated across the empire. First the body had to be brought back to Rome, if the emperor had died elsewhere, with a long cortège and honours from all the cities along the route. An enormous pyre was built of layer upon layer of precious scented woods and perfumed materials, with columns, balconies and terraces rising to where the embalmed body lay. It was then set ablaze. When the fire reached the top, a trapdoor opened, and an eagle was released from a cage. That was the moment at which the emperor became a new god.

It seems a long way from the sexual embrace to the scented pyre, but sex and death were entwined in Roman thought. The tragedy of love interrupted by death, or the heroic saving of the

object of desire from a terrible fate were then, as now, a common-
place of romantic fiction. The various fates of the human body
in the amphitheatre were another reason for reflecting on the
two themes together, and gladiators were regarded as sexually
very potent. This is an area that is hard to read from the surviving
evidence. To encourage good luck and frighten off the evil eye,
you might have hung by your front door a kind of bronze wind-
chime: four bells were suspended from a prancing penis-headed
lion, which has a penis as a tail – one from its neck, one from
each of its back paws, and one from its own erect (human) penis.
But in another version the bells dangle from a gladiator, armed
for the wild-beast hunts of the arena and slicing at a panther.
The snarling head rearing up to savage his face is, however, the
tip of the gladiator's own huge penis.

However we might read the gladiator, the panther and the
penis, the Romans of Hadrian's time saw a close link between
sex and death. The two ideas certainly came together in what
the world thought of Hadrian's passion for his lover Antinous.

Artemidorus' dream-interpretations naturally illuminate
some everyday ideas about sex and morality. They confirm
that views of sex were usually quite matter-of-fact, no doubt
because of its easy availability. His generally relaxed attitude
still recognised an order of moral desirability. It wasn't by any
means a world in which anything went. Artemidorus was much
concerned with dreams about having sex with your mother – it
is one of the longest sections of his *Dream Book* and is where
he includes most detail about the positions used in Roman sex,
a unique text that confirms the often explicit paintings of Roman
interior décor. The only position he approves of is 'flesh to
flesh', or the 'natural' position, or 'according to Aphrodite's
law'. The others are very bad signs: from behind; standing up
and holding her up; with her kneeling; with her on top, strad-
dling the dreamer. Strangely enough, he thinks that there are
circumstances in which dreaming of making love to one's dead

mother can be a good sign. Oral sex with her, though, is a truly terrible sign.

Dreams of unnatural sex fill a separate section, and include intercourse with oneself (masturbation is not, however, mentioned), lesbian sex, sex with a god, necrophilia and bestiality. He was perplexed by a man who dreamed regularly of oral sex: disaster should have followed but had not. Then he discovered why: the man actually *did* it.

Sex was so visible a part of Roman culture because it was for sale. The sex scenes in Roman paintings are often set in premises let for the multiple recreations of the Roman street-corner – gambling, snacking and drinking. Prostitution was a recognised profession, taxed and regulated by the authorities, mainly because it was a potential source of disorder. But beyond the formally registered whores, other women sold sex as an essential means of survival. The desperate poverty of the cities, and the institutional horror of slavery, made everyday non-marital sex such an accepted feature of life.

Outsiders, such as Jews and Christians, rejected the indulgence of town existence and had a different view of freely available sex. However, the main Greek and Roman tradition accepted that excess was bad, as was giving way to powerful emotion or losing control of physical impulses – especially if it subverted the order of social status. The invention of the sleazy sexual world of the tavern, though, offered excitement to the upper classes whose behaviour was mimicked in such places. The upper-class woman turned whore was a favourite fantasy, and anecdotes were repeated with relish of the lively festivals when Caligula, Messalina or Nero encouraged men and women of the senatorial and equestrian orders to conform to the norms of the back-streets rather than traditional Roman restraint.

Which brings us back to Hadrian and Antinous. Was this another monstrous tale of imperial sexual transgression? Like his predecessor Trajan, Hadrian's orientation seems to have been exclusively homosexual. It was perfectly normal for men to be bisexual: Domitian, for instance, had affairs with a number of senators' wives, an energetic taste in concubines (he liked to depilate them, according to Suetonius), enjoyed swimming with 'the prostitutes who are especially heavily in demand', and had a passion for a beautiful young freedman eunuch, Earinus ('Springtide'). But all the (relatively limited) sexual innuendo about Hadrian concerns men and boys, especially in Trajan's entourage. Here the traditional Greek pattern of older men courting teenage boys flourished, with the palace pages' training school as one focus. Trajan's officials often shared his taste. A man he appointed to govern Egypt provoked outrage by his blatant affection for a well-born seventeen-year-old: 'He dined with him nearly every day, sometimes with his father, sometimes not; when people gathered to pay their respects in the morning, there he was, coming out of the prefect's bedroom, and causing offence by the way in which he would roar with laughter with the chamberlains on duty; his gestures and smirk were disgusting, and he humiliated the prefect's debtors by miming what he had been up to with the prefect.' The scandal, notably, was not about the sex but about the boy's insufferable behaviour and the political offence it gave.

The fact is that homosexuality was an elaborate pastime elevated to the same level as the other cultural activities that made élite life distinctive – philosophy, poetry, fine food, hunting and the baths. When participants in a revolt against Domitian were being tried, a beautiful young senatorial officer escaped by pleading that the only contact he had had with the leader of the insurrection was as his lover.

Antinous was different from the young male favourites of earlier emperors. A slave sex-partner, male or female, had an especially low status, as a plaything, a toy, an indulgence, an object: they had no choice in the matter. Antinous, however, was freeborn, and much younger than his admirer, which meant that his relationship with the emperor was a voluntary but unequal one, and cast Hadrian as a great Greek statesman and philosopher of the Athens of half a millennium earlier – exactly as he most wanted. From the physical angle, it goes almost without saying that the emperor, the 'Lover' in the formal terminology of ancient Athens, took the active role, and Antinous, the 'Beloved', the passive. The only question was how long the classical Greek pose could last. Antinous would not remain an ephebe for ever.

Hadrian and Antinous hunted together. When they arrived in Egypt in 130, they went out on an expedition to dispose of a man-eating lion, and a local poet made a fine account in Greek epic style of their adventures, with Hadrian putting Antinous in a dangerous position and saving him at the last moment from the monster. The courtier-bard presented a banquet-crown of Egyptian lotuses, which he said would now always be known as an Antinous-crown, because its colour came from the lion's blood as it sank into the sand. Nothing else is known about the sexual, emotional or intellectual dimensions of the relationship until, a month or two after the lion and lotus episode, it came to its extraordinary conclusion.

The world could accept a bit of philosophical play-acting, and an emperor with a long-term boyfriend. The lad was not Roman, but he was not a slave. In the past emperors had been much more ingeniously offensive, and had disturbed the social order much more alarmingly. What was so intriguing and shocking about Antinous was that he drowned in very strange circumstances in the sacred river Nile, and that his life appeared, willingly or unwillingly, to have been sacrificed in a strange religious or magical deal for his beloved Hadrian's future wellbeing.

XII

WHAT HUMAN BEINGS
NEED MOST IS GODS

Hadrian was extremely attentive in his performance of Roman religious rites, and despised those of other peoples.

HISTORIA AUGUSTA

The most conspicuous aspect of Roman religion was the sheer number of gods. There were scores of divine figures from different places and times and it was common to recognise that they came in uncountable numbers. Of course, people didn't know them all, so to be on the safe side it was often advisable to make dedications 'to the god or goddess who protects this place'.

It is quite hard, from today's perspective, to work out what people thought gods were. Some elements of Roman religion are familiar from twenty-first-century religious systems, above all that gods are vastly more powerful than humans, and that they are associated with everything in nature that is beyond comprehension. Some familiar concepts were not prominent: the creation of the universe and humanity, their ultimate destiny, were not nearly as central to most ancient religions as they are in Christianity. It was easiest to give gods a human form and see them as superhuman, but from the start worshippers sensed that this must be inaccurate and inadequate. Absolute and abstract concepts, such as fate, order, justice and some more philosophical postulations on the nature of infinity were part of the picture, but the balance that existed in ancient Rome between imagining the gods as a race of all-powerful superhumans and considering transcendence and abstract theology is virtually impossible to recover.

Within the multitude of gods, known and unknown, certain figures were much more frequently venerated and discussed than others. It was normal to propose a list of twelve, but this had no formal theological implication. The personalities of individual gods or goddesses were built up over many generations, in a slow evolution that started before classical history began. Above all, they were shaped by religious practice. A deity was defined by the types of prayer, the form of the sanctuary, the ritual acts, the normal form of statues and pictures and so on. Among these ritual acts were sacred narratives, which told of a god's virtues, achievements and generosity.

Stories about the deeds of the gods were an intrinsic part of ancient literature from Homer onwards. In fact, the literary gods parted company, in a sense, with the religious gods. Poets – including Homer – told of the gods' adultery, deception, violence towards each other and humans, which were quickly seen as discordant with religion, and as encouraging people to do these things too. The holy man Apollonius thought that Aesop's fables were better for people than Greek tragedy.

The gods might take on individuality from being associated with distinct people, communities and places. A ruler, an island, a family, a mountaintop, a village and especially a city had a special link with a patron-deity. If they became famous, the patron added an extra element to their portfolio. From these ways of describing gods emerged the familiar couplings: Hephaistos and fire, blacksmiths, volcanoes; Poseidon and the sea, horses, earthquakes; Artemis and wild animals, hunting and the wilderness. But to say 'Artemis was the goddess of hunting' doesn't do anything like justice to a complex divine personality. It was as true to call Artemis 'the goddess of Ephesus' or Poseidon 'the god of the isthmus of Corinth'.

Take Aphrodite. She was invoked as the daughter of the king of the gods, Zeus, and represented as a beautiful woman; her worship concentrated on sexual desire. She was said to be married to Hephaistos, and *The Odyssey* features a burlesque scene in which her cuckolded husband uses his ingenuity to trap her under a net when she is in bed with Ares, the god of violence in war. Greek observers thought this scandalous. Aphrodite was serious: sexual desire mattered. She had other important roles too, such as protecting seafarers; she was one of the main deities in Cyprus and Sicily, and in several important cities. In Cnidos she was represented with a world-famous statue so beautiful and realistic that men were said to have fallen in love with it. Copies were made in hundreds, and many survive from the villas and houses of rich Romans.

The Romans had been in close contact with the Greek world for centuries and the two cultures shared much the same set of divine personalities, but they used their own names for them: Zeus was Jupiter; Artemis, Diana; Hephaistos, Vulcan; Aphrodite, Venus, and so on. They continued the never-completed process of elaborating their characters. Aphrodite-Venus was never the same after she was adopted as the foremother of an important patrician family, which was standard practice among ambitious aristocrats, and not just in Rome. But this family eventually produced Julius Caesar, who gave his name to Rome's emperors, and Venus was now a patron of the city that had conquered the world. It was only under Hadrian, though, that she acquired a suitably grand sanctuary there, the gigantic joint temple shared with the goddess of the city, Roma.

Gods and goddesses of Venus's stature were often known as the Olympians, because they were imagined – by Homer again – to live on the inaccessible summit of the highest mountain in Greece, Olympus. Zeus was the greatest Olympian, and gave the name of the mountain to the sanctuary in southern Greece where he was worshipped with his wife Hera, the queen of the gods. Olympia, where the games took place every four years from 776 BC, became a key religious place for Greeks, and many others too.

In 509 BC the Romans built their first vast temple, the Capitol, on a little hill above the Tiber. It was also, they said, the first time they had set up statues of gods. Those they chose to worship were a selection of the most famous and powerful personalities of the moment in Greece. They chose Athene, whom they called Minerva, a warrior and famous for patronage of all intellectual pursuits and craftsmanship; she was also the city goddess of the two most important communities in Greece – Athens, which bore her name, and Sparta. They chose Hera, queen of heaven and protectress of a swathe of other rich and powerful cities, and called her Juno. Then, with a certain *chutzpah*, they chose Zeus, who ruled gods and men, and whose sanctuary and games at Olympia were famous. He became Jupiter the Best, the Greatest, the God of the Capitol.

These three divinities, worshipped side by side in the massive temple in the heart of Rome, became the guarantors of Roman political and military success, and the protectors of the citizens and their activities. Around the time of Hadrian some regimental commanders in newly conquered Dacia set up a succinct dedication: 'To Jupiter, Best, Greatest, Capitoline; to Juno of the People, the Queen; and to Minerva who shares in the counsels of Jupiter'. A disapproving account of over-enthusiastic popular piety reveals a different picture: the crowd of devotees at the Capitol ceremonially dressing and adorning the images as if they were living grandees. Many Romans found it offensive to tell certain types of story about the gods, and it was only at the end of the Republic and under the emperors that Roman authors began to talk about the gods in the spirit of Greek literature. But the same sneering description of the devout rituals of ordinary folk adds something unexpected. There were even women worshippers, it said, who thought – in the spirit of the myths in which the gods had sex with mortals – that they might be attractive to Jupiter and win his love.

The Greeks surrounded the important and familiar gods with a crowd of other divinities. There were half-divine mortals, the so-called heroes; there were the lesser divinities of springs, groves, rivers and caves. They had also developed a habit of linking concepts with the gods, such as harmony, victory, peace, and endowing them with religious honours. And, like other peoples of the time, they sometimes honoured their most successful generals and most powerful kings as gods.

The Romans, too, had a host of minor divine personalities, such as Consus, the god linked to the games in the Circus Maximus, or Flora, goddess of spring fertility, whose festival was particularly frisky. The Romans liked abstracts too, and dedicated temples to Hope, Mind, Loyalty and Harmony. But they went a stage further, and gave a divine aspect to every action and every thing – door-opening and door-hinges; Aius Locutius, who was considered the personification of the speaking voice; the gods who protected roads, crossroads, doorsteps, houses, and the particular divinities of each man and woman – the male divine spirit was known as Genius (the origin of our word), the female Juno.

The Romans liked to think that they were outstandingly conservative in religion. Observing religious rites and rituals in precisely the right way was extremely important. Every tiny detail had to be performed according to rigidly prescribed methods. The way a sacrifice was made, the exact wording of an incantation, hand gestures during prayer – if even the smallest thing deviated from correct practice the whole process had to begin again, even if the ceremony had been going on for days. Such mistakes could be expensive, as new sacrificial animals had to be found.

The springtime festival of the Lupercalia evoked the city's founders Romulus and Remus, and how they were suckled by the she-wolf. The cave below the Palatine Hill was preserved as a shrine. The rite involved half-naked young men, prancing around the city with lashes made of goat's hide, and flicking people, particularly women, with them. The touch of the hide was said to bring fertility and prosperity, and the custom dated from the early history of Rome. It was still taking place more than a millennium later. Nearly two hundred years after the empire became Christian, a disapproving letter from the then Pope warned Rome's youngsters that they should not do anything so lascivious and reminiscent of the old religious system.

Despite the conservatism of some, new things were always happening in religion. The Romans had happily shared in the development of the gods and goddesses of the Greeks and their neighbours, and they went on introducing new ones. The more the merrier. Capturing the gods of the enemy was traditional Roman behaviour: if the divinities could be persuaded to come and live on Roman territory, they would no longer support Roman opponents. The offering made by a Roman general during a war in southern Asia Minor in the first century BC has survived: 'Whether it is a god or whether it is a goddess in whose protection the town of Old Isaura has been up to this point, Publius Servilius fulfilled his vow.' Servilius took the extra name Isauricus to honour the victory that followed.

It was also worth inviting powerful divinities to Rome in more peaceful conditions, even if their cult was unusual by comparison with other Roman religion. Rome had welcomed the cult of the Great Idaean Mother of the Gods from what is now Turkey and given her a temple in the precinct of Victory. Her cult involved self-castrating eunuch priests, and flourished in Rome, despite its foreignness. Like many others, it was popular with the huge communities of outsiders who played an ever important part in the life of the city.

The accumulation of deities resembled the collection of wonders and works of art, which acted partly as powerful supernatural signs and partly as rational proof of Rome's reach and clout. The statue of Aphrodite from Cnidos ended up in Rome. The emperors Caligula and Nero, who were both interested in sex, had an image of Aphrodite's son and ally Cupid moved to Rome on separate occasions (the moderate Claudius returned it in the meantime). The people of Thespiai, from whom it was taken, were sure that this was why those emperors' sex-lives were so uniquely unpleasant. Statues were powerful.

The Great Mother was represented only by an uncarved upright stone. This was one of seven talismans that were supposed to protect Roman power. The others were the ancient terracotta chariot of Jupiter from the roof of the first Capitoline temple; the ashes of the Greek hero Orestes; the sceptre of Troy; the veil of Iliona; the ancient statue of Minerva, which had also come from Troy, and was cherished in the temple of Vesta beside the sacred hearth of the city where the fire never went out; and the shield that fell from heaven as a good omen when Romulus founded the city – which was kept in a little building in the forum, called the Palace, alongside several replicas so that no one would know which one to steal. It was also said that Rome had a secret name, and that as long as it was never divulged the city would be safe. A last trace of these ideas is found in the medieval prophecy that the world would last as long as Rome, and that Rome would stand as long as the Colosseum.

The Romans believed that the favour of the gods had given them their powerful universal empire and that this power was maintained by their unique understanding of how to deal with religion, which was displayed in ritual conservatism or in their care over such matters as public executions. This wasn't just a matter of invincibility and historical destiny: every aspect of Roman life, law, custom, institutions, they argued, was excellent because of divine good will, and was designed to preserve that benevolence. So, the high profile of religion gave a tremendous boost to their political reputation. It was a central part of the one-upmanship that maintained the imperial order.

Over the years of the conquest of Italy and the rest of the Mediterranean, many others came to believe in these claims, which in turn made the Romans ever more confident in making them. Eventually their expertise in the world of the divine and their glorious destiny came to be universally accepted. One consequence was that any challenger to Rome's dominion had to take this on.

Every Roman citizen was considered an expert on the gods. Each family head conducted religious rites on behalf of his household, worship in which women and men, slave and free, all played their part. In theory, citizens were equal, but Romans knew that some were superior in birth, wisdom, morality and in the favour of the gods. They were the aristocrats, for whom the usual term was the 'Good'. Greek (and no doubt other) states also had aristocracies that claimed the moral high ground. But they seldom made the claim in such a religious way as the Romans.

Roman religious superiority was a major part of the success of this ideology. It was quite explicit: the Romans were the 'most religious of human beings', and that was what gave Hadrian the excuse to despise other forms of worship – while being intrigued by them. Religion was regarded almost as a science, the product of discovery and long refinement, and there were specific experts too: the point of Roman religion was to make sure that what happened was beneficial, so much was connected with discovering the future. The augurs, for instance, were a priesthood devoted to a form of divination in which the sky was the object of study. Anything that moved in the heavens, especially birds, could reveal the gods' intentions and be the basis for decision-making.

To make the observations systematic, the sky was divided into a notional grid, taking a particular line of sight as the starting-point. This religious practice is certainly linked with the development by the Romans as early as the fourth century BC of techniques of dividing up conquered land and allotting the countryside to new proprietors.

However arbitrary, in the end, the axioms were on which these religious sciences rested, the development of the discipline involved reason and the marshalling of experience, knowledge and skill. Like literary and artistic expertise, religious knowledge could not be made up as you went along: it really had to be understood and mastered, and that, in a perverse way, provided intellectual credentials for political participation in the old

Roman system. Alongside powerful foreign gods, the Romans had collected other prophecies, the most famous of which were the Greek texts called the *Sibylline Books*, access to which was tightly controlled. The study of what the markings on the livers of sacrificed animals might mean or interpretation of the antics of sacred chickens when they were first let out of their basket were other examples of Roman divinatory learning. But religious science extended also to making Roman diplomacy more effective through insisting that it was based on an insider knowledge of the will of Jupiter, the responsibility of experts called *fetiales*, the Treaty Priests.

Few people doubted that the gods affected daily life, the fate of people and communities, or that effort and ingenuity would help to secure a good outcome. At the same time, everyone knew that the gods were capricious and that answers to prayers were unpredictable, if not unreliable, in a way that was reminiscent of the impotence of the individual in the face of the imperial government. People often spoke of their reactions to the gods and to the emperor in a similar way. A senator wrote of how he remembered making speeches praising Hadrian in the Senate but without true affection for him: he was too alarming, too serious, too great – it was more like praying to one of the grim gods who need propitiation rather than love, such as Father Dis, god of the underworld, or Mars, the god of the soldier on his way to war.

Not only was there a divine patron for every possible activity. Religion was an activity that was visible everywhere. One of the things that ancient states spent most time and money on was religion. This was unavoidable even for the most absolute ruler. But even by ancient standards Rome was exceptional: when the emperor Augustus had a ritual to perform at dawn, his biographer tells us, he went to stay at the house of an ex-slave near the sanctuary as he hated to get up early. Augustus liked to be seen as dutiful, but was not, so far as we can tell, especially pious. The matter-of-fact tone of the anecdote shows how normal this was.

As emperor Augustus was also high priest, so he had more high-profile religion to perform than most people. It seems curious to us that the absolute ruler should also be a priest, but it was normal in the ancient world. Sometimes a particular cult called for an outsider as priest, or even a slave. The priest of Diana in her sanctuary at Nemi, beside a crater lake deep in the Alban Hills outside Rome, was a runaway slave who won the priesthood by murdering his predecessor, and kept it until he was despatched in the same way. But priests (and priestesses) were often members of the upper class. At Rome, the numerous official priesthoods had been very like the other official posts in the Republic: the high priesthood was even elected, and there was bribery as in the other elections. The most successful politicians, drawn from the echelons of society considered virtuous, were also the most prominent religious experts.

An important religious role was reserved for six patrician women: from puberty, the priestesses of Vesta tended the sacred fire on the hearth of the city of Rome, in a small temple beside the forum, which no man might enter, and guarded certain sacred objects, including the talismanic statue of Minerva from Troy. They were vowed to celibacy until the menopause, when they were released from their vows and resumed normal life. But during the time of their fertility, if anyone was unchaste she would be buried alive. A celebrated example of that took place in the reign of Domitian, just twenty-five years before Hadrian's accession. As well as being more despotic than senatorial opinion could tolerate, Domitian was a stickler for religious propriety. Cornelia, the senior Vestal, was accused of unchastity, and condemned unheard. Her reaction was logical: 'How can the emperor think me unclean? While I have been in charge of the worship of Vesta, he has conquered and celebrated triumphs.' At the time senators thought she might have been guilty, but they later claimed that they were shocked by Domitian's sadistic enthusiasm for the traditional punishment. Public opinion was inclined to think that his wars were more about spin than military necessity. As she was going down into the underground room in which she would be sealed with some food and a light (so that technically her death was no one's fault), Pliny relates that 'her dress caught, and she turned to free it. The executioner [the Latin word means 'meat-maker'] offered her his hand, but she shrank away, keeping her clean and chaste body from his disgusting touch, preserving her holiness to the very last minute.'

Domitian was using the powers of the high priest (*pontifex maximus*), who, as one of the College of Pontiffs (the name means bridge-builder and is linked with the annual rebuilding of Rome's ancient wooden bridge across the Tiber), was held to be a general authority on religious matters. There were other colleges of priests: a board of fifteen in charge of rituals, the augurs, who watched the heavens for portents, and the committee of seven, who managed the sacred banquets on the Capitol in which real food was placed before the images of Jupiter, Juno and Minerva, and the whole Senate joined in with the meal alongside them. One year mice nibbled the gods' olives – a terrible omen. And there were the Ploughfield Brethren, who met in a sacred grove down the Tiber and sang a hymn in a Latin so old it could hardly be understood. By Hadrian's time, they were all senior senators, and although the point had originally been to promote agriculture, their ritual calendar was now filled with celebrations of the imperial family and its doings. The emperor was automatically co-opted to this brotherhood, and the rites of the Arvals are one of the first things Hadrian is attested as doing after his arrival in Rome in 118.

The main gods each had a personal priest, and the Priest of Jupiter was the most important. He had to be a patrician, and it was difficult to find anyone to do the job, which entailed a ferocious series of ritual obligations that applied to his children and his wife – he had to be married using the ancient specially binding spelt ceremony and had to resign if he was widowed –

but, most of all, to his own behaviour. He was not permitted to see an army with its weapons, dogs, ivy, yeast or flour. It is not known why these items were considered so inauspicious. His bed-legs had to stand on little pots of natural soil. He couldn't spend more than three days at a time away from Rome. He wore a curious pointed hat, which looked a little like a baseball cap without a brim but with a prong sticking out from it, called an *apex*. It was said that every day was a feast-day for the priest of Jupiter. The reason? He was a living statue, 'a sort of holy and living image of the god'. It was yet another of the Romans' ways of showing how closely they were linked with the gods who looked after them.

Prayer and sacrifice were the central religious acts in the ancient world. Without prayer, the gods would not know the needs and disposition of the worshipper. Prayer told the gods why they should help humans, and how. Worshippers recounted the virtues and generosity of the god, and expressed the devotion, gratitude, merit and need of the petitioner. Prayer could be expressed in many forms, in public: the Romans stood to pray, using special gestures, including spreading the arms or putting a fold of the toga over the head, or by the dedication of something that conveyed an ongoing message to the gods, an inscription with invocatory words, or a monument to commemorate a vow and its fulfilment.

Sacrifice was the payment rendered for an expected service from the gods. The Romans were quite literal about the bargains they struck with the gods, and the almost mechanical pay-off they expected for ritual acts of prayer and offering. But they were also aware that the favour of the gods was unpredictable, and depended on more than the precisely correct observance of a ritual. The character and morality of petitioner and community came into it, although the ethical dimension in the relationship between humans and gods was far less developed than it is in either the Old or New Testament. Sacrifice means 'making holy', and the principal rite of ancient religion was the slaying of an animal, made holy to the gods by the act.

It had to be done in the right place. It was recognised that the gods could be anywhere, and later that they were everywhere – but also that there were especially sacred places. Some were forbidden to humans, marked out and fenced off, such as areas where lightning had struck, or where natural wonders were to be seen. More common were the places where the gods were at home in buildings people had made, the temples in the sanctuary complexes, houses of the god, as could be seen by the principal statue, visible and venerable.

An altar for sacrifice stood in front of the temple, which was a potent location for prayer, and the protection for the cult-statue, where honours could be paid to it, such as bathing, anointing and clothing. Here, too, the most valuable offerings could be kept safe: temples had thick walls, and (usually) one stout pair of doors. Although they might be very large and house various activities (the Roman Senate regularly met in temples), they were not places of congregational worship in the style of synagogue, church or mosque. Some were so holy that access was restricted – some were forbidden to men or foreigners – but most were readily available.

Temples were of a fairly standard form, the most common being rectangular with columns across the front, sometimes all round, and a pediment over the main entrance on one of the short sides. Every city had several, sometimes dozens, of buildings of this kind, and each had one particularly fine sanctuary for its principal protectors, which might become celebrated far beyond its location. Close to Tivoli on the edge of the plain outside Rome's gates, the city of Praeneste, now Palestrina, honoured First-born Fortune, eldest of the gods. There was an oracle here, and the sanctuary, rising on terraces up the mountainside above the town, was one of the grandest in Italy. The Jewish Temple in Jerusalem was the symbolic centre for Jews dispersed across the Mediterranean, and supported by offerings sent from every region. The Ptolemys in Alexandria founded a sanctuary for a new god, Serapis, woven from a combination of

Greek religious practice and Egyptian tradition. The Serapeum of Alexandria became one of the holiest temples of antiquity. When Heliopolis, now Baalbek, in Lebanon, became a Roman city, its god was identified with Jupiter, and his temple was rebuilt on the largest possible scale. The worship of Jupiter of Heliopolis spread far and wide in the empire. Something similar happened on a smaller scale in Rome's western provinces. Where a local god had an important healing cult, the place became a Roman centre: the god was identified with one from the Mediterranean tradition, and in the new hybrid form acquired devotees in distant places. At Grand in France the springs and caves of a limestone district attracted religious awe; Gallic Grannus was linked with Apollo, and Apollo Grannus became a famous healing divinity. On a smaller scale, something similar happened at the hot springs of Bath, where a fine Roman-style sanctuary celebrated the British deity Sulis as Roman Minerva.

Despite the popularity of the standard type of temple, there were also exceptions: open-air temples and round ones (Hadrian's Pantheon combined elements of both); mountaintops and caves; ground-plans and elevations that fitted special ritual needs or local traditions other than the Greek and Roman mainstream. Their settings were diverse too. Usually a temple had to be in a precinct, to mark out the sacred from the profane and to protect the valuable offerings. But there were large or small precincts, with gateways, pilgrim hostels, processional routes, bathing-places for purification, sacred groves and gardens, residences for priests, dormitories for receiving holy dreams, dining rooms for sacred banquets, archives and storehouses, sheds for processional vehicles, architects' workshops for the endless maintenance of buildings that might be as large and complex as a medieval cathedral.

The procedure to be followed in a sacrifice was precisely detailed. Flour or meal was sprinkled over the forehead of the animal, and the grandee who was performing the ceremony gave the animal a ritual tap with a sacrifical implement. It was then killed by ritual attendants, who had been trained in the business of slaughtering. The victim was then cut up. Certain parts, not necessarily the choicest cuts, were burned on the altar and dedicated to the gods. The rest was cooked and distributed to the participating and often large crowd. The sacrifices of powerful rulers might involve the killing of a hundred cattle (a 'hecatomb') or more, but sacrifice had many varieties and gradations. In many sanctuaries bloodless offerings were made, usually sweet cakes, and the commonest sacrifice of all was the libation: a drop or two of wine was poured on to the ground for the gods before a family began their meal.

A private sacrifice might be made on any auspicious or appropriate day, but there was also an official calendar of festivals in which sacrifices were prescribed to a particular deity. These might also involve competitions, processions and displays. Just as the great festival of Zeus at Olympia occasioned the Olympic Games, in Rome the great festivals were marked by spectacles in the theatres and chariot-racing in the Circus Maximus. The oldest and greatest of the festivals was the *ludi Romani*, the Roman games to honour Jupiter, Juno and Minerva, the three gods of the Capitol. It took place every September and lasted two weeks, and every day there were performances in the theatres, gladiatorial combats, circus games, as well as sacrifices. Other important festivals included the Quinquatrus in honour of Minerva in March, the Megalensia in April, for the Great Goddess, and the games of Apollo in July.

Religion was visible everywhere. In Hadrian's world statues of every size and material – wood, stone, marble, bronze, silver and gold – were to be seen all over the cities. In today's museums there are hundreds of the portable images that were kept in shrines or household sanctuaries. There were pictures on tableware, cheap or fine, or the walls of houses – the picture of a huge snake on the wall of a kitchen was intended to propitiate the Good Spirit.

The images reflected the ways of describing the gods: some were pictures of the gods of literature; some were marked out by their pose, their clothing or the items they carried, as the deities of a particular sanctuary. Some attempted to convey the complex ideas of overarching godhead that had become more popular as communications improved and horizons widened.

But representation of the divine was always potentially dangerous. The Jews had forbidden images, and the Romans also believed that they too had once, in their very early history, thought it inadvisable to represent the divine in human form. In the eastern Mediterranean state that succeeded the Roman empire in the early Middle Ages, the influential iconoclast movement attempted to purge Christianity of this legacy of ancient religion. At the same time, Islam was insisting on the same restraint as ancient Judaism. All these people believed that any image of the world of the gods might have significance and power. Most of the deities of Greek and Roman religion were represented in anthropomorphic style. Only in Egypt were deities represented as animals – crocodiles, ibises or jackals.

In this varied and richly textured religious life, personal experience played an important part. Plenty of things were going on, after all, that could not be explained. It is hard to glimpse what people felt, but when they recorded a religious act, such as a dedication in fulfilment of a vow, they often included a statement of why they had done so – an indication of the will of the god in a vision, a dream, or through some form of divination or oracle.

Here is a dedication made by a prosperous ex-slave in the time of Augustus:

To the eternal god Jupiter, Juno the queen and Minerva, to the Sun and Moon, to Apollo, Diana and Fortune, to Wealth, Isis, Devotion and to the divine Fates, that all may be well, propitious, and happy with Caesar Augustus, his rule, the Senate and people of Rome, and the nations. At the happy opening of the new year

[AD 1, as it happens], Lucius Lucretius Zethus, former slave of Lucius, set up this Augustan altar the bidding of Jupiter.

At the top, someone else has added later 'to Mercury', and at the bottom, 'health in seed-sowing; victory of the people'. Even dedications on stone were not final.

So religion occupied every point on the spectrum of possibility, big and small, private and public, with every possible variety of prayer, temple, sacrifice and rite. One final variation was esoteric versus transparent. How much were people supposed to know about the gods and how to worship them?

Most religion was practised in the open, but a few sanctuaries were run by small communities and few people knew what happened at the festivals, which were open only to carefully prepared initiates, who were then under oath not to reveal what went on or what it meant. The Greek word for 'initiation' gives us 'mystery', which was used to describe these branches of ancient religion. In antiquity the most famous mystery religion of all was the worship of Demeter and her daughter Persephone, usually called the Maiden, at Eleusis just outside Athens. These goddesses were honoured for teaching humanity how to grow cereal crops – the name comes from Demeter's Roman name, Ceres – and the mysteries no doubt concerned this, but the secret was well kept (Athenian law punished leaks with death) and we cannot be sure what happened. It also offered initiates a particularly blessed afterlife, which was not, of course, a prominent feature of the religion of ancient cities. In Hadrian's time the Eleusinian festival was the most crowded of Greek religious occasions.

It was the duty of a householder to ensure that religious observance was not shirked. The huge staffs of slaves and ex-slaves on Roman estates and in the larger town-houses, the tenants of the apartment blocks and the workforces of warehouses or workshops produced worship strongly coloured by the traditions of these people's homelands. Mithras was historically a Persian god, but his worshippers in Hadrian's Rome had little knowledge of or contact with Persia. Instead, they took certain images, symbols and interpretations from that tradition, and built them up into a new, complicated and distinctive form of worship. There were seven grades of initiation, and worship took place in small halls, often underground, decorated to look like natural caves. At one end, the cult-statue depicted the young god Mithras, a force for good in the universe, slaying a bull, which stood for evil and was being attacked by other animals at the same time (a scorpion is always depicted biting his genitals). The cult was largely male, and especially popular with Roman soldiers: a Mithras temple has been found on Hadrian's Wall and another in London. In Rome, artificial caves were created from rooms in tenement blocks, or in the basement of public buildings, such as the great baths. Several of Rome's early medieval churches were built on these sites. Practice was variable and often arcane, as the following graffiti from the wall of a Mithras cave in an apartment block in Rome make plain: 'The livers of birds taste sweet, but Care reigns'; 'And those hast saved us by the shedding of eternal blood'; 'Accept the burners of incense, Holy Father, accept the Lions, through whom we offer incense, and through whom we ourselves are made an offering'; 'Hail to the new Lions, now and for many years to come!'. The 'lions' were initiates into a higher grade of devotee: this religion was secret. The word used, *Nama*, meaning 'hail', can still be heard today in invocations in Hindu temples.

The worship of Mithras took place on private property, away from the public eye. Other religious practices which appealed to the poor or to slaves developed cult-places in similar locations. Certainly the physical setting for Judaism and Christianity in Roman towns was similar, although it was people from the Jewish communities of the eastern Mediterranean who made up the worshippers. It was a natural consequence of Constantine's recognition of Christianity that churches became public monuments. Until then, like synagogues, they had been suites of rooms in private properties. The change was unprecedented: a religious movement made the leap from obscurity and a precarious existence in private to a place of honour in the public life of the empire.

XIII

RELIGIOSISSIMI MORTALES
(THE MOST RELIGIOUS OF ALL PEOPLE)

The emperor Alexander Severus wanted to build a temple to Christ, and enrol him among the gods. This is said to have been an idea of Hadrian, who ordered temples without images to be set up in all the cities (they are called Temples of Hadrian to this day, because they have no other deities). He didn't go through with it, because the diviners worked out that, if he did, everyone would become Christian and all the other temples would be abandoned.

ALEXANDER SEVERUS' BIOGRAPHER

The huge resources of Hadrian's empire were not used for scientific research – to push back the frontiers of human knowledge in ways familiar to us. All the energy went in directions to which modern societies do not give the same priority. The subject of universal enquiry was theology and religion, and providing good new answers was enormously important. Roman expertise in religion played differently in a world in which the Romans were no longer recent conquerors, and in which community allegiances had become much more fluid. There were increasing numbers of alternatives available, other places to which even ordinary people might turn to win the favour of the gods for themselves. The research method adopted was comparative, and the winning systems were those that successfully brought together the most powerful and charismatic elements from the most diverse backgrounds.

Sometimes the authority was traditional enough: the Greek oracles now found themselves asked about new theology.

However, their individual status was shifting: Apollo's shrine at Delphi was still famous, but the temple of Apollo at Claros, near Ephesus in Turkey, was in the ascendant. When Apollo was asked about the God of the Jews, he responded: 'Those who know the mysteries should keep this secret. But if you know little and understand less, learn that Jehovah is the highest god, Hades in winter, Zeus at the beginning of spring, the Sun in summer, and Jehovah in the autumn.'

The new religious experts came in many different guises, and the charismatic holy man was becoming a more prominent figure, either wandering the world or setting himself up in one place that became a centre for pilgrimage. A man called Alexander established himself in a small town on the south coast of the Black Sea, with a divine serpent called Glykon. He attracted a huge following, and even persuaded a Roman senator to marry his daughter on the ground that she was the daughter of the Moon. A satirical attack on him as a charlatan has survived, but his home town was renamed Ionopolis, now Inebolu, after the snake.

A different kind of charisma belonged to the Silent Philosopher, Secundus, who outwitted Hadrian. The tale went that Secundus had been sent away to be educated, and was unsettled by hearing that every woman had her price, and began to doubt his mother. He returned home unannounced and, having grown up since his departure, was not recognised. He took a room in his father's house and bribed the slave-girl to arrange an assignation for him with his mother, claiming to have fallen in love with her. Then he sent in supper for two. In bed, however, he turned away, and in the morning revealed his identity. His mother was devastated – not unreasonably – and hanged herself. Overcome with guilt, Secundus vowed perpetual silence and became a wandering philosopher.

When Hadrian summoned him during a visit to Athens, he would not tolerate the man's voluntary silence: 'I do not want any man to live who refuses to speak to the emperor Hadrian.' He set up a test: the executioner must try to persuade Secundus to speak and execute him if he did so. Secundus refused, and

Hadrian conversed with him in writing. The philosopher's message to him was appropriately gloomy: for all his power, the emperor was nothing before the face of the universe, and even his long journeys were easily outdone by the Sun and the Moon. Soon everything he had achieved would come to nothing. It was familiar realism, which was soon to be echoed by the philosopher-emperor Marcus, next but one to rule Hadrian's empire.

Here are two maxims that circulated as examples of Secundus' wisdom.

What is woman?
A man's desire, a wild beast that shares one's board, the worry with which one gets up in the morning, intertwining lust, a lioness sharing the bed, a clothed viper, a battle willingly chosen . . . a daily loss, a storm in the house . . . an excessive burden, a nine-wind tempest, a venomous asp, a necessity for the procreation of men, a necessary evil.

What is a gladiator?
Death on show, a sacrifice made by the giver of the games, gluttonous appetite, doom to order, a bloody craft, the error of fate, quick death, destiny at the sound of the trumpet, ever-present death, a bad victory.

Holy men might be either religious experts or philosophers, or they might combine the two, like Apollonius of Tyana, who had stood up to the tyrannical emperor Domitian. Some philosophers developed sceptical positions, and there was even a little serious atheism, but it was a dangerous line to take, given the continuing almost universal prevalence of the idea that prosperity depended on propitiating the divine. There was nothing that could be called secularism. A similar role to that of the more obviously holy men was played by experts in scientific systems that provided technical advice on how to cope with the universe, such as the interpretation of dreams. There were treatises on what each element in a dream meant – according to the social position of the dreamer. We have made frequent use of observations of both Apollonius (according to his ancient biographer, Philostratus) and Artemidorus of Daldis, whose *Dreaminterpretations* is the only example to survive from the period. The two most influential systems were astrology and magic, both of which were rapidly becoming ever more popular in Hadrian's lifetime.

These systems of explanation appealed in part because they made universal claims. They did not depend on a person's birth-community but were accessible (for a price) to everyone everywhere. Globalisation meant that local experiences were fed into the same system, which in turn meant people realised that religion was comparable and differences were ironed out: the cult of the same god in different places began to look more similar. Written accounts of religion helped standardise local behaviour. Famous religious centres acted as authorities on questions of religious propriety, especially those like Delphi that had oracles. It was inevitable, as the world shrank, that religion should become more universal and more abstract, and theology became more ambitious at explaining the supernatural. The world was centralised under Rome: the universe became centralised too. Ahead lay ideas of a central divinity – perceived as either an overarching principle of higher status than the familiar gods (perhaps Fortune, Fate or Eternity) or one of the more important gods (perhaps Zeus/Jupiter) of whom all the others were manifestations. Or perhaps it was the One God, all the others being either lesser spirits (good or bad) or even figures of speech.

The Virtues of Isis, preserved on a dedication from what is now western Turkey but said to have been copied from a temple in Egypt, claimed for the great goddess, one of the supreme deities, that, among other things,

> I gave and ordained laws for men which no one is able to change.
> I showed the paths of the stars.

I ordered the course of the sun and moon.
I brought together woman and man.
I revealed mysteries to men.
I made an end to murders.
I compelled women to be loved by men.
I assigned to Greeks and barbarians their languages.
I ordained that nothing should be more feared than an oath.
No one is held in honour without my knowing it.
I am in the rays of the sun.
I am the queen of seamanship.
I created the walls of cities.
Fate hearkens to me.

For all the appeal of the universal, the most popular religious/scientific ideas were the ones that had a distinctive exotic background. Both magic and astrology were strongly linked to the ancient civilisation of Egypt, then as now a subject of great fascination – but in the Greco-Roman world also considered barbarous and repellent. And magic was also linked to Judaism.

Egyptian and Jewish religion were based on voluminous writings, in whose interpretation wisdom could be sought. It stood to reason that anything as holy, old and complicated as the inscriptions on the walls of Egyptian temples, or the Greek translation of the Old Testament, must be potent and effective. Egyptian religion, principally in the form it had taken since Alexander under the Greek pharaohs, the Ptolemies, was widespread in the Mediterranean, centring on the cult of the god Serapis, and, above all, on Isis, while during the first century AD there is evidence of conversion to Judaism, even among the Roman élite. What did the leaders think officially of these religious powers?

Roman religious experts had to decide what to do about other people's observances, inside and outside the empire. If they were similar to what Romans did, what did it mean, and should anything be done about it? Did a striking difference mean that another community had discovered something that should be added to Roman knowledge on how to deal with the divine? Or should it be sharply rejected as antipathetic to Roman ways?

Roman priests were among the most influential decision-makers in the field of cultural policy. The acceptability or not of religious behaviour was the language in which Romans expressed decisions about whole cultures. There was some toleration, linked to the ideas of good and responsible government that circulated in the age of Hadrian, but there were many cases of intolerance too. Isis and Serapis had been expelled from Rome but allowed to return, and were now well established in the heart of the city. The Great Mother had been integrated fully into the Roman system, but the eunuch priesthood was strictly controlled. In the north-western provinces of Gaul and Britain, some local priests, the druids, had been suppressed, mainly because they were implicated in resistance to Rome. Boudicca, the queen of what is now Norfolk, had risen against Rome in AD 60 while the governor was campaigning against druid centres in Anglesey.

The Roman pretext for intolerance was unusual and unacceptable religious practice, such as the animal imagery used in Egyptian religion. The druids were accused of human sacrifice, and it is true that, before the Roman conquest, the Gauls had developed a distinctive way of celebrating victory: they pinned the corpses of their defeated enemies to trellises in ritual enclosures, then sat down to feast among them. Remnants of these monuments have been excavated in the last decade. But human sacrifice was not alien to Roman religion: in times of danger to the state a ceremony involved burying alive a Gaul and a Greek in the cattle-market in the centre of Rome as a sacrifice that would persuade the gods to protect the state against emergencies. In gladiatorial games, too, there was an element of human sacrifice. As with all spectacles that took place on religious occasions and were held ultimately to honour the gods, a fight to the death in public between men was an offering, as was the strangling of the enemy general in the prison under the Capitol after a triumph. If the alternative religious power offered by a

rival system couldn't be assimilated, as so many religious practices had been, it had to go.

There had been a famous crackdown on the worship of
Dionysus in south Italy in 186 BC. Dionysus' worship was known
for its overturning of order, and its links with wine and drunkenness. The meetings were said to be held underground and after
dark, and they were organised by women. Three hundred years
later, the situation was worse: across the empire, in every city,
in every region, there were disaffected people – the poor, the
unfortunate, the oppressed, people who remembered independence from Rome. It was people of this kind, collected in masses
by widespread mobility in the empire's cities, who were so
attracted to alternative religion, which posed a threat to the
Roman order. In this deeply religious world, violent change was
thought to be brought about by the gods: it was best to be on
the right side, and to know what was going to happen.

Predicting the future was the most important of all the forms
of religious expertise, which was why the Romans had domesticated so many ways of doing it. At the level of high politics,
predicting the death of the emperor was, of course, a serious
act of treason. But at its most dangerous, in the empire at large,
prophecy might invite people to attempt to bring about change
with violence, and not to wait for the gods to act. In the druid
world some priestesses prophesied the fall of the Roman empire
and encouraged resistance. During the civil war between would-
be successors to the Emperor Nero in AD 68–9, the Roman Capitol
burned down, which was taken as a sign that the empire's collapse
was imminent.

The last book of the New Testament, Revelation, is known
(after the Greek word for 'revelation') as apocalyptic prophecy,
and sprang from the Jewish prophetic tradition. In Egypt, in the
second century BC, the Jewish community circulated predictions
about how the evil city that ruled the world would be burned and
completely destroyed; a new golden age would follow. They had
meant Alexandria, but it was easy to reinterpret the idea to fit

Rome, and natural when the last Roman conquests had made the world into one superpower. Revelation itself is explicit about the fate awaiting the city of Rome.

One strain of apocalyptic prophecy maintained that the destruction of the great evil city and the dawn of a new golden age would take place when the Dog Star rose on the eastern horizon at the same point as the sun. That was the traditional date on which the life-giving Nile flood was expected, and also a day of mystic meaning in many traditions linked with Egypt. In AD 64, that day fell on 19 July – and in the evening the worst fire in Rome's history broke out. Three-quarters of the city was wiped out, with many of the ancient temples, built in wood and terracotta. The entire quarter known as the Sacred Street, which led up on to the Palatine Hill from the forum, was destroyed.

Emperor Nero blamed the Christians and many were burned alive as a suitable punishment. But all Christians at this date were from Jewish communities, and it was in those communities that prophecies of this type circulated. It was too much of a coincidence that the city's catastrophe should have happened on the right day.

However, many people blamed Nero for the fire because he gained much from it. Until then aristocratic credentials included owning a home on the Sacred Way, so after the fire, its aristocratic past was obliterated. That suited Nero's agenda: he took over swathes of the burnt-out area for his Golden House.

The ancient Jewish state, as old as any in the Mediterranean world, had revived after political disaster on the fringes of the great kingdoms that split the empire of Alexander at the end of the fourth century BC. In 150 BC it had been a heroic rebel against Greek power; by 50 BC it was a heavily Hellenised state; and by 10 BC the despotic rule of Herod the Great had turned it into a highly centralised monarchy, loyal to, and much favoured by, the imperial Rome of Augustus. The emperor and his family were celebrated in Judaea with new cities and monuments that drew heavily on the ways in which Greek kings and city aristocrats, Roman generals and statesmen promoted themselves. Most importantly, Herod rebuilt the religious heart of the Jewish people, the Jerusalem temple, on a magnificent scale, its surroundings on the Temple Mount like the citadel of a fine Greek city, with great colonnades and courtyards, beetling terraces, punctuated with awe-inspiring towers. By his death in 4 BC, Jewish religious and intellectual culture, and the sense of pride and identity that went with it, were flourishing.

The Jewish kingdom was important because there was only one way from Egypt, with all its wealth and population, to the buoyant and productive cities and plains in what are now Syria and Iraq. That route went through the city of Gaza, which was then, as now, not a Jewish community. However, all the approaches to Gaza from the east crossed the tangle of highlands and fertile valleys that were the ancient heart of Israel.

The Jews mattered to the world outside because they were based on the fringes of the Mediterranean heartland and had thrived on the demand for mercenary soldiers for the wars that followed the break-up of Alexander the Great's empire. Many peoples supplied such troops, and many veterans settled in the places where they had served, adding to the social diversity of an already kaleidoscopic Mediterranean. The Jewish contingents had a strong sense of their own community, and their religion gave them a compelling reason for retaining a more than sentimental link with their homeland and, above all, with Jerusalem and its temple. These diaspora centres – especially Alexandria, where Jews mixed with a wide range of gentile groups, albeit uneasily – were formative in Jewish cultural life.

The leaders of the Jewish state had three bargaining chips: the vital geopolitical location of Jerusalem; the complex and close-knit culture of the revived Jewish state; and the fact of a substantial diaspora that retained the key organising principle of allegiance to its place of origin. But, as is the way with bargaining, these advantages could lead to suspicion, jealousy and hostility as well as to negotiation and accommodation.

In AD 6, ten years after Herod's death, Augustus turned Judaea into a Roman province. It was run rather worse even than most other provinces at that time, which was well before anyone had formulated notions of the lustre of the age or thought that meticulous government was important, and there was a long series of disturbances and revolts. But until 66 there was no reason to think that anything out of the ordinary was going on there.

It was different in the world of the diaspora, where almost all Jews spoke Greek, and many Jewish philosophical works were composed in that language. In Egypt under the Ptolemies, in the third century BC, the Jewish Old Testament had been translated from Hebrew into Greek by a team of seventy scholars. Jews and others mixed constantly, and it was here that people had access to, and became interested in, Jewish ideas. Many educated people found the Jewish scriptural tradition impressive, its ethical teachings philosophically persuasive, and its monotheistic views suited the trend in religion of the time. At the same time, Jewish community values could seem alien to Greeks and Romans. The synagogue's role in social welfare seemed repugnant to Artemidorus, the dream-interpreter, who linked it with beggars and the destitute: 'No one visits the synagogue who isn't worried; and beggars are completely hideous and indigent.' Dreaming about them was a really terrible sign, particularly if they came into your house or on to your property. 'Beggars are like death: if you give to them you get nothing back.' It is clear that there were major social tensions around the mixing of Jewish and non-Jewish communities, especially in Alexandria, but in other cities too. We hear of rioting in Rome itself. The level of emotion and violence on both sides in clashes of this kind was high. The combination of a distinctive – and persuasive – religious tradition with a dangerous political affiliation, especially when it was spread across the entire Mediterranean area, was likely to cause hostility in the authorities. As Apollonius, the holy man, is supposed to have said: 'The Jews rebelled long ago not only against the Romans but against all human beings – a people that has discovered a way of life which allows no mixing with others, and who do not share our food, libations, prayers or sacrifices, are more alien than the barbarians.'

The electrifying possibilities of religion, ethics and social politics around Jewish and other immigrant communities in the cities of this highly mobile empire were demonstrated by a movement that began in the 30s AD. Its followers called themselves Christians, after the title given to their founder Joshua (Iesous, or Jesus, in Greek and Latin), son of Joseph, a Jewish holy man: Christos, the anointed one, indicating the Messiah long predicted in the Jewish scriptures. He was born in the hill-country of Galilee, to a middling-status artisan family in a large village. In Trajan's reign, descendants of his cousins were said to be living as small-to-middling farmers in the Palestinian countryside.

Christians appear in two contexts at about the same time, in the 50s and 60s AD: first, in the story told by the historian Tacitus of how Nero punished them for the Great Fire; and second, in a series of theological, philosophical and pastoral letters to groups in cities scattered across Greece, Turkey and even in Rome. They were written by a Jewish Roman citizen from a family in the textile business in Tarsus, southern Turkey. Originally named Saul, he became more widely known as Paul. His letters show how quickly Christian groups had formed and sub-divided, and shed considerable light on what they believed about Jesus, who had been condemned as a subversive and put to death by the Roman authorities in Judaea. The subsequent reappearance of Jesus and the concomitant belief in his divinity, with all its implications, were already central to a tradition that was clearly vigorous and locally capable of winning many adherents. Perhaps Artemidorus had a distant sense of the upheaval to be caused by such claims: 'Dreaming that the dead are resurrected means trouble and loss. Just imagine, for a moment, what chaos there would be if the dead were actually raised!' At the same time narratives of the life and sayings of Jesus were in circulation, which are the basis of the slightly later New Testament gospels. That of Luke, for instance, dates from after the Romans destroyed Jerusalem in AD 70 because it reflects the mood of despair that affected the Jewish community after the razing to the ground of the Jewish temple.

Paul's letters and the gospels also reflect a radical set of social teachings that deliberately overturned most of the then norms of life in proclaiming the equality of all humans, slave, free, men and women, before God, and in disregarding the hierarchies of status and power that were so basic to ancient life. It seems that in early years, in a spirit of apocalypticism, a further triumphal return of Jesus and the end of time were expected in the immediate future. This encouraged the development of already uncompromising demands on the faithful to practise austerity and personal devotion. Paradoxically this made Christianity more appealing, gave it power and authority, and set it apart from the vast majority of ancient religions and communities, including many of the Jewish groups within which it had originated. Paul had insisted that the distinction between Jew and Greek no longer mattered. At the same time, Christian sages made rich and creative use of the Greek versions of the Jewish scriptures, which they saw as foretelling the life, death and resurrection of Jesus. 'Our fathers wrongly and capriciously translated the books into Greek so that you could take possession of them and silence us,' a Jewish writer said later. On the other hand, an annual festival on the Lighthouse Island at Alexandria commemorated the translation, and it was much frequented by Jews and non-Jews alike.

The Jews were not the only group in Hadrian's empire to belong everywhere and nowhere: a gap existed between Christians and the rest of the world, to which the Letter of Diognetos attests:

> For the Christians are distinguished from other men neither by country, nor language, nor the customs which they observe. For

they neither inhabit cities of their own, nor employ a peculiar form of speech, nor lead a life which is marked out by any singularity. The course of conduct which they follow has not been devised by any speculation or deliberation of inquisitive men; nor do they, like some, proclaim themselves the advocates of any merely human doctrines. But, inhabiting Greek as well as barbarian cities, according as the lot of each of them has determined, and following the customs of the natives in respect to clothing, food, and the rest of their ordinary conduct, they display to us their wonderful and confessedly striking method of life. They dwell in their own countries, but simply as sojourners. As citizens, they share in all things with others, and yet endure all things as if foreigners. Every foreign land is to them as their native country, and every land of their birth as a land of strangers.

This was ominous for Rome. It was bad news for Christians too. They were disliked by Jews who regarded them (rightly, by the second century) as dissenters from central beliefs in Jewish religion and politics, while appearing cynical appropriators of Jewish scripture and tradition. But meanwhile they remained closely enough linked with Jews in the eyes of others to be implicated in the terrible Jewish revolts that came in the reigns of Trajan and Hadrian.

By Trajan's time, if not before, Romans in government circles were linking serious public-order problems, particularly in the provinces, with Christians. Pliny, as governor of the area where Istanbul is now, wrote to Trajan asking for guidance on the tensions surrounding Christian communities. It was alleged, because they worshipped in private, that Christian rites included sexual depravity and cannibalism. Pliny investigated these stories, and reported that there was no evidence to support them, but that sales of sacrificial meat had plummeted because Christians would have nothing to do with sacrifices to traditional cults. That in itself caused economic problems, but Christian denial of the principal religious system was much more serious. Most people believed that it was vital for the maintenance of order and continuing prosperity, so Christians were persecuted – by their neighbours and the state – for fear that the gods would become hostile if traditional worship was abandoned.

Christianity took longer than Judaism had to reach the wealthier sections of society, but it spread across the empire, and following in Paul's footsteps, attempts were made to maintain a common order among Christians. The communities were in active contact with each other across long distances. Their conformity in thought, belief and rite has been exaggerated by Christian historians, from the fourth century AD, but there was enough uniformity to frighten Roman officials.

Christian communities came to practise one skill that had some appeal to others, and was shared by some of the wandering holy men: exorcism. Apollonius and his companions travelling on a moonlit night saw an *empusa*, an evil demon, changing its shape and flickering in and out of sight. Apollonius knew what to do: insult and abuse caused it to run off shrieking. On another occasion he stopped a young man marrying an *empusa*, which had been fattening him up to devour him. At this time, the world was beset with fear of evil spirits, who must be warded off, or could be brought into one's service.

The author of the life of Apollonius was sceptical about magic, and said that merchants and athletes looking for unfair advantage in competition were the people most likely to resort to it. Lovers cast this spell, invoking Isis. First, light a brazier:

all the flaming, all the cooking, all the heating, all the steaming, all the sweating, that I [the male suppliant] bring about on this light brazier, you will induce in the heart, liver, navel and belly of [name of the beloved], until I bring her to the house of [name of the male suppliant] and she puts what is in her hand into my hand, what is in her mouth into my mouth, what is in her belly on to my belly, what is in her female parts on to my male parts – quick! Quick! Now! Now!

When Apollonius was brought to trial, the emperor's attendants were told to remove from him any amulet, book or note-tablet.

When the emperor Antoninus died, one of his heirs revived the age-old hostilities with Parthia. Nothing was achieved, except that the soldiers brought back plague, which devastated the Mediterranean world. The new disease provoked a new response: in western Turkey, Apollo's famous oracle at Claros ruled that the catastrophe must be put down to magic and treated accordingly. Artemis 'shall ward off evil and dissolve the lethal spells of plague, melting the moulded models with torches of pitch in nocturnal flame, the evil signs of the craft of the magus'.

Remedies like this had been practised for many generations, but they had flourished as an alternative to official forms of supernatural help, and often in secret. Of course, the Roman authorities were wary. Here again was a rival way to resolve a problem, which the empire claimed already to achieve satisfactorily: in its dealing with the gods, it could predict the future and thus avert or curtail disaster. Magic was, like the Roman state, spectacular, awe-inspiring, linked with the divine, ancient, wrapped up in mysterious facts and words, hard to learn, exclusive and possibly efficacious. Magicians and magic were tightly controlled by law, and those who mattered politically were damaged by accusations of involvement with or dabbling in them. But the oracle about the plague confirms to us that it was becoming harder to draw a line between magic and religion.

The death of hundreds from plague helps to explain people's recourse to magic but it was also linked to the seismic shift in attitudes towards the central structures we keep meeting. Just as the empire had become big enough and integrated enough for the plague to become a pandemic, so its central ideas became, for all Hadrian's frenetic travelling, too monolithic to work. After another two centuries, the whole empire turned to one of the main alternative systems of power and religion, when Constantine made Christianity the religion of power and empire, and changed its nature in the process.

So, by the second century, Judaism and its derivative Christianity foreshadowed later challenges to the unique authority of Greco-Roman culture. This clash of values was in its first, convulsive phase during Hadrian's lifetime. During this period, the traditional religion faced challenges as the world that had known only one religion, with more or less powerful deities and more or less acceptable practices, moved towards the adoption of two. The dedications that follow were made by imperial functionaries in northern Spain:

> To Holy Serapis, to Isis of the Ten Thousand Names, to the Unconquered Maiden, to Apollo Grannus, and to Mars the Cloaked, Julius Melanio, Procurator of the Two Emperors.

> To the Gods and Goddesses to whom it is lawful and proper to pray in the pantheon, Publius Aelius Hilarianus, son of Publius, Procurator of the Emperor, with his children, for the Wellbeing of the Emperor.

They demonstrate how well stocked the religious supermarket was, and how impossible any coherent policing of a boundary between traditional and novel cults. The deities of the first inscription are from an amazing collection of localities – Greek Egypt (Serapis and Isis), Athens (Persephone of Eleusis) and Celtic Gaul (these forms of Apollo and Mars). In the second, the official's name shows that his father had probably been a slave in Hadrian's household. He has taken a short-cut approach and used the idea of a pantheon to establish a universal way of coping with religious variety. But the telling words are those that betray a careful bureaucrat's sense that there are now unacceptable deities who must be excluded. Some forms of religion have been outlawed.

XIV
HADRIAN, PRIEST AND GOD

> All the forbidden magical rites he will share.
> He will turn a teenager into a god.
> He will overturn everything holy and good . . .
>
> SIBYLLINE ORACLE

Hadrian liked the occult. The text of a torn document, found in the bone-dry sands of Egypt, shows him investigating with his usual thoroughness and professionalism.

Pachrates, the prophet of Heliopolis, displaying the power of his godlike magic, revealed the spell to the emperor Hadrian. It attracted in one hour – caused illness in 2 – destroyed in 7 and sent the emperor himself dreams as he thoroughly tested the whole truth of the magic within his power. In admiration of the prophet, he ordered him to be given double fees.

What you will need:

    a fieldmouse deified [drowned] in spring water
    2 moon-beetles, deified in river-water
    a river-crab
    fat from a virgin nanny-goat
    dung from a dog-faced baboon
    2 ibis eggs
    2 drams storax
    2 drams myrrh
    2 drams saffron
    4 drams Italian galingale
    4 drams uncut frankincense
    one onion

Pound all the ingredients in a mortar. Keep in a lead box.

Instructions for use: take a little of the mixture, light a charcoal brazier, go up on to a high roof, and make the offering as the moon rises. She comes at once.

The incantation: 'Let all the darkness of the clouds be scattered for me – let Aktiophis the goddess shine for me – let her hear my holy voice. I come announcing the blasphemy of [target's name] the defiled and unholy woman . . . Go to [name] and take away her sleep, and put a burning heat in her soul, punishment and frenzied passion in her thoughts, banish her from every place and every house – bring her here to me!'

Then sacrifice, groan loudly, and climb down backwards. Pay attention to the person you have summoned! Open the door for her, or the spell with fail.

Magic of this kind is strongly redolent of all the secret alternatives to mainstream religion that were so significant in Hadrian's world – but in this case the practitioner was said to be the man who was in charge of the religious decisions of the Roman state. In the late Republic, political competition had drained much credit from the traditional aristocracy. The priesthood and its prerogatives were used for some blatantly political manoeuvring, but religion retained its appeal. The system had never depended on the élite priests: others could perform sacrifices and most other rituals of the cults. In any case, a solution to the problem of religious authority had been formulated: when Augustus had set up the imperial system, it was inevitable that religious power ended up in his hands. It was far simpler for everyone if there was one central expert and point of power. All of the old priesthoods survived, and Augustus revived some historical and obscure ones, such as the Ploughfield Brethren and the Treaty Priests, and found a patrician willing to become Priest of Jupiter. He made a point of allowing a former rival, now in exile, to keep the title of high priest, but when he died,

Augustus took it too. From then on, all emperors became high priest as part of the job. That was what gave Domitian the authority to condemn the Vestal Virgin to be buried alive without a fair trial.

Hadrian, too, became high priest, responsible for maintaining the tradition of Roman religiosity and ensuring that state and people retained the favour of the gods. This made him a social engineer: he took any decisions about what was Roman and what was not, and policed the relationship between 'Roman' and other labels such as 'Greek', or 'Gallic'.

At the same time, Hadrian was a god. Divine honours had been voted to emperors for centuries, and it had been routine to worship them since Augustus. This was reasonable as well as traditional: no one could do more for the people to change the world in which they existed than the emperor. Order, memory, peace, prosperity, stability, law, security might result from prayers to him, or his representatives, as much as from the less tangibly present gods. And worship of the emperor was a unifying religious act: it honoured the power that held together the universe and the world. Only very unpopular or unsuccessful emperors missed out. Hadrian had dutifully deified Trajan and followed him in proclaiming the womenfolk of his family goddesses. When Hadrian died in 138, there was considerable opposition to his deification, but his successor, the dutiful Antoninus, ensured that it went through.

Human gods are naturally problematic. As one sceptical philosopher wrote a generation before Hadrian, if you want to know whether or not the emperor is divine, ask the man who empties his chamber-pot. Most of the subjects who worshipped the emperor as divine day by day never came near seeing him. The Greek rationalistic philosophy in which Hadrian had been educated was generally dismissive of worshipping people, and the most intractable problem with such worship was death, which was why formal deification was held over until that bridge had been crossed. At least that sort of new god was not going to die any more. But to Jews and Christians the idea of worshipping people was anathema, even if it was just a way to express loyalty to the Roman empire.

Hadrian's own religious leanings, so far as we can tell, fitted well with the times. He is on record as having invested huge energy and expenditure in projects that expressed the universality and unity of vision of the world's religions. The Pantheon in Rome and the sanctuary of Olympian Zeus in Athens, meeting-place of all the Greeks, are more spectacular examples than any religious buildings constructed by other emperors. The Pantheon was intended to emphasise that Rome was a religious capital for the world, not just the home of the gods who had given the Romans world empire.

Hadrian's passion for knowledge and understanding, such a prominent character trait, did not stop with routine secular subjects like the finances of state or the architecture of the vault. His taste for the esoteric was also characteristic of his age. In the heat of the end of the summer of 124, he was, for instance, initiated into the Mysteries of Eleusis, at Athens. Other prominent Romans had been initiated too, but in his case it is tempting to link it with his great interest in Athens and its ancient history, and in unusual religion, especially when it was linked to death and the hereafter. Appropriately enough, when his reign was described in a Greek prophecy that purported to be one of the famous Sibylline oracles, it was said of him that 'This emperor will take part in all the forbidden initiations of magic.' The spell quoted on pages 253–4 shows that this was a widely held view of Hadrian. He was presented with a text of the mystical teachings of Pythagoras, which the holy man Apollonius had brought out of an oracular chasm in central Greece. It was kept in one of the many imperial villas in Italy, the seaside palace that Nero had built on the cliffs at Anzio.

Hadrian's great-uncle had been adept at astrology, and was reported to have predicted his young relative's elevation as emperor. Hadrian, too, was interested in astrology, and purported to have cast the horoscopes of many of his contemporaries. A horoscope of Hadrian survives but it is doubtful that it much resembled any composed before he became emperor. The position of the planets in the heavens at the moment of his birth is precisely detailed, and it goes on:

> The person whose horoscope this is was adopted by a relative who was emperor. After two years at his side he became emperor himself. He was an intelligent and educated man, to the extent of being honoured with temples and sanctuaries. He lived with one woman, from her maidenhood, but had no child. He had a single sister. He fell into dissent and conflict with his family. Around his sixty-third year he died, dropsical, of a respiratory attack.

The astrological working is set out at great length, then a little more detail: 'He was of a good, large build and brave and well favoured in appearance because the two lights (the Sun and Moon) were in a masculine and human-form House (Aquarius); and intelligent, educated and profound because Mercury follows Saturn in the eastern part . . . and attends upon the Sun.' He is further described as 'opinionated, a man of grand designs, a giver of gifts, quick and effective, a great benefactor, venerated by multitudes, but beset by termagants and plotters, his intelligence offset by a lack of benevolence and a tendency to be deceitful.'

It was, however, the demise of Hadrian's lover Antinous that confirmed Hadrian's interest in the mysteries of death, yet there was almost nothing to explain: an accidental death, and an extravagant response by a flamboyant emperor. If Hadrian could deify his mother-in-law Matidia, why not his much-loved boyfriend? But the world took it differently. It happened in Egypt: Hadrian was interested in specifically Egyptian magic, and death was one of the concerns of new currents in religion.

The imperial household was cruising on the Nile at the end of the annual flood during the festival of Osiris, who was honoured for the gift of the Nile waters – although this year the flood had been worryingly low. As the boat passed Greater

Hermopolis, Antinous vanished overboard. His drowned body was later recovered and embalmed in the Egyptian style.

Observers scoffed at Hadrian's emotional reaction. 'He wept for him as women do,' sneers his biographer, who also speaks of Antinous' well-known beauty and Hadrian's 'excessive pleasure' in the relationship. If that had been all, the story would have been soon forgotten. But Hadrian made Antinous a god. Then he founded a city in his name: Antinoopolis. This wasn't a knee-jerk reaction: he had thought hard about it. Antinoopolis was an Egyptian Athens. Several aspects of the city's laws and organisation were taken straight from the classical city. There were ten major sub-divisions of the citizen body, recruited from the Egyptian population with tax-breaks, and these were broken up into local districts.

INVENTING ANTINOUS' MEMORIAL CITY

Who the Districts were named after	*Who or what the wards were named after*
Hadrian	Zeus, King of Gods and Men
	Olympus, the Greek heaven
	The Capitol, sanctuary of Roman imperial power
	Saviour of the Universe
	The Leader of the Dance of the Muses, goddesses of art and culture
Antinous and Osiris, the dying and resurrected god of Egypt	Bithynia, homeland of Antinous
	Hermes, its patron
	Cleitor and Parrhasia, cities of Arcadia, mythical homeland of the people of Antinous' town
Athens	Artemis, goddess of the Athenian ephebes
	Eleusis, centre of the Mysteries
	Erichthonios, protector of the Acropolis
	Marathon and Salamis, the great battles which saved Athens from the Persians

Aelius family	The sacred bull of the Egyptian god Apis
	Dionysus, god of wine and freedom
	The City as an idea
Matidia, Trajan's niece	Demeter, goddess of Eleusis
	Thesmophoria, her festival
	Kalliteknios, Persephone her daughter
	Marciana, Matidia's mother
	Plotina, Trajan's wife
Nerva, Trajan's adoptive father	Founder of the adoptive line
	Bringer of Peace
	The hearth of the city
	The ancestors
Paulina, Hadrian's sister	Isis, great goddess of Egypt
	Her great festival
	Sibling-hood
	Brotherly, sisterly love
Sabina, Hadrian's wife	Harmony
	Marriage
	Hera, queen of heaven and goddess of marriage
	Trophonius, a Greek oracle
	Phytalos, a figure at Eleusis
Augustus, founder of the empire	Apollo, his protector god
	Asklepios, god of healing
	Castor and Pollux, children of Zeus
	Herakles, son of Zeus
	Caesar, the imperial title
Trajan, Hadrian's predecessor	The Possessor
	Bringer of victory
	The Roman army

A whole universe of what Hadrian and his advisers thought important appears here, and it tells us two important things about Antinous' deification: he was seen as Osiris, the brother of Isis, the god who had drowned, been dismembered, then revived by his divine sister, and he was presented as one of the emperor's family. They are all here – Plotina, Sabina and Paulina. The other recently deified members of the imperial household stand out too: Nerva, Trajan, Marciana and Matidia.

Hadrian seems to have been preoccupied with what happened to the great after death. Imperial deification was supposed to be the consequence of great benefactions to humanity. Many people were sceptical about it, but a Christian pamphleteer used it as a way to help people understand the resurrection of Christ. And put side by side with the resurrection of Osiris, deification looks like a statement of what Antinous could expect in his new state. That might simply have resulted from the depth of Hadrian's grief, combined with his interest in religion that could predict the future and what happened after death, an interest many shared at this time. On Cyprus Antinous was worshipped as the equally beautiful young Adonis, another deity whose death and re-appearance were celebrated every year. Later, Christian writers were particularly fierce in their denunciation of the god Antinous. The young man who had died for his friends but lived on was, after all, a central theme of the Easter liturgy, and they found misunderstandings frequent and distressing.

Contemporary rumour suggests puzzlement: many thought there was more to Antinous' death than an accidental tragedy. The idea that a willing victim might sacrifice himself for the community, or for the good of another person, not just by heroism but in a kind of deal with the gods, was well known so some said that Antinous' death was the result of a strange pact or sinister ritual. Magicians, the story went, had told Hadrian he could prolong his life if he could find a willing substitute to die for him. No one would oblige until Antinous offered himself. Hence Hadrian's spectacular gratitude.

In the Black Sea, some way off the delta of the Danube, lies the White Island, where the greatest of the heroes of Homer's poems was worshipped. It is a strange place, one of several islands that the great heroes were thought to have found: remote and frequented mostly by seabirds, hard for navigators to locate, the kind of place where mariners saw strange sights. The heroes manifested themselves as the strange atmospheric effects in the rigging of the ship that later ages would attribute to St Elmo. Here, Achilles could be seen through the mists, practising his swordsmanship or running along the sand. Some said that Helen of Troy had ended up here too, in a satisfying but deeply uncanonical rendering of the mythical cycle so as to give a kind of happy ending – the sounds of lovemaking were audible to more imaginative seafarers. By Hadrian's time, there was a temple on the island, visited by worshippers eager to experience dreams in which Achilles appeared to them.

In his tour of inspection of the coasts of the Black Sea, the governor Arrian made a point of including Achilles' island, to turn a very gracious compliment to Hadrian within months of Antinous' death. Arrian tells Hadrian that it is Achilles' lover Patroclus, not Helen, who shares the White Island with his hero friend:

> I am personally convinced that Achilles was a unique and exceptional hero. The evidence is his nobility and his beauty, and the strength of his spirit; the fact that he left human life young; Homer's poetry about him; and most of all that he was a lover, and a loving comrade, and wanted to join his lover even in death.

Arrian is not shy of the subject of the emperor's homosexuality; nor of the topic of the death of Antinous.

The emperor's sexuality, like the emperor's grief, were topics for a wide audience, and the language in which they had to be discussed was, naturally, that of the classics. Greek literature provided the decorous models and phrases in which the delicate topics of the present could be expressed safely, eruditely and movingly.

The cult of Antinous was taken up with predictable enthusiasm. An ancient Greek city remembered that it could claim to be the base from which the settlers of his home town had come, and discovered a mythical ancestress called Antinoe. Their festival of Antinous as Dionysus was particularly vigorous. It is not known whether they had time to reap the benefits of telling Hadrian about this before he died. Likenesses of the beautiful youth were made and dedicated all over the empire, and many have survived, though they shade into idealised types of young male loveliness. 'I never met Antinous,' says a writer a generation later, 'but he is everywhere in paintings and in statues.' He was describing the five-yearly festival at Mantinea, where Antinous appeared as the god Dionysus, closely identified with Osiris. In the finished city of Antinoopolis there were grand colonnaded streets, with hundreds of columns and a bust of Antinous on each one.

Hadrian came back to his villa outside Rome four years later, and built a tomb-monument to his dead lover right beside the main entrance into the villa at Tivoli, so that every visitor passed it. Here, too, it seems Antinous was represented as Osiris, the god who had drowned but was reborn.

The man who mourned Antinous was the ruler responsible for deciding how to cope with the religious changes of the age, and with the problems of the communities of Jews and Christians. Trajan's answer to Pliny's query about the Christians had been that they should not be persecuted. A few years later, Hadrian wrote in similar vein to another governor, discouraging informers and malicious prosecutions. Toleration and detachment fitted the image that the imperial government wanted to project.

The spread of Christianity means that a large selection of texts illustrating the clashes of Christians with the authorities has survived. A record from Africa exists of a public trial. The words of the examining judge and the defendants seem fairly represented. A group of men and women, whose names sound part Roman, part African, faced the provincial governor in the city of Carthage; the ancient metropolis had been destroyed and rebuilt by Rome to serve as the capital of the province. These people were free but not members of the élite except for the judge Saturninus, a high-ranking senator.

In the consulship of Praesens (for the second time) and Claudianus, on 17 July, Speratus, Nartzalus, Cittinus, Donata, Secunda and Vestia were put on trial in the [governor's] council chamber at Carthage. The proconsul Saturninus [P. Vigellius Raius Plarius Saturninus Atilius Braduanus Caucidius Tertullus] said,

'You can secure the indulgence of our lord the emperor if you return to you sense.'

Speratus said, 'We have never done any wrong; we have lent ourselves to no injustice; we have never spoken ill of anyone; but we have been ill-treated, we have given thanks, because we honour our emperor.'

The proconsul Saturninus said, 'We, also, are religious, and our religion is simple; and we swear by the genius of our lord the emperor, and pray for his welfare, as you too ought to do.'

Speratus said, 'If you grant me your undivided attention, I will tell you the mystery of simplicity.'

Saturninus said, 'I shall not grant you a hearing if you speak evil about our sacred rites; but swear rather by the genius of our lord the emperor.'

Speratus said, 'The empire of this world I do not recognise; but rather I serve that God whom no man has seen nor can see with human eyes. I have not committed theft; if I buy anything, I pay the tax, because I recognise my lord, the king of kings and emperor of all peoples.'

The discussion turns on the relationship of these people to the emperor and his power in the world. The defendants are keen to show that they are good citizens – but as far as the governor is concerned, they are good citizens for the wrong reasons. Like ordinary provincials, they obey authority because they recognise the power of a 'divine emperor'. They speak of him in language identical to that which the governor and his staff might use. But the defendants are referring to a transcendent god not currently present in human form on earth, while the governors are referring to Marcus Aurelius. Both sides claim religious expertise. Both claim common sense and intellectual superiority. The

Roman authorities were right to be wary of these groups because they expressed themselves in a fashion that parodied or appropriated the language of everyday political loyalty.

A similar narrative depicts the trial of Polycarp, Bishop of Smyrna, by the governor of Asia, in AD 155. The setting is the city circus, and Polycarp is speaking to the Roman notables and to an audience of thousands. His loyalty is being tested: the horrifying punishments of Roman law are threatened.

> And when the proconsul yet again urged him, and said, 'Swear by the fortune of Caesar,' he answered, 'Since you are uselessly pressuring me to swear by the fortune of Caesar, and insist that you don't know who and what I am, I here declare confidently – I am a Christian. And if you wish to learn what the doctrines of Christianity are, name a day, and you shall hear them.' The proconsul replied, 'Persuade the people.' But Polycarp said, 'I consider it right to offer an account to you, for we are taught to give all due honour to the powers and authorities ordained by God. But as for *these*, I do not think them worthy of receiving any account from me.' The proconsul then said, 'I have wild beasts at hand, and will throw you to them unless you change your mind.' Polycarp replied, 'Call them then, for we are not accustomed to repent of what is good in order to adopt that which is evil.' Again, the proconsul said to him, 'Since you despise the wild beasts, I shall have you burned alive, unless you change your mind.'

Polycarp remained adamant.

> The proconsul was astonished, and sent his herald to proclaim three times in the midst of the stadium, 'Polycarp has confessed that he is a Christian.' When this proclamation was made by the herald, the whole multitude of pagans and Jews, who dwelt at Smyrna, cried out with uncontrollable fury, and in a loud voice, 'This is the teacher of Asia, the father of the Christians, and the overthrower of our gods, he who has been teaching many not to sacrifice, or to worship the gods.'

The third story of Christian–Roman confrontation takes us into a world of miracle and dramatic revelation. The tale of the holy Christian woman Thecla is an example of the racy fictions that circulated widely in the empire, sexy, violent and tinged fascinatingly with the excitement of new religious knowledge and the clash of old and new. Thecla is converted to Christianity by Paul, on his journeys in what is now Turkey, falls foul of the authorities, but becomes a heroine for the women of the city where she is to be exposed to wild beasts in the arena. The people shout, 'Bring in the woman guilty of sacrilege!' and call down divine wrath on the city: 'May the city perish for this lawlessness – slay us all, Proconsul! A bitter sight, an evil judgement!' Thecla is befriended by the savage lioness to which she is tied for the procession into the arena – the animal licks her feet, and kills the first bears and lions sent in to maul her, but dies in the process. The women weep because Thecla has lost her protector. There is a lake of savage seals in the arena (a sure sign that the author was from the interior, and knew little about the sea . . .) into which Thecla now dives: the seals are killed as if by lightning. Ever more predatory animals are released, but the women throw bunches of exotic flowers into the arena and they are subdued by the sweet scent. Just as maddened bulls are to be deployed the governor ends the show, so impressed by Thecla that he releases her. She rejoins St Paul and eventually dies peacefully after a life of Christian evangelism.

We can only guess when Hadrian first heard of Christians as a group distinct from Jews, perhaps during his governorship of Syria, if not when he was in Pannonia. During his youth in Rome people were certainly talking to senators about the appeal of Judaism, and particularly to their wives. We cannot know how far his own interest in the secret, the learned, and the religion of the afterlife led him to explore any mainstream form of Christianity, or in derivatives as practised covertly in the eastern Mediterranean, and especially Egypt, which we know as Gnostic. Later Christian writers claimed that Hadrian's enthusiasm for old, secret religion in Greece influenced others to attack the Christians, and perhaps it is more likely that his interests disposed him against them. A later observer, Hadrian's biographer, claimed that Hadrian considered setting up a Christian sanctuary, but was dissuaded on the ground that too many people would convert. That is a fantasy, though, from the last age of ancient religion, when its desperate supporters clung to improbable prophecies, such as that the new faith was doomed to disappearance 365 years after the Crucifixion.

There was a plethora of exotic religious expressions around an increasingly ordered Christian doctrine. In the early third century, a cunning individual called Alcibiades, a native of Apamea in Syria, came to Rome, bringing a book by a just man named Elchasai that he said he had received from Parthia. Its contents had been revealed to the author by an angel ninety-six miles high, sixteen miles broad, and twenty-four miles across the shoulders, whose footprints were fourteen miles long and four miles wide by two miles deep. This was the Son of God, and He was accompanied by his sister, the Holy Spirit of the same dimensions. Alcibiades announced that a new remission of sins had been proclaimed by the third year of Trajan (AD 100), and described a baptism that should impart this forgiveness even to the grossest sinners. For all sins of impurity, even against nature, a second baptism was enjoined 'in the name of the great and most high God and in the name of His Son, the Great King', with an adjuration of the seven witnesses written in the book, the sky, water, the holy spirits, the angels of prayer, oil, salt and earth. Then the text moved on to medical therapies: one who had been bitten by a mad dog should run to the nearest water and jump in with all his clothes on, promising the seven witnesses that he will abstain from sin. Forty consecutive days of baptism was recommended for consumption and for the possessed. Followers of this tradition still practised this treatment generations later, when descendants of Elchasai, two sisters, Marthus and Marthana, were still alive, revered as goddesses. The dust from their feet and their spittle were used to cure diseases.

We can only imagine what educated Romans, or Hadrian

himself, made of religious behaviour of this kind – a mixture of scepticism and awe, most likely. Elchasai was said to have been Jewish, and there is no reason to think that outsiders were much concerned with the niceties of doctrine that distinguished mainstream Jews or Christians from these colourful deviations. Which made it all the more likely that their opinion of the mainstream was shaped in part by information about the fringes. And in the case of the Jews, Hadrian's opinions and how they were formed is a subject of considerable importance.

XV

THE SON OF THE STAR

Hadrian ruled in the most humane possible way.

The situation of the Jews in Hadrian's empire was the product of a sequence of disasters that went back to the middle of the first century. Judaea had been a Roman province since AD 6, and had suffered serious unrest ever since. The troubles culminated in a wholesale rebellion against Rome, a bloody war, and the siege and sack of Jerusalem, with the levelling to the ground of Herod's Temple, in 70. Hindsight makes it seem that all the troubles in the region had built up for sixty years to this disaster, but in all probability many parts of the empire were just as ineptly run as Judaea for most of that time. But by the 50s and 60s a uniquely repressive climate had developed.

In the Roman empire order and stability were maintained through endless little displays of submission and expressions of respect, constantly recalibrated and always in need of tuning. In this tricky negotiation, the rich always played the part of brokers: they had local influence, and peace was overwhelmingly in their interest. But they competed with each other, in their influence over the local poor and for the rewards of loyal connection with Rome, and their mutual jealousies ruled out a united front.

It was in the spring of 66 that violent uprisings in Judaea demonstrated how fragile Rome's control was. The provincial governor seized a large sum of money from the Temple treasury. The population responded with violent satire: they passed round baskets pretending to collect donations for the impoverished Roman administration. The governor responded by initiating random atrocities, including the flogging and crucifixion of a number of Jewish Roman citizens and the sacking of part of the city by troops.

The next day a detachment of the Roman army was due to arrive in Jerusalem. Normally such an occasion would have merited a welcome ceremony in which the city's population would greet the arriving Romans with garlands, speeches and public expressions of joy. The temple priests, in an effort to prevent disaster, managed – despite the previous day's atrocities – to ensure that this gesture, however hollow, took place. But the soldiers knew they were marching into trouble, and refused to play their part in the charade. Convention demanded that they should respond to the loyal acclamation with carefully rehearsed gestures and shouts of apparent friendliness. However, truculent and edgy, they ignored the welcome. The crowd took offence, dropped the veneer of obedient enthusiasm and expressed their true feelings. The soldiers responded in kind. Violence escalated and the governor, with his garrison, prudently abandoned Jerusalem.

When it is said that the cities of such-and-such a region were at peace for ten generations, the perpetual possibility of a local crisis over slights and provocations is often overlooked. In Judaea, the fighting spun out of control into a full-scale war in which at first the rebels were successful. But the Romans instituted a major push against them and, helped by in-fighting between the leaders, recovered effective control.

The rebel factions were confined to Jerusalem, where they fought each other with real savagery. Relatively low-profile disengagement over a period of months should now have been possible, no doubt with reprisals and punishments in the Romans' grim, routine fashion. If the reoccupation had been carried out in a relatively low-key way by a local commander, it might have taken place without trouble. But it was now that another disastrous step was taken, which raised the conflict to an even higher level of political sensitivity, vulnerable honour and violence.

The last heir of Augustus, the infamous Nero, on whose behalf the war against the Jews was waged, had been driven to suicide by news that Romans in the provinces had rejected his rule. In the chaos of civil war between claimants to be emperor that followed, Vespasian, the commander of the army in Judaea, decided to join in the race to be emperor. He won – and instantly became worthy of increased publicity. The gallery to which he and his son – another commander in the fight against the Jews – were playing suddenly became the entire empire and all of its soldiers. The commander of the army in Judaea was an outsider, from the first generation of the Flavius family to be senators. He had a lot of persuading to do: the conflict in Judaea had to become heroic – historic, even – and the siege of Jerusalem epic. Troy, Tyre, Carthage, all the great sieges of history, were summoned in support. Jerusalem was described as 'far and away the most famous city of the whole East', and an entirely false statement was inscribed on a triumphal arch in Rome that the conquest of the city had been 'attempted without success – or not even attempted – by all the generals, kings and peoples of history'. The sequel, the siege of the last remnants of the rebellion at Masada, was another opportunity for the display of shock and awe as vast military engineering works were carried out in the extreme conditions of the desert bordering the Dead Sea. These were siege works, isolating the fortress and giving access across ravines to the almost inaccessible crags above.

Meanwhile, the new emperor made the most of his sensational victory, which helped to distract everyone from the civil strife that had just ended. Many potentially discontented soldiers could be kept busy: the spoils of prosperous Judaea were their own reward. The talents of the new dynasty were on display: the emperor's son had been chiefly responsible, in person, for the destruction of Jerusalem. One of the most regrettable and disgraceful episodes of the recent conflict had been a struggle in

Rome during the civil war in which the most important and sacred Roman temple, the Capitol, had been destroyed in an accidental fire. Subjects of Rome up and down the empire thought that this meant the end for the rule of Jupiter's people. The razing of the Jewish temple no doubt helped to restore the balance. The successful commander made a triumphal progress through Palestine, Syria and Lebanon, with a huge festival in each city he visited at which his prisoners were compelled to fight to the death in the arena. Seven hundred of the most impressive-looking were kept for his eventual triumph in Rome. Some lived on in Italy: we have a poignant epitaph to a woman described simply as 'a prisoner from Jerusalem'.

Victory over the Jews was commemorated, with characteristic cultural cynicism, with the construction in the centre of Rome of a gigantic temple to Peace. The other, more appropriate, monument was the amphitheatre we call the Colosseum, dedicated in 80, with a spectacle at which unprecedented displays of recreational warfare and slaughter were staged. The Colosseum was built (unusually for the great edifices of Rome) with slave labour – the prisoners of the Jewish war. When it was opened, Hadrian was six.

It is scarcely surprising that aggression of this kind led to abuses; more surprising that some of Rome's rulers attempted mitigation. It was only to be expected that palliation did not achieve much, and predictable that resentment, resistance and violence should swell in provinces with substantial Jewish communities. It was towards the end of the reign of Trajan that the cataclysm burst.

Worst hit were Egypt, the fertile part of modern Libya around the city of Cyrene, and Cyprus. In these regions, Jewish communities had lived for generations alongside other groups but with a long history of tension. It was a substantial part of the eastern Roman empire, and among its richest, most populous areas. The level of violence is evident from accounts of atrocities and the vivid sidelong allusions to the atmosphere of fear and disruption that survive in snippets of papyrus preserved in the aridity of Egypt. In the end, it was estimated that across the region 220,000 people had been killed by the rebels.

Indeed, sickening violence is about all we know of this episode, of which ancient writers tell us hundreds of thousands died. The figures are likely to have been inflated, and tales of atrocities inflicted by the rebels are hard to judge. One remarkable detail is that the Jewish rebels of Cyrene made their victims fight in the arena. It must have seemed appropriate to make their foes suffer from their own depraved entertainment and outweighed the rebels' hypocrisy in adopting the demeaning punishments they so despised and hated.

Artemidorus, the dream-interpreter, met a young officer serving in Cyrene at this time. He dreamed that the letters IK and TH were inscribed on the blade of his sword. It turned out to mean 'Death to the Jews in Cyrene', as the officer succeeded brilliantly in defeating the rebels – but, as Artemidorus pointed out, no one could have predicted *that* from the dream. The reprisals were horrific. This catastrophe was one of the reasons why Trajan could not succeed in his Parthian war, and he reacted with predictable anger to the disruption of the whole of his eastern strategy. Arrian later wrote in one of his histories: 'Trajan came to the conclusion that he should, if it were practicable, exterminate the [Jewish] people, but if not, at least by smashing them down stop their excessive, reckless violence.'

In fact, it is pretty clear that there was a connection between the invasion of Parthia and the revolt . The idea of the Kingdom of the East had a long pedigree in popular consciousness, involving Old Testament evocations of Assyria and Persia, and the sense that somewhere there was an adversary of the Greeks (Alexander) and the Romans (who had been rather less successful than Alexander in their wars in this area). Some even linked this idea – that there might be a state that would do to Rome what Rome had done to others – with a belief that, against all chronological likelihood, Nero might be about to return from his hiding-place in the east. Forty years before in western Turkey, a man called Terentius Maximus had announced that he was Nero – he hadn't committed suicide, after all. He made his way eastwards to the banks of the Euphrates, gaining followers all the way, and was even taken up for a time by the Parthians. Now Trajan was bringing about the longed-for confrontation, and there was every hope that he might lose.

In accordance with the spirit of impending catastrophe, the rebels in many places destroyed symbolically significant monuments in the cities they seized – temples, tombs and other public buildings. Revealingly, they even took the trouble to destroy the pavement of Roman roads, understanding that roads symbolised the might of Rome. The systematic alienation of the Jews since the fall of Jerusalem had succeeded in creating within the empire a general consciousness of and a hostility to the civilization which supported the Roman Empire and the emperor himself. This took the form of a solidarity that had not existed before between peoples outside the empire to the east. Of course, some Jews had distanced themselves for centuries from Greek culture and the religious divide was nothing new, but, especially in diaspora communities, there had been little sign of such cultural aggression until this period.

The whole saga is depressingly familiar. The state, anxious that its subjects might combine against it, got in first with coercive behaviour and ensured that its rallying was as effective and motivated as possible. The Romans' suppression of the Jews in AD 70–74 and appropriation of the conflict for imperial high politics created a still more serious problem a generation later: the revolt was no longer contained in a single region of the empire, but was spread through so many regions and cities that it came to bear a strong likeness to Roman power. The diaspora war of 114–17 was a completely new *kind* of problem for the Romans: never before had they faced an enemy ranged across so much of their territory or such integrated and impassioned ideological opposition.

All hostilities bring about change on both sides: the Romans' abuses of the Jews changed the Jews. But the war in which the Romans suppressed the revolt of AD 66–74 changed the Romans too. The Jews had created an anti-Roman ideology before a Roman ideology had been invented. Now, in countering the anti-Roman movements, they made a new Greco-Roman cultural and ideological statement. For us it is most closely associated with Hadrian.

During the years of the revolt Hadrian was in the east, and saw at first hand what happened on Cyprus. The war that had ended in the sack of Jerusalem had brought a new dynasty to power in Rome – now, half a century later, Trajan's successor too came to the office of emperor straight from appalling conflict within the empire. It is no surprise that he abandoned Trajan's plans to rival Alexander or that he resolved the provinces needed more direct attention from their ruler. In 123, when he was travelling in the west, he heard of a crisis in Parthia and immediately rushed east. As he looked at the ruins of the city of Salamis on Cyprus, he saw the need to forge a new public expression of the unity that was the object of the rebels' hatred – the combination of ancient classical culture with modern Roman power.

It is also, sadly, hardly surprising that he did not introduce a conciliatory policy aimed at mitigating the hatreds of the eastern Mediterranean. Far from it. During the 120s, Hadrian's travels might have impressed the regions of the empire with the reality of the Roman imperial system. Much less helpfully, it was during this period, inspired perhaps by all the other refoundations he had done, and above all by his having been the second founder of Athens itself, that he formed the bright idea of refounding Jerusalem – but as his own Roman version of the famous metropolis. It is just possible that he thought this might be a positive step: back in the age when the Romans had conquered the Mediterranean, they had made an example of two famous ancient cities, Carthage and Corinth, destroying them both within a single year in a calculated display of terror. Many Romans had been shocked by this, and almost exactly a hundred years later Julius Caesar set in motion the formal creation of a new Roman-style Carthage and Corinth. This was a sort of apology: the new cities were emphatically Roman and for Roman benefit but they were allowed to pay a certain cultural homage to their vanished predecessors, particularly in their religion. Perhaps Hadrian thought the same privilege should be extended to Jerusalem. Aphrodite of Corinth, Baal and Tanit of Carthage were re-instated, in Roman guise, in the city pantheons Caesar had set up: would the God of the Jews be included in the cults of the new city Hadrian built, Aelia Capitolina, named for his family and the great god of the Roman state, Jupiter Capitolinus? Certainly Jupiter received a great temple in the new city. Why did no one tell Hadrian that elision and cross-fertilisation between cultic ideas was alien to Jewish theology and cult? Perhaps he knew perfectly well how offensive the refoundation was. Perhaps he was continuing deliberately to rub salt into Jewish wounds. That view is supported by the care with which he fostered the recon-struction of the ancient Greek religious buildings of Cyrene, which had been a deliberate ideological target of the Jewish rebels there. The great doors of the Jerusalem temple, carefully preserved after the sack in 70, were redeployed with deliberate offensiveness in a restoration of the holy temple of the Samaritans, whose deity was now reworked as Highest Zeus – at Hadrian's expense. One of the things that the clever high priest of the Roman people understood was religious symbolism.

Whatever he thought he was achieving, the effect was the same. This was the trigger for the last of the three great conflicts between the Jews and Rome, the revolt of Simon bar Kosiba, which depopulated the region.

In 132, fifteen years after Hadrian's accession, his subjects in an important province took up arms against Rome in a care-fully planned rebellion. It involved an entire region and its people, from rich women of property to the landless poor. Worse, the disaffected from many parts of the empire flocked to take part in the conflict motivated, it was said, by greed but probably also by hatred of Rome. The leader of the rebellion proclaimed himself king, and took the charismatic sobriquet 'Son of the Star'. Freedom from Roman oppression was the theme proclaimed by the rebels, who began to count their years on a new calendar from the moment they declared independence. They got half-way through year four.

In the revolt's opening days, the Roman authorities were inclined to make light of it, but were soon compelled to take it extremely seriously. The governor of Britain, the toughest and most experienced general of all, Julius Severus, was summoned, and Hadrian himself led to war the armies whose morale and preparation he had fostered so carefully. Fifty fortresses and 985 villages were destroyed.

The rebellion was without question the thing that went most wrong in Hadrian's empire, but it was only the last act in a drama whose main part had been played out just as he came to power.

The revolt took place in Judaea, and the rebels were the Jews. The freedom of Israel was proclaimed in Hebrew on coins; Son of the Star was the messianic style of Simon bar Kosiba, who reigned briefly in Jerusalem. The coins also proclaimed the authority of a priest called Eleazar; and this was the hour of glory of one of the most learned rabbis of the age, Akiba, who was caught by the Romans and torn to pieces with sharp iron combs. The strategy of the uprising, apart from the seizure of Jerusalem, was to fortify as many small centres of resistance as possible, and contest each to the end – the plan which had worked so well back in AD 66. The rebels probably hoped for risings across the eastern Mediterranean, as had happened twenty years before: but perhaps Hadrian's assiduous visiting of the provinces, and the repressions that had followed the revolt of Trajan's last years made this impossible, and fighters from what was left of disaffected sections of the diaspora communities seem to have made their way to Judaea rather than resisting at home.

When they ran out of hilltop villages to defend, the Jewish rebels turned to the desert of the south and east, and defended little strongholds in caves in the sides of wadis. Their papers and their bones have been found in the dust. The rebellion was fired by religious fervour, and pursued with the desperate tenacity we associate with religious causes. Perhaps they hoped that their example would spread, or that Rome's enemies beyond the frontier would draw off strength from the reprisals. Neither was fulfilled. And the inherent weakness of the strategy was revealed when, the stores having been exhausted and the land left untilled, the defenders were weakened by malnutrition, which left them open to disease. The Roman commanders had the resources and the patience to reduce one guerrilla centre after another, killing as they went, until nothing was left.

After the end of the revolt, in 135, no Jew was allowed to enter Jerusalem, now undisputed as the Roman city Aelia Capitolina, named for Hadrian's family and Rome's great protecting god. A monumental arch commemorated the revival of the Roman province, which was no longer called Judaea but Palestine Syria. Jews everywhere were subjected to discrimination and oppression.

Roman records traditionally made a point of enumerating the enemy's losses rather precisely, and the figures for the forts and villages are probably an approximation of the truth. The picture they give of a land of villages fits with other evidence from before the revolt, and is likely to be right. The same Roman account also said that 585,000 Jews died in the fighting, and an indeterminable number of others 'by starvation, disease and fire'. You can never rely on casualty figures – too many people have an interest in rounding them up or down – but these accord with the numbers of inhabitants per village. We can be certain that hundreds of thousands of civilians were killed – in cities and villages far from the edges of the empire and any real or imagined barbarian threat.

The Romans did not conceal that many of their soldiers had

been killed too. Usually commanders adopted a particular formula to begin despatches to the Senate: 'It is good you are well; I and the army are well.' Hadrian omitted it: Roman losses were heavy.

The slaughter of so many thousands of people was a familiar Roman strategy. A people in what is now Libya had revolted against Domitian, massacring Roman tax-collectors, defeating the general sent against them, and having a whale of a time with his copious stores. The consequence: total destruction, even of non-combatants. 'I have stopped the Nasamones existing,' said the grandiose emperor, claiming, as he liked to, essentially divine power. But though we reach for the word 'genocide', and the Romans, on occasions like this, were undoubtedly aiming at precisely what that term implies, there was one significant difference, although it hardly makes any difference to the horror. It was the political and social community that was to be destroyed through massacre and enslavement. Genetic or racial definition did not play a large part. Domitian's agents spent no time enquiring after people with unacceptable levels of Nasamonian descent. And it was often possible to lose the offending identity and become something else. When Trajan said that the Jewish people should be obliterated, his ferocity and cold-bloodedness were appalling, but the idea was a quite different one from the Final Solution. An edgy, squeamish Roman view recorded two generations later put it well: Judaea was now a terrible place both because of the odd ways of the Jews, and because of the awfulness of what had been inflicted on them.

The suppression of Judaea was always going to have important consequences because of the bargaining factors that the Jewish state possessed. The troubles of the years before the Jewish revolt had echoed across the diaspora. Alexandria in Egypt had seen especially violent conflict between the Jewish and Greek communities; the Jews of Rome, in various sub-groups, including some who had started calling themselves Christians, also caused significant disturbances. But things were now going to be much worse, because a huge political edifice had been built on top of a legacy of hatred, victimisation and bloodshed. The Romans could have kept the Jewish revolt at the level of just another piece of disobedience, to be rewarded with extreme and exemplary punishment – but they could not resist the temptation to turn it into an Event on the larger stage of Roman imperial history. For a while they had their reward: the Flavian dynasty (Vespasian and his two sons Titus and Domitian) enjoyed considerable popularity for twenty years or so. But they had upped the symbolic charge of this stand-off so much that it was only a matter of time before someone – full of the hatred generated by the memories of real atrocity – saw also the potential political impact of attempting to reverse the Flavian victory. Instead of the dull recrudescence of old grievances, the normal outcome when revolt is suppressed with terror, the Romans had ineptly given these enemies the opportunity to claim that they were pursuing more dramatic and shocking goals than old vengeance – rather, that they were striking, once again, at Roman power itself.

The message was underlined by a special form of oppression developed by the Flavian emperors. They specialised in taxation – indeed, were lampooned for their meanness – and devised a special tax for the crushed Jews. Observing that Jews everywhere had formerly paid a contribution annually to the temple, they now demanded the continuation of the payment, but the money now went to Rome's temple, the newly rebuilt Capitol, seat of the supreme deity Jupiter. The measure reveals Roman fears and preoccupations: the cohesion of the Jewish community, expressed in its fiscal organisation, was a rival to the Roman state itself. But it was also exquisitely offensive: reminding Jews every year by exacting a substantial payment that their holiest place had been profaned and destroyed. There is no doubt that the tax was widely collected. Equally, no doubt, it was evaded. But the Romans had a way of establishing which men were eligible:

forced inspection to discover who was circumcised. Quite apart from the loss of dignity and the opportunity for brutality, this made circumcision into an increasingly conspicuous issue, and linked it as a sign of Jewishness with the memory of Rome's destruction of Jerusalem and with the ongoing humiliation and burden of the Jewish tax. Nor was the playing out of this oppressive drama a dialogue only between Rome and its Jewish subjects. Everyone was always alert to the latest shifts in the honour and dishonour charts. The issue was obvious to onlookers from all the other communities that lived among the Jews of the diaspora. They were encouraged to take sides.

It seems almost enough to chronicle the oppressions, the fears, the hatreds, the reprisals and the anger. But the fate of the Jewish communities needs to be seen as part of at least two wider pictures.

One is the open cultural frontier of west Asia. Here it was not possible to pretend that beyond Roman power there was nothing except barbarism and poverty. Parthia and its neighbours were cultured, populous and rich, and many of their peoples were very like the subjects of the eastern parts of Rome's own empire. Anything that happened here could threaten to alienate further or even detach the richest parts of the empire. Not just a thousand wealthy cities in Turkey, Syria, Jordan, Libya, but the vital heartland of Egypt, hub through which the wealth of the Indian Ocean was flowing ever more lucratively, granary of the eastern Mediterranean and now of Rome itself. Only a hundred years after Hadrian, new aggressive rulers of the house of Sasan, from the Iranian plateau, threatened all that Romans had feared: they set themselves up as the civilised power, divided the world into 'us' and 'them', 'us' being the Aryans after whom Iran is named, 'them' being its opposite, An-Iran, the non-Aryans, the great Satan. They knew their history as well as any Roman or Greek speechmaker, and proclaimed a return to the empire of Xerxes, which had all but swallowed up the Greek world to which the Romans of the empire looked back with such sentiment.

The other part of the picture is the ever-precarious unity of the Roman empire. It was a loose collection of ideas and ways of thought without any firm ideological basis. Neither religion, ethnicity nor culture offered the conviction and zeal that make communities resilient. There had been nothing essentially incompatible between the loose Roman framework and Jewish culture: incompatibility had been painstakingly created by aggression and cruelty, until Jewishness had been turned into an alien and repugnant allegiance, but one that was, unlike all the other alien and repugnant people of the empire and its environs, united, proud and now desperate. That made the Jews threatening beyond brigands or barbarian kings. And it created a legacy of conflict and fear that was to pattern the relationship between the state and the tenacious offshoot of Judaism that proclaimed its allegiance to Christ.

XVI

THE END

When he was dead, much was said against Hadrian by many people. The senate wanted his acts to be annulled. If Antoninus had not insisted, he would not have been made a god.

HADRIAN'S BIOGRAPHER

In late spring 134, Hadrian was back in Rome with two years in which to enjoy the villa at Tivoli relatively untroubled by crises, domestic or foreign. In January 136 he celebrated his sixtieth birthday. This was a significant year: when Augustus was approaching that age, he had called it the climacteric, and it was the moment he had selected to put the keystone into his arch of titles and powers and became 'Father of the Fatherland'. It seems that Hadrian began to think seriously about what would happen after his death. He had only two close relatives now, Servianus, his sister's widower, and Fuscus, the son of Servianus's daughter. Servianus was almost ninety. He had held the consulship for a third time, a special honour, in 134. Now Hadrian, concluding his reign with atrocities as he had begun it, compelled Servianus and Fuscus to commit suicide. It was the Roman emperors' usual disposal method for people of the highest status.

At first sight this seems arbitrary and whimsical, and was certainly unexpected, even though Hadrian and Servianus had not always been on good terms, but it can be viewed in a slightly different light. Suppose that Hadrian really believed in the principle of adopting the best man for the job. This might have been the only time when it was achieved in all Roman history, if we recall that Trajan had left his predecessor, the aged emperor

Nerva, no real choice, and that Hadrian himself had been the preferred candidate of the ladies in Trajan's court – not that he would have seen himself as anything other than the best man for the job. Servianus and Fuscus had to go because they would have formed the centre of a faction that claimed to believe blood mattered. The best man – whoever he turned out to be – should not have to face that sort of competition.

The strategy Hadrian followed had people guessing. It still does. It involved two senior, well-born, rich and successful figures, whose names were Aelius and Annius. Hadrian thought of the more distant future too, as Augustus had, and planned the adoption of the next generation as well, building into the system Aelius' son Lucius, aged less than seven, and daughter Ceionia, and Annius' grandson Marcus and granddaughter Faustina. It helped that Marcus, then fifteen, was betrothed to Ceionia.

Hadrian's Plan A was to make Aelius his successor, with his son Lucius and his son-in-law, Marcus Annius' son, in the wings. He adopted Aelius in mid-136, gave him a major selection of the imperial powers and sent him to the Danube. But Aelius suffered from tuberculosis – there is a religious offering for his better health from a soldier on Hadrian's Wall – and when he returned to Rome to give a formal speech on New Year's Day 137, he dropped dead before he could speak. It was around this time that Sabina, too, died; her deification was one of Hadrian's last public acts in Rome.

Plan B came into play. Hadrian retained the two back-ups, Lucius and Marcus, from Plan A. But as his actual successor he now adopted Aurelius Antoninus, husband of Annius' daughter Faustina. The ceremony took place on 25 February.

By then Hadrian was feeling unwell, and had effectively retired from the public eye, leaving Antoninus in charge. His medical condition deteriorated rapidly; he went to the curative waters of the notorious resort of Baiae near Naples and died there on 10 July 138. Antoninus took over, and reigned in peace and harmony for twenty-three years. In 161, he was succeeded, as Hadrian had planned, by Lucius, then Marcus. Lucius died in the winter of 168, Marcus in the spring of 180, the much-lamented and universally acclaimed Good Emperor Marcus Aurelius, the philosopher king.

His disposal of the succession to the Roman empire, so as to give it an unparalleled reputation for stability and good government for forty-two years after his own death, is far from the least of Hadrian's achievements, but no one has ever been able to work out what he was up to. Ancient gossip said that he liked the looks of Aelius, who had a reputation for being a luxury-loving cipher. Modern speculation once made Aelius Hadrian's bastard, but it is no longer thought likely that Hadrian fathered a child. More recently, the family ties between all these people have been teased out, along with their inheritance of huge fortunes and their connections with Spain. But Spain meant nothing now to Hadrian. It is more plausible to think that Hadrian saw these people, with their cultured and literary tastes – especially Marcus, already outstanding at fifteen – as the best people for the job. That was certainly what he said he was doing, when he addressed his council on his sixty-second birthday, 24 January 138, and he can hardly be blamed for choosing people like himself. What he did not do was put blood before what he thought to be merit.

Marcus was so much the right person for the job that he was reluctant to move to the imperial palace from the estate in the suburbs that had belonged to his mother. He was not pleased to be adopted, and had already, at fifteen, a keen sense of the evils of absolute power.

The cities of the empire, which had seen so much of Hadrian and the armies, remembered him as one of the greatest emperors. There was never again quite such a liberal benefactor of so many individuals and communities. He acquired a positive place in folk tradition. At the centre, the story of his last days was told in a rather different spirit. Two emperors had died in distant villas, probably of old age. Seven had died violently. Trajan had died far away. Only Vespasian had died near the capital, comfortably, with a joke on his lips: 'Bother me, I think I'm turning into a god.' It was rather different for the taverns and bath-houses to hear rumours of an emperor tortured by illness, longing for death and unable to rest.

In modern times, Hadrian has had a different kind of reputation. He has acquired a name as a thinker, an aesthete, and as a man of Feelings, with Soul. This must be in part because he was one of two Roman emperors whose remarks about their soul are preserved. Hadrian's imperial 'grandson', Marcus Aurelius, wrote a series of subtle reflections on his own identity and its ethical implications. Hadrian's reputation for self-examination depends largely on a peculiar little poem he is said to have written shortly before his death. It has a mawkish quality, only slightly exaggerated by Margaret Hodgson's translation:

> Poor little, lost little, sweet little soul,
> My body's companion and friend,
> Where are you going to now, little soul,
> Pale little, stiff little, bare little soul,
> Now that the jokes have to end?

His usually not unsympathetic biographer says, with a curl of the lip, 'He also wrote verses – not much better – in Greek.'

Alongside the other facets of the unconventional Hadrian – the obsessive memory, the passionate competitiveness, the strange hobbies – there was clearly a feeling that he was an unhappy figure, bad for other people and for Rome, since unhappiness was unlucky. While other gallery pictures of emperors explore their gluttony or sensuality, their cruelty or their odd tastes, Hadrian became an image of loneliness and pain, which has moulded some treatments of him in the twentieth century – for example, Marguerite Yourcenar's *Mémoires d'Hadrien*. A school exercise, purporting to be Hadrian's last ever letter to his successor Antoninus, was circulated for pupils to practise accurate copying of a piece of edifying Greek:

That I am escaping from life not before time, not losing my reason, nor in a way which provokes pity – nor unexpectedly, nor without due reflection – is what I most of all want you to know. Though I shall seem to be unfair to you (as I know by experience) my constant companion in my need, reassuring me and urging me to take it easy.

Less pleasantly, one of his last victims, the ninety-year-old Servianus, cursed him to wish to die but live on. This was remembered and quoted, and the tale of Hadrian's horrible, dropsical decline bore it out in detail. Hadrian, it was said, tried to have himself killed, but failed, in an apt illustration of the practical limits of even the most absolute power.

It is also appropriate that he should have seen the soul continuing the imperial travels into still more remote and uncharted provinces, less so that his reign should be seen as a time of jokes. None of the usual jokes in future, he tells it.

Julian, the fourth-century emperor who tried to turn back the clock and abandon Christianity, wrote a satirical account of his predecessors. The scene is heaven, and each emperor turns up to a banquet with the gods to decide whether any dead Roman ruler is truly worthy of a place among them. After Trajan comes 'an austere man, practised in all the arts, and especially in music, gazing at the heavens, and dabbling in the forbidden arts'. He is looking for someone. But he is told brusquely that he won't find Antinous there, and disappears, never to be seen again.

Hadrian's reign marks, almost exactly, the height of the expansion of the network of compromise and co-operation that kept the empire stuck together. In his childhood, the benefits of mutual support by civic élites were still spreading, as newish towns in north-west Europe became more established, as the last kingdoms left independent in the eastern Mediterranean were incorporated into the empire, as a few last communities along the frontiers became integrated into Roman ways of running themselves. The end of his reign saw a level of routine violence across the empire greater than had ever happened before, and which ran on through reign after reign thereafter. The curve of integration had been topped, and the downturn was gradual at first; it would be much steeper later.

A simple pattern of co-operation and competition had been an unstoppable success at integrating the Roman empire. The big men of Community A and Community B agreed that they were a good thing. They offered their colleagues in Community C a chance to join in and receive a share in the self-esteem. On top of the feel-good factor, the élites of the communities agreed to support each other in case of insubordination. The empire used honour and fear in equal measure to create a system of mutual support between the upper classes. While the idea proliferated, replicating itself across the Mediterranean, its own success was guaranteed. But as soon as it stopped, the attraction faded. Eventually union with the universal system of values ceased to be a good way for élites to maintain themselves. The cohesive force of this simple mutual-benefit society was far more important to the Roman empire than the swordsmanship of the soldiery.

But it was never an overwhelming force. In city after city, region after region, it could be and regularly was challenged by local upheavals, but it was strong enough, and the system was vigorous enough, for net consolidation to continue. Its eventual weakening, caused simply by the fact that there was nowhere else for it to expand into, destroyed the coherence of ancient civilisations far more effectively than barbarian invasion. All that was left was a sense of shared belonging to Christendom, and that could be attained without much in the way of political commitment beyond the frontiers.

What keeps big systems integrated? Can they go on getting bigger and bigger? How much do communications media matter? How far can globalisation go? How does systems-failure begin to appear? From the reign of Hadrian, the Roman empire, gigantic system that it was, stopped getting bigger, more integrated, more complicated, stopped providing so many opportunities, stopped improving the possibilities of change and innovation. Maybe it was enough that the positive trends faltered; maybe they started to go into reverse. No one noticed for generations, but the pace and nature of change had altered for ever. The big labels, Greek, Roman, Christian, remained but concealed increasing chaos.

'They' became more and more of a problem. They came through the frontier belts, they emigrated *en masse* into the heart of the provinces. They attracted notoriety because they were barbarians. The first, from the north, to be seen in Italy, except as slaves, attacked Aquileia, one of the greatest cities in northern Italy, in 170, only a generation after Hadrian's death. Roman management of peoples on the fringes – border management, selection occupation, controlled resettlement, exemplary massacre, occasional aggression – broke down. Little by little the effort to maintain Roman institutions was abandoned in province after province.

The Roman province in Britain lasted until the fifth century, and was indeed quite prosperous in the fourth. It was around the time that the city of Rome was captured by outside enemies for the first time in eight hundred years that governmental links and Roman military authority ceased. The break was announced in traditional form. Emperor Honorius wrote letters to the officials of the individual cities of the province, advising them chillingly to look after themselves.

A monk writing in Britain in about 540 told the sorry saga in colour: 'Then Britain was despoiled of all its armed soldiery, all supplies for the army, all its rulers – terrible though they had been – and a very numerous generation of men in their prime. They sent ambassadors to Rome with letters begging for help . . .' An expedition was sent, which destroyed a great number of enemies and freed the Britons. But it returned home, and the barbarians came back. 'Then another group of troubled ambassadors were sent. They tore their clothes. They poured dirt on their heads. Like frightened chicks looking for a hiding-place under the protecting wings of their parent, they begged for help, to prevent their wretched land being completely obliterated.'

Another expedition did still more harm to the foes of the Britons. This time the Romans said that

> they could no longer be annoyed by putting on such time-consuming missions and wearing out a very large and effective army and the standards of Rome against weak and disorganised brigands. The Britons should look after themselves. They gave them advice and handbooks on self-defence. They said farewell, intending never to return.
>
> Disgusting throngs of Scots and Picts now eagerly emerged from the coracles in which they had sailed across the sea, like the teeming worms that wriggle out of holes in the rocks when the weather grows warm. They were more inclined to cover their faces with hair than their private parts with clothes. The garrison on the Wall was too lazy to fight, and too unwieldy to retreat.
>
> Massacres followed. Famine followed the massacres. A last appeal went to Rome: 'The barbarians drive us to the sea – the sea drives us back to the barbarians – we are drowned or slaughtered!' But no help ever came again.

The original abandonment was not like Hadrian's abandonment of Mesopotamia, a calculated piece of imperial policy. It came because in the first decade of the fifth century, even with the barbarian worms wriggling all round, the leaders of the Roman army in Britain would not give up their ambitions to rule the north-western provinces or Rome itself. It was to support the bid for power of a ruthless commander that the last soldiers of Rome left Britain. The break-up of the Roman empire was caused as much by the failure of consensus among a ruling élite as by the destructiveness of outsiders.

But 'they' were inside too. It's wrong to separate out 'barbarian invasion', because of where these raiders came from: the empire was just as incompetent at coping with massive internal unrest. The loss of probably many more than half a million subjects in the Jewish disasters of Hadrian's lifetime and just before was the worst example of simplistic brutalism in dealing with dissent and unrest, which ran deep in Roman state thinking. It had an unexpected effect. Unlike all the other victims of Roman genocide, the Jews had a religious and cultural ideology that had spread widely in the empire and, with its offshoot Christianity, formed a counter-culture, something that no ancient state had ever had to deal with before. Its existence was dangerous to the Greek and Roman mainstream. The Jewish rebellions and the persecution of Jews and Christians turned it antagonistic. The result was dissension, conflict and violence in communities across the empire, which further weakened the consensus that kept the empire together.

The consensus and the city life it maintained were robust. It took the ancient world half a millennium to disappear, to mutate into fragmented early medieval states, in which cities and city-élites functioned differently. Indeed, most of the cities disappeared, even in the biggest of the early medieval states, the Roman empire of Constantinople, which we usually call Byzantine. Public buildings were too expensive to maintain, let alone build. The rich felt safer in fortified estates in the country, each family defending its own land in its own stronghold. So the inclusiveness which had spread down from the wealthy in ancient towns disappeared: there was less to trickle down, and nowhere for it to happen.

Despite its failure to keep the Roman empire intact, the ideology of imperial power was robust too. For centuries the Byzantine empire remained a highly organised complex of institutions, with an extraordinarily powerful monarch, supported by a cradle of culture and law inherited from the Roman past. The Catholic Church, its bishops and the See of Rome retained the sense of imperial inclusiveness and authority they had acquired when Constantine accepted Christianity. When new experiments in overarching, continent-scale order were made, they drew on both traditions: the Holy Roman Empire endured until 1806. The conception of transcendent order, which united the furthest-flung outposts of rapidly expanding Islam in the eighth century, and brought Spain, Egypt, Syria and all that lay between them into a single framework, resembled the Roman empire in many ways. Finally, in a different world, new dominating powers in the European tradition expressed their aspirations in the vein of the diligent functionaries of Hadrian's age – Pliny, Arrian, Frontinus and Hadrian himself, unwearying, pernickety, interfering, prickly, pedantic, learned and informed by a philosophical spirit of justice and decency, however erratic their delivery of it – and displayed their power in the emphatic language of Roman symbolism, with eagles and Capitols and *fasces*.

LAST WORDS

Marcus Aurelius, Hadrian's grandson by adoption, and the next emperor but one, wrote:

Do not be anxious. Everything is in accord with the nature of the universe. In just a little while, you will be nothing, like Hadrian.

FURTHER READING

If the reader wants to pursue Hadrian further, the Biographer's *Life of Hadrian* which we so frequently cite is easily available in the Penguin Classics *Lives of the Later Caesars*. For the other main ancient account in Books 65 to 70 of Dio's *History*, the only convenient English version is that of the Loeb Classical Library (Harvard University Press). Philostratus' account of the wanderings of the Holy Man Apollonius are also translated in the Penguin Classics series. Josephus' *Jewish War* provides a chilling eye-witness chronicle of the early phases of the disasters recounted in our book.

Elizabeth Speller's *Following Hadrian* is an evocative introduction to the period. For those who wish to consult a definitive and fully detailed account of the reign, *Hadrian: The Restless Emperor* by Antony Birley will answer all queries. Miriam Griffin's excellent account of Nerva and Trajan in the *Cambridge Ancient History*, second edition, Volume 11, explores some of the contradictions which are our theme in this account. For the brutal realities of Roman attitudes to outsiders, Brent Shaw's sobering chapter in the same volume is strongly to be recommended.

Margeurite Yourcenar's anguished Hadrian makes an admirable subject for a great historical novel, but hers is not our view of the emperor. Royston Lambert's *Beloved and God* explores the relationship of Hadrian and Antinous with more care and historical sensitivity than the sensational title suggests.

INDEX

INDEX